Shakespeare's Daughters

Shakespeare's Daughters

SHARON HAMILTON

McFarland & Company, Inc., Publishers
Jefferson, North Carolina, and London

LIBRARY OF CONGRESS CATALOGUING-IN-PUBLICATION DATA

Hamilton, Sharon, 1943–
Shakespeare's daughters / Sharon Hamilton.
p.   cm.
Includes index.

ISBN 0-7864-1567-3 (softcover : 50# alkaline paper)

1. Shakespeare, William, 1564–1616 — Characters— Daughters.
2. Shakespeare, William, 1564–1616 — Characters— Fathers.
3. Domestic drama, English — History and criticism.   4. Conflict
of generations in literature.   5. Fathers and daughters in literature.
6. Daughters in literature.   7. Fathers in literature.   I. Title.
PR2992.D38H36   2003   822.3'3 — dc21   2003001316

British Library cataloguing data are available

Cover art: Ophelia *by John William Waterhouse, 1894 (Eyewire);*
Shakespeare *(Art Today); detail from* Under the Lemon Trees,
Bordighera *by Claude Monet, 1884 (PicturesNow.com)*

Manufactured in the United States of America

*McFarland & Company, Inc., Publishers
Box 611, Jefferson, North Carolina 28640
www.mcfarlandpub.com*

For my Dear Ones: Emily, Kate, and Abby

Contents

but usually not from the perspective of the daughter. The father, patriarch and power figure, tended to be the focus. I was curious about the daughter's reactions to various kinds of paternal treatment, authoritarian, benevolent, or oblivious. In the comedies, I realized, the effects of a deleterious relationship could be overcome by the influence of happy chance or a powerful champion. In the tragedies, with no lucky factors to counter the father's control, the ultimate effects are disastrous. For example, in three plays that depict a daughter who rebels against her father's will and chooses a suitor of her own liking, the daughter in the comedy, Hermia in *A Midsummer Night's Dream,* attains the wish of her heart; the young woman in the tragedy, Desdemona in *Othello,* suffers isolation, abuse, and ultimately death; and the tragicomic daughter, Jessica in *The Merchant of Venice,* attains the husband she loves but at the cost of her own and her father's tranquility. For a few of Shakespeare's daughters, such as Lear's Goneril and Regan, the issue is not only domestic but also political power. Already married and supposedly content, they are spurred to heights of ambition and malice by their father's sudden unfounded favor. Other daughters, well-loved as children but rendered fatherless by circumstance, prove resilient and independent, and even, at their strongest, able to assume the parental role themselves. Ironically, among their number is Lear's youngest daughter, Cordelia, whose devotion to her father abides even through his rash rejection and abuse.

I knew early on that I wanted to address such thoughts to a broad audience, not simply a small community of scholars but also the large body of ordinary playgoers and readers. Parents and children ourselves, we turn to Shakespeare's plays seeking what only great literature can provide: wisdom about the human heart and eloquent words to sustain us in dark moments and enhance our times of triumph and celebration. Among his other achievements, Shakespeare was an icon-maker. Once acquainted with his works, we discover that his lines and characters enter our minds unbidden to enrich our daily round. Nowhere is he more astute than in his portrayal of fathers and daughters, and the factors that foster or undermine that bond. This book is meant to record some of my own illuminations on Shakespeare's art, and to share them with fellow members of his vast audience.

I would like to express my gratitude to the many teachers who have enhanced my own understanding of Shakespeare, among them Leo Cierpial, Edmund Creeth, Charles Shattuck, Allan Holaday, Jan Hinely, Kristin Linklater, Tina Packer, Gail Price, Alan Dessen, Rex McGuinn, Sarah Ream, Adrienne Thomas, and Miriam Gilbert. To those I would add readers who provided sage counsel and encouragement about the manuscript:

David Cavitch, Herbert Coursen, Miriam Gilbert again, and my late husband Morse Hamilton. I am grateful to the many students who have provided inspiration, insight, and candor and, in the best tradition of education, taught me. I am indebted, too, to the actors, directors, and set designers, amateur and professional, on stage and in film, who have given life to these luminous play scripts. Finally and most importantly, I want to celebrate the memory of my own father, Spiro Saros, and express my thankfulness to Emily, Kate, and Abby, who, individually and together, continue to bless me with the invaluable gifts of a daughter's love.

Introduction

It is a wise father that knows his own child.
The Merchant of Venice, II.ii.70

Why is there such a resurgence in Shakespeare's popularity? What has he, a writer who lived four hundred years ago, to offer the modern movie and theater goers who flock to his plays? Perhaps the most important answer is a deeper insight into our feelings and motives, and into the consequences of treating others in particular ways. Such factors are crucial to the family relationship that Shakespeare depicted in play after play: that between father and daughter. Juliet and Capulet, Miranda and Prospero, Ophelia and Polonius, Rosalind and Duke Senior, Perdita and Leontes, Cordelia, Regan, Goneril, and Lear — the variety and vitality of Shakespeare's daughters may surprise even modern audiences with a new consciousness of women's roles. Shakespeare's canon, as actress-director Tina Packer points out, contains seven times as many roles for men as for women.* Not only in the theater but in Western culture generally, the relationship between father and daughter was long missed or ignored by historians, philosophers, and anthropologists. Instead, Lynda K. Boose notes, "the father and son [were] the pair most frequently in focus, and the mother and son the second," an emphasis that can be seen as "a paradigm of women's relations to male culture."† Shakespeare did write in the context of a patriarchal society. That is reflected particularly in his history plays, where the major family relationship *is* that between father and son. But in the comedies and tragedies, where war and dynasty provide a backdrop to domestic issues, the daughter occupies center stage.

History probably influenced the prominence that Shakespeare gives

*Noted in *Women of Will,* her performance and commentary of scenes from several of the major plays, summer 1991.
†"Introduction," *Daughters and Fathers,* eds. Lynda K. Boose and Betty S. Flowers (Baltimore: Johns Hopkins Press, 1989), pp. 1–2, 7.

5

to the father-daughter relationship: for the greatest part of his career, the most important member of his audience was a brilliant queen, daughter of the century's other most powerful monarch. The socio-economic aspect of marriage no doubt also played a part: in civil life the union of families has long been the major event, and therefore a popular subject with play-goers. As the fortune he earned as a shareholder in the Globe company attests, Shakespeare had a keen eye for the box office. Psychological forces may have contributed: a suitor represents the father's rival for his daughter's affections—the man who will win her and carry her off. By exploring his own "feminine side," Shakespeare could have the gratification of playing all three roles. Finally, biographical factors certainly had an influence: Shakespeare and his wife, Anne Hathaway, had three children, Susanna, and twins, Hamnet and Judith. Only the girls survived to adulthood; Hamnet died at eleven. It is notable that in the plays, many of the boys are precocious and fragile. The princes in *Richard III*, young Arthur in *King John*, the boy Macduff, Prince Mamillius in *The Winter's Tale* all die young, the touchingly brave victims of tyrants. His own loss, of the sort that befell so many Elizabethan parents, may have given Shakespeare special insight into bereavement, and, perhaps, deeper regard for the bond between father and daughter. In his life, as in his nation's, it was the daughters who represented the future.

For whatever political or personal reasons, Shakespeare explored the father-daughter bond again and again. According to the typical pattern, a middle-aged to old man, usually a widower, has an adolescent daughter just emerging into young womanhood. The daughters are protected for a time — the manor house or the castle contains the whole world in their girlhoods. The plays take up the stories when the women are on the verge of leaving that insulated circle. The main conflict is over the choice of a husband, and the outcome, happy or unhappy, depends heavily on the father's treatment of the daughter: Does he see her as an object whose value on the marriage market will reflect well on him, or as an individual with feelings and needs of her own? How well does he understand her? How willing is he to trust her to make this choice? The issue, in other words, is control. If the father hampers or humiliates the daughter, she must circumvent him in order to assert her own identity. The results of her rebellion will be remorse, alienation, perhaps death. But if he honors her feelings and sanctions her decisions, the rewards will be mutual affection, hope, and fruitfulness.

What Shakespeare implies in play after play is that no matter how well-intentioned the father or how seemingly ideal the suitor, if the girl's heart is not engaged, the match cannot work. This truth emerges in the comedies as well as the tragedies. To Lord Capulet in *Romeo and Juliet*, Paris is the perfect fiancé; to old Egeus in *A Midsummer Night's Dream*, it is Demetrius. Each father becomes outraged when his daughter rejects his choice. But they are not Shakespeare's spokesmen. That role belongs to the lovers. As young Lysander quips to his rival: "You have her father's love, Demetrius, / Let me have Hermia's; do you marry him" (*A Midsummer Night's Dream*, I.i.93–94).*

In other plays, the daughter chooses the man, but her father rejects him. The reason may be the suitor's social status, race, or religion. No matter: the results are equally unhappy. Not only Juliet but Ophelia, Desdemona, and even Shylock's daughter Jessica might have fared happily had their fathers been more accepting. Instead, the men issue orders and threats; they badger, trap, accuse, scorn. It is not that they do not love their children: the love, in every case, is intense. But it does not inspire either empathy or candor. All Shakespeare's tyrannical fathers— Egeus, Polonius, Brabantio, Capulet, Shylock, Lear — value pride in their familial authority and social image over their children's feelings. They insist above all that the daughter be Good — i.e., obedient and chaste. To put it another way, the Good Girl must be conveniently free of will, in both the usual sense of volition and the peculiarly Elizabethan one of sexual drive. The girls with nerve — and that group includes most of Shakespeare's heroines— refuse, rebel, run off. Forced to choose, they pick husband over father as, Desdemona reminds Brabantio, tradition and "duty" dictate they should. The daughter is "bound" to her father "for life and education," but Biblical injunction and social precedent make her allegiance to her husband still more compelling:

> ...so much duty as my mother show'd
> To you, preferring you before her father,
> So much I challenge that I may profess
> Due to the Moor, my lord [*Othello*, I.iii.186–89].

Not only "duty" but emotional development necessitates this stance. Parents have to raise their children to go away from them. Then as now, the rites of passage, choosing a mate, a career, a place to settle — to which modern families would add a college — require benevolent support and, often, sacrifice, on the parents' part if the child is to flourish. Shakespeare saw that in his day a father was in a privileged position to grant that support, and that a daughter's need for it is as keen as a son's. The father may hold

---

*All quotations are from the Pelican editions (Penguin Books) of the plays.

the power, but it is power that he abuses at his peril. His own happiness as well as his child's depends on acknowledging her wishes and needs.

Shakespeare embodies these insights in a pageant of fathers and daughters, happy and unhappy. His view of human nature is not sentimental, but neither is it cynical. Many of his examples are negative — warnings rather than models. Ophelia, the one Shakespearean daughter who acquiesces to her father's demands, ends up tragically "divided from herself and her fair judgment." The hapless onlooker who gives this description of her notes that without an independent will, we are less than human — "pictures or mere beasts" (*Hamlet*, IV.v.85–86). "Pretty Ophelia," the "picture" of daughterly obedience, becomes, in Gertrude's account of her drowning, "incapable of [realizing] her own distress" and sinks to "muddy death" (*Hamlet*, IV.vii.177, 182).

If Ophelia's docile outlook is not typical of the oppressed daughters in Shakespeare's tragedies, her fatal destiny is. No amount of logical explanation or eloquent pleading arouses the father's sympathies. The young woman is rejected, isolated, and eventually destroyed. The father, forced to face the cost of his intransigence, suffers bitterness and, in some cases like Lear's and Brabantio's, literally heart-rending sorrow. In the comedies, through magic or sudden changes of heart, or both, father and daughter are saved. Such daughters as Hermia, Celia, and Hero end up both reconciled to their fathers and wed to their true loves.

Not surprisingly, the comedies and the romances abound with benevolent patriarchs who promote a relationship based on affection and mutual self-esteem. The prime example is *The Tempest*. Prospero raises his daughter Miranda to choose the very course he would approve of, but then grants her the freedom to make the choice herself. Those are the hallmarks of a salutary bond: nurturing, bestowing blessing, letting go. The resolution benefits not only the daughter but her family and her society.

For marriage is a communal as well as a private act. The couple cannot thrive in isolation. For the love's resolution to be happy, it must be blessed by and bless the entire household or court or country. In Shakespeare's plays the heroine's ultimate gift is to bring about communal healing. She bestows it by helping others, too, attain truth of feeling. Shakespeare implies that the good father not only expresses but practices the values that he wants his child to emulate. At great cost to his own comfort, Prospero chooses generosity over egotism, candor over affectation, compassion over coercion.

Such a spiritual legacy may also be conveyed by a father no longer present to act as mentor. In *As You Like It*, for example, Rosalind's father, Duke Senior, has been exiled to the wintry depths of the Forest of Arden. Still, his credo is: "Sweet are the uses of adversity" (II.i.12). This is not Pollyanna optimism: like Prospero, the Duke has known betrayal and deprivation at a brother's hands. But that experience has not left him bitter and self-pitying. He values loyalty and generosity, and he has a keen sense of others' worth. When the desperate young Orlando threatens the rural court with violence, it is Duke Senior who subdues and then aids him. The young man proves worthy of the rescue, and of winning the heart of Rosalind, the Duke's only child. During their courtship, she, in turn, gives ample proof of empathy, resilience, and daring. In other words, Shakespeare shows not only that women have strengths of character but that they can receive those traits, inherited and acquired, from their fathers. Like father, like daughter.

How did Shakespeare, who wrote for an all-male repertory company, create heroines who continue to play so convincingly, while such creations of his contemporaries as Thomas Kyd's Bel-Imperia and John Webster's Duchess of Malfi usually appear only in the confines of study? One explanation is their three-dimensionality: Shakespeare's women are complex, assertive, agile of mind and body. Their wit and forthrightness have sometimes been attributed to the accident of theater history that the roles were written for boy actors. But this explanation ignores the fact that the same casting practice applied to the plays of Shakespeare's rival dramatists. More important, the parts do not feel, to actresses or to audiences, like males in drag. Juliet, Viola, and Rosalind seem so "feminine" that the discovery that they were played by boys on the Elizabethan stage usually shocks modern audiences. Shakespeare made the sexes distinctive.

Twelfth Night suggests such a distinction in the portrayal of the twins Viola and Sebastian. Although the plot depends on their being young enough to look androgynous— no more than fourteen or fifteen — Sebastian is much more aggressive and vigorous. The cowardly Sir Andrew discovers this, to his terror, when he challenges the wrong twin to a duel. The few Shakespearean heroines who display military prowess, Joan de Pucelle in *Henry VI, Part 1* and Goneril in *King Lear*, for example, are made objects of amazement or mockery. At the same time, Shakespeare implies that most traits of character are shared by the genders, and that in a crisis anyone, male or female, may be capable of courage and cunning. The duels that such women as Rosalind, Portia, and Beatrice win so handily are those of wit and will. Shakespeare gave his heroines an array of strengths: grace, eloquence, resourcefulness, prescience, imagination — perhaps above all intelligence. Sebastian's description of his sister Viola could apply to all these young women: "She bore a mind that envy could not but call fair" (*Twelfth Night*, II.i.26).

The conventions of Shakespeare's day are of course dated. Marriage is no longer a woman's main means to adult status and, in the West at least, few fathers choose their daughters' husbands. Some feminists go so far as to denigrate the very institution of matrimony as a patriarchal anachronism. From this point of view, the old matchmaking "happy ending" is anathema, the betrothed daughter the hapless bargaining chip between father and suitor. Marriage has been and continues to be a means of oppressing some women, but any human pairing carries the potential for abuse — parent-child, sister-sister, boss-employee. Nor does any form of relationship, including marriage, necessarily create unhappiness.

Meanwhile, people continue to marry, to raise children, and to seek understanding of the stresses involved. Many threats to well-being that seem modern — teenage suicide, divorce, venereal disease, alcoholism — are even older than Shakespeare's time. In contrast, many of the institutions that once governed human behavior — the church, the village, the extended family — have weakened or disappeared. Yet even in our marriage-shy age, Shakespeare can speak to us, and clarify feelings if not offer easy answers.

One reason is the intensity of Shakespeare's focus. His characters live not in the expansive landscape of novels but in the limited world of plays. We do not see the whole fabric of the heroine's life. The action is limited in time and place: We need not reflect on the future course of Portia and Bassanio's union or the possibility that several of the couples "hasting to the ark" after the final dance of *As You Like It* will be sparring partners in later years. Like all works of fiction, plays afford us the luxury of hindsight. We can trace actions to their causes, see motives and circumstances with a clarity and simplicity that real life seldom allows. Freed of mundane trivia and telescoped in time, plays let us understand why certain lives turn out as they do. The endings of the comedies are cheering, of the tragedies moving or shocking, but both have a gratifying inevitability. The tragicomedies alone leave us uneasy — and make us sense the consistency of tone in the other plays.

Shakespeare's voice continues to engage us because he gave his daughters as well as his fathers depth and variety and at the same time made them familiar enough to seem universal. The drama critic Michael Billington, commenting on the success of several foreign-language productions, calls Shakespeare "a cosmic mirror in which each culture finds its own reflection."* This is not to suggest that as we read and envision these figures or watch actors embody some magical combination of the characters and themselves, we all see the same thing. Not only different cultures but different members of the same audience will see the plays with a difference. Shakespeare has become, in Marjorie Garber's wry term, a modern "fetish,"

The Guardian, reprinted in *World Press Review* (July 1992), pp. 24–25.

to which each generation of readers and playgoers turns for enlightenment and confirmation.* The more the reader or playgoer has experienced, the richer will be his response. *The Winter's Tale* is a more poignant play for someone who has lost a wife or child or seen friends go through a painful divorce; Juliet's suicide is agonizing to viewers who have not only lived through adolescence but, like the senior Capulets or the Nurse and the Friar, raised teenagers of their own. The situations differ but the analogies hold. When comparable events occur in our actual lives, Shakespeare may provide us with words that clarify or console.

Perhaps the key to Shakespeare's continuing appeal lies in his relationship to his own public. He did not write solely for a particular class or outlook. His earliest editors, John Heminges and Henry Condell, addressed *The First Folio*, the first collection of Shakespeare's plays and poems, "To the great Variety of Readers." Long-standing members of the Globe company, Heminges and Condell had performed for audiences that ranged from royalty to rude mechanicals. Their late colleague's plays, they asserted, were meant for the whole spectrum, "From the most able to him that can but spell." This book, intended for those whose curiosity about Shakespeare has been piqued and who want to deepen their understanding, is a tribute to that broad-based legacy. It seeks to explore the many variations that Shakespeare wrought on the father-daughter theme. I begin by comparing the two pairs that strike me as both most similar and most diametrically opposite: Capulet and Juliet, Prospero and Miranda. Then I consider several stances that daughters in the play take toward their fathers: rebelling, acquiescing, assuming the father's role in his absence, and forgiving and healing. The annotated index is intended both to describe these patterns more fully and to allow readers to select the plays and the relationships that most interest them. To elaborate on Ben Jonson's compliment, Shakespeare was not for an age or a gender but for all time and people. We are all Shakespeare's sons and daughters.

---

*"Shakespeare as Fetish," *Shakespeare Quarterly*, volume 41 (Summer 1990), pp. 242–50.

1

The Father as Inept or Able Mentor: *Romeo and Juliet* and *The Tempest*

> I have done nothing but in care of thee, my dear one, thee, my
> daughter. *The Tempest*, I.ii.16–17

Shakespeare created two of his most memorable father-daughter pairs at the beginning and end of his career. The fifteen years that separate the probable date of *Romeo and Juliet* (1596) from that of *The Tempest* (1611) correspond roughly to the age of each young heroine. Juliet and Miranda have a great deal more than age in common: they are beautiful, intelligent, refined, and compassionate. Each is an only child, used to being the focus of parental indulgence and approval. They are portrayed at the moment of first love, and both unwittingly choose as the object of that love the only son of their father's bitterest enemy. Both prove fiercely loyal lovers.

Their fathers, too, have similarities. They are old: Capulet can no longer dance at his own parties, and Prospero anticipates, even in triumph, that "every third thought shall be [his] grave."* Both feel the burden not only of years but of worldly cares. Capulet is married to a "jealous hood"† (V.iv.13), and he has borne the deaths of all his other children — his "hopes." Prospero is a widower. Both are noblemen who have paid a bitter price for the luxury and privilege of their rank. Lord Capulet is beset by the violence of a civil feud in which he heads one of the rival families. Prospero, erstwhile Duke of Milan, has suffered betrayal and exile at his

---

*All quotations are from the Pelican edition, Northrop Frye, ed. (New York: Penguin Books, 1970).

†All quotations are from the Pelican edition, John E. Hankins, ed. (New York: Penguin Books, 1970).

once-loved brother's hands. Each man claims that the major goal of his life is to secure his daughter's happiness, in the form of marriage to a worthy suitor. But Juliet ends up a suicide, Miranda a radiant bride. Shakespeare implies that the crucial factor in each young woman's fate is her father's treatment.

On the surface, the lot of the usurped Duke seems harsher, and his daughter's chances for happiness more tenuous. He and Miranda are believed dead and, in fact, are confined to a remote island. He is his daughter's only companion, teacher, and role model. The Capulets, in contrast, hold a prominent place in the busy current of Veronan high society. Juliet has the potential benefit of four parent-figures— her nurse and her father confessor as well as her actual parents. But circumstances prove less fateful than character.

Why is Prospero so much more successful a father than Capulet? The Veronan lord is the consummate man of affairs, extroverted, pragmatic, used to issuing orders and getting prompt results. Like many successful men, he values above all the externals: rank, wealth, and decorum. He is proud of Juliet's spirit and wit, traits she has certainly not gotten from her rigid mother. But he is wary of emotion, particularly self-doubt, fear, and tenderness. Capulet covers up his discomfort with volatility — angry words or energetic actions. He rushes around issuing orders and doling out tasks because if he stops, he'll have to look inside both himself and his child. He also clings to a self-flatteringly authoritarian concept of the father/daughter bond: His role is to lavish on her every material comfort and to make all her major decisions; hers, to reflect well on the family — to look lovely and obey.

Capulet prides himself that in choosing Juliet's future husband, he is acting in her best interests, but he is blind to her point of view. Rash and imperious, he credits neither her objections to his favorite nor her wisdom about the nature of love. It does not occur to Capulet that parents can learn from their children. Complacent and pragmatic, he reflects the values of the community in which he wields power. It takes losing Juliet to make him see beyond ambition and reputation, to recognize her incalculable value as an individual. At the end of the play, that searing realization is reflected in his language. Capulet's typical tone is blunt and self-assured. Only when Juliet lies dead is he moved to introspection and to poetry.

Prospero is Capulet's diametrical opposite: intuitive, imaginative, iconoclastic. He has eschewed politics, Capulet's native element, at the cost of exile and, nearly, of death. But that experience has not made him alter his estimation of the wages of power. Instead, he has created a private commonwealth, become the "god of [the] island" to which he and Miranda were driven. He has raised his daughter alone, without either the family or the society that surround Capulet. Granted, Prospero is a magician who can call on the supernatural for aid. It is inconceivable to picture Capulet in a world that contains Ariel, or to imagine the old lord conjuring up the spirits of Iris and Ceres for his child's entertainment. But Prospero's powers are not absolute, and his resolution of Miranda's fate depends more on empathy and sacrifice than on force.

Prospero's years of struggle have made him more practical. He realizes that if his daughter is to mature and prosper — his name suggests his character note — she must return to the world she barely remembers. His suffering has taught him above all the unique value of this child. In the beginning of their exile, her love and optimism sustained him. Now he is determined to secure her happiness. Like Capulet, he has a fantasy concept of his daughter's future. The difference is that he wants to make sure that it is well founded and that she shares it. For Prospero, youth equals inexperience but not ignorance, especially of one's feelings. He guides but does not coerce his daughter, living by the precept that Capulet only mouths: if a match is to be happy, it must be made with the woman's free "consent." Prospero remains true to the assurance he gives Miranda at the play's outset: "I have done nothing but in care of thee, / Of thee, my dear one, thee my daughter" (I.ii.16–17). The personal pronoun echoes like an affirmation of Miranda's unique and treasured self.

Prospero has sometimes been accused of being manipulative and tyrannical in pursuit of Miranda's marriage. But such charges ignore both her acquiescence in his course and the cost to Prospero of attaining it. He must renounce his hard-won powers, forgive his most implacable enemies, and forgo his beloved daughter's company. Unlike Capulet, Prospero does not need anguished grief to be moved to poetry: it is his natural idiom. His dialogue, with its falling cadence and evocative imagery, contains some of the loveliest speeches in Shakespeare, including the monologue traditionally called the playwright's farewell to his art. In that parallel, and in his ability to create compelling illusion, Prospero is often seen as Shakespeare's self-portrait of the artist. He is also the Shakespearean father at his wisest and most benevolent.

Romeo and Juliet

One of the most painful scenes in Shakespeare is Lord Capulet's berating of Juliet. When I first read it, at Juliet's age, I felt only the scalding force of the father's rage — wave after wave of insults, threats, and curses.

Without understanding what some of his words meant, I was all too clear about their tone: he hated her, his only child, to the point of wishing her dead. And what had Juliet done to provoke this volcano? Said politely that, at fourteen, she was not yet ready to marry — an opinion that Capulet himself had expressed to her suitor, the County Paris, only two days earlier. I understood, too, the enormous gap between the reasons she was giving him and her actual predicament: secretly married to Romeo, the son of her family's great enemy, Juliet cannot obey her father's wishes without betraying the precepts of society and religion: bigamy is both a crime and a sin. Her private scruples are even more compelling. The timing of the confrontation is particularly cruel. Juliet has just consummated her marriage and bade her young husband a wrenching farewell. Romeo is making his way out of the Capulet orchard even as her parents enter her room. To so enamored a bride, the thought of admitting a second "husband" to her bed is repellent.

But Juliet never ventures to reveal her true situation to her father, and in that secrecy, too, my adolescent self identified with her. Who could expect such a tyrant to listen, much less sympathize? If Capulet is this furious at her request that he delay the marriage to Paris, what would he say to the news that she has made it impossible — and by marrying a Montague? Juliet is convinced that, to her father, she has done the unforgivable. I agreed with her completely: better to keep the secret, to remain true to Romeo and to her own integrity, even at the risk of death. At that point, I naively assumed that Shakespeare was Capulet, that the playwright was speaking through the enraged man. Only later did I realize that, of course, he was as much the daughter as the father, that he felt Juliet's hurt and fear and wrote the scene so that I would feel them, too.

The quarrel escalates to the point that Capulet issues Juliet a stark ultimatum: "An you be mine, I'll give you to my friend; / An you be not, hang, beg, starve, die in the streets" (III.v.193–94). This is the marriage mart, with the daughter as commodity. Either she agrees to be sold to the highest bidder or she loses all value. How have they come to this terrible impasse? What has happened to turn this child from the pride of her father's life to the object of his unmitigated fury?

From the beginning, Juliet, like Miranda, is identified in the cast list through her relationship to her father: she is "daughter to Capulet." But in feud-torn Verona, "Capulet" is not simply a family name: it is a prescribed set of loyalties, an implied code of behavior. As the Prologue tells us, it is the "continuance of their parents' rage" that will prove fatal to the lovers. In fact, the first time that we see Lord Capulet, he is calling for his sword and claiming that he must wield it to counter "old Montague," who, he charges, "flourishes his blade in spite of me" (I.i.75–76). Choler and impulsiveness are his character notes. But as he later admits to Paris, that show of force was largely bluster: Keeping the peace, he confides, is no great burden for "men so old" as he. Toward his daughter, Capulet's rage knows no such limits.

The Montagues, in contrast, never show anger towards Romeo; in fact, they scrupulously avoid intruding on his privacy, even when he is causing them pain. Lord Montague is concerned about Romeo's "black and portentous humor" (I.i.139) and has "importuned" him to reveal the source of his melancholy. His motive is not idle curiosity but compassion. He assures Benvolio: "We would as willingly give cure as know" (l. 153), and then leaves Romeo in peace to talk over his troubles with his friend. Whether because a son in this society is given more latitude or because they are naturally understanding, the Montagues grant Romeo trust and independence. Juliet's parents give her neither of these boons.

It is not that Capulet does not love Juliet: the play is his tragedy as well as hers. But he does not show that love in ways that benefit her. He is enormously proud of her grace and eloquence, but that very pride contains the seeds of her destruction, for it is largely the pride of ownership. Capulet himself would never put the case in such crass terms. He sees himself as the indulgent patriarch whose only concern is for his daughter's happiness. He plays that role when Paris first comes to pay court. Capulet refuses the eager suit by describing Juliet in tenderly protective terms: "My child is yet a stranger in this world," not yet "ripe to be a bride" (I.ii.8, 11). But almost at once he changes his mind, either because he does not want to put a damper on romance or because, as he later tells Juliet, this is too rich an offer to lose.

He feigns humility about Juliet's looks, advising the young count to compare her to the other ladies at the feast and "like her most whose merit most shall be" (l. 31). In fact, Capulet, cosmopolite and ladies' man, knows that Juliet is a striking beauty. The plot depends on the instantaneous passion she inspires in both Paris and Romeo. In spite of the father's qualms about her youth, he cannot resist showing her off and observing the young man's reactions. He gives Paris permission to "woo her," "get her heart." That done, he says, "My will to her consent is but a part" (ll. 16–17). The rhyme suggests his complacent belief in this liberal attitude — as long as he can designate the suitor. Having approved of Paris's qualifications, he is ready to grant the girl freedom to second his choice.

At the play's outset, Juliet is too naive to oppose such a plan. She is the "lamb" and "ladybird" (I.iii.3) of the Nurse's pet names, a girl eager to please the parents who have indulged her. When her mother introduces the idea of marriage to Paris, Juliet responds politely to what for her is merely a theoretical situation: "It is an honor that I dream not of" (l.66). Clearly, this is a subject that discomforts both mother and daughter. Lady Capulet was herself married very young — as she tells Juliet, she was only about fourteen when she bore *her*. Her husband is roughly twice her age. (At the ball he hosts, Capulet recalls dancing at a fete that occurred some thirty years before.) That early marriage "marred" (I.ii.13) his wife, he hints to Paris, and certainly Lady Capulet seems stiff and repressed. The necessity of discussing sex with her pubescent daughter brings on waves of embarrassment, and Lady Capulet takes refuge in a formal tone and euphemistic phrasing. Since Juliet has never met Paris, the Lady describes his "beauty" in a series of conventional metaphors. He is a "flower," a "fair volume" unbound and awaiting a wife to provide a "cover" for the "golden story" of their love (I.iii.85–92). It takes the earthy Nurse, whom the awkward mother has invited to join the tête-à-tête, to undercut the pretty image with ribald candor. She reminds us — and Juliet — what conjugal love really entails: "happy nights" and, for the woman, "growing bigger" with child (ll. 105, 95). Perhaps the discrepancy in the Capulets' ages accounts for the tension in their marriage, the resentful subjugation of wife to husband, and for the coldness of the mother toward her only child. Their experience of the harmful effects of premature marriage does not, however, dissuade either parent from urging Juliet's subjection to that fate.

Juliet is embarrassed, too, by both her mother's awkwardness and the delicacy of the subject. But she sees no objection to the plan and gives the Good Girl's answer that her mother is waiting to hear: She will "look to like," as her mother bids, but make no deeper commitment than "your consent" permits (I.iii.97–99). The "your" is plural: Juliet realizes that Lady Capulet is acting as her husband's emissary.

Falling in love with Romeo dashes the scales from Juliet's eyes and galvanizes her will. It makes her see beyond the petty enmity wrought by the feud. After she discovers the devastating fact that her new love is "Romeo, and a Montague," she wills him fancifully: "Deny thy father and refuse thy name" (II.ii.34). Unaware that he is eavesdropping on her "counsel," she maintains: "Thou art thyself, though not a Montague." She, in turn, offers to shed her old identity: "be but sworn my love, / And I'll no longer be a Capulet." Juliet also comes to understand the generosity essential to love, romantic and familial:

> My bounty is as boundless as the sea,
> My love as deep; the more I give to thee,
> The more I have [ll. 133–35].

The aim should be to give everything that will enhance the beloved's well being. The giving is its own reward. Juliet's father, for all his years and experience, is oblivious to those precepts.

Meanwhile, Capulet is pursuing his own scheme for Juliet's future. When Tybalt is killed, instead of delaying the marriage, the old Lord decides to hasten it. A practical man, he is not deeply grieved by his nephew's death: "Well, we were born to die" (III.ii.4), he says with facile stoicism. He is annoyed by the inconvenient timing, but agrees at first that Juliet must be granted one night, at least, to mourn her cousin. As Paris begins to take a respectful departure, however, Capulet suddenly disrupts the decorous arrangement. While before he argued with the ardent suitor that Juliet should be allowed two more years to mature, now he rashly accepts the proposal. He admits that he is making "a desperate tender / Of [his] child's love." But he adds immediately: "I think she will be ruled / In all respects by me; nay more, I doubt it not." The tentative claim has become a strident assertion. Lady Capulet's silence suggests that she is used to bending to her husband's will.

In Capulet's mind, County Paris has all the qualifications—rank, wealth, and appearance:

> A gentleman of noble parentage,
> Of fair demesnes, youthful, and nobly trained,
> Stuffed, as they say, with honorable parts... [ll. 181–83].

This suitor is a great bargain, a unique "tender" of "fortune" that Juliet — or rather Capulet — cannot refuse. Ironically, this description would fit Romeo as well as Paris, with the added advantage that the alliance could be the means of ending the pernicious feud. That, in fact, is Friar Laurence's avowed purpose for agreeing to perform the secret rite. Could Capulet heed his daughter's pleas, universal happiness would be the likely outcome.

Capulet has an inkling that Juliet will not welcome these hugger-mugger arrangements. The sign is that he goes into his Lord of the Manor mode, sending his wife on ahead to announce the decision, issued in a series of imperatives: "go you," "bid her," "a Thursday tell her / She shall be married to this noble earl" (III.iv.15–21). Lady Capulet recites to her daughter the official line: Juliet's "careful" father has arranged for her "a sudden day of joy" (III.v.108–09). Once Juliet has cut through the sugar coating and discovered the bitter facts, she protests vehemently to the haste of the match and asserts that she feels no attraction for the suitor she has met only once. Better be wed to Romeo, she tells her mother in a bold double entendre, "whom you know I hate." But Juliet's purported freedom of choice, so lately touted by each of her parents, is now only a memory.

When she asks Lady Capulet to tell her "lord and father" that she does not wish to marry "yet," the mother washes her hands of the matter: "Tell him so yourself / And see how he will take it at your hands" (ll. 125–26). The sarcastic tone suggests that she has experienced before her husband's reaction to opposition.

Juliet tries in every way she can to tell her father — without telling him why — this marriage is repellent to her. Capulet notices that she is crying copiously, but he merely tries to tease her out of her sorrow. He has convinced himself that a little wedding cheer is just the thing to ease Juliet's grief, supposedly for Tybalt. When his witticisms fail, he returns to the purpose of the family conclave and demands: "How now, wife? / Have you delivered our decree?" (III.v.138–39). As his choice of words underlines, this is a command issued from on high. For response, he expects not only acquiescence but "thanks."

Juliet is well aware of his expectations, and she tries to balance candor about her true feelings with sensitivity to his wounded pride. When, at last, she refuses outright, he explodes. From his point of view, he has done everything possible to fulfill his paternal duty: all his "care," he claims melodramatically, "hath been to have her matched" (ll. 179–80). Not, it should be noted, married to one she loves but "matched" with a prestigious mate. In his frustration, Capulet loses all sense of proportion. He calls this supposedly beloved child a "wretched puling fool," "a whining mammet." He mocks her voice and her objections: "'I'll not wed, I cannot love; / I am too young, I pray you pardon me'" (III.v.187–88). The girl's pallor, caused by her sleepless wedding night and the shock of this crisis, evokes not pity but scorn: "you tallow-face!" "you green-sickness carrion!" he shouts. Even Lady Capulet is taken aback: "Fie, fie! Are you mad?" she protests. He admits, with an oath, the truth of her charge, though he lays the blame for his outburst on Juliet's refusal: "God's bread! it makes me mad" (III.v.177). He utters the terrible wish that "God" had never "lent" them "this only child," an ominous curse that echoes his wife's "I would the fool were married to her grave!" (l. 141).

As his tantrum comes to a climax, Capulet puts his claim of ownership in the harshest terms: Juliet is either "his" to "give to [his] friend" or her own to "hang, beg, starve, die in the streets" (ll. 193–94). The hyperbolic verbs suggest how out of control he is: each one stabs. Some might argue that Capulet is no different from other fathers in Shakespeare's day: that he had not only the power but the duty to arrange his daughter's marriage. But the play does not support that reading. It criticizes the cruel manner in which he imposes his will, in the shocked protests of both Lady Capulet and the Nurse. More important, it shows the dire results of his treatment in Juliet's suicide. Shakespeare is no advocate for Capulet's embodiment of the pater familias.

In fairness, it must be conceded that Capulet has no idea of Juliet's real motives for refusing Paris's offer. She never confides in her parents, and he has no such magical device as Prospero's cloak for eavesdropping on her courtship. But neither does he have the magician's empathy. It is clear why Juliet feels driven back on her own small resources. When she tries to "beseech ... on [her] knees" his "patience" to let her "speak but a word" (III.v.160–61), he silences her with a threat: "Speak not, reply not, do not answer me! My fingers itch." Some stagings of the scene have shown Capulet in fact striking his daughter. But such physical violence under-cuts the emotional pain he is inflicting. A slap, frank and direct, might have been easier for her to bear than the scalding torrent of blame and abuse. Capulet's final pronouncement reveals the real basis for his rage: "I'll not be forsworn." He has given Paris his word as a gentleman. Maintaining his reputation as generous host and undisputed head of his clan means more to him than succoring his only child.

Juliet, as the Chorus implies, has few "means" (II.Cho., 11) for break-ing out of the strict course that her father has set her. She is either at home or at church, and she is subject to his rule. But she keeps striving for some control. After Capulet has stalked off, she turns to the parent who might still intercede in her behalf: "O sweet my mother, cast me not away!" It is the most intimate and piteous tone that Juliet has used toward her. She asks her only to "delay this marriage," and she concludes with a veiled threat of suicide: if she is forced, her "bridal bed" will be in Tybalt's "mon-ument." But Lady Capulet is either too status-conscious or too afraid of her husband's temper to heed her: "Do as thou wilt, for I have done with thee," she says, and leaves the chamber. In her hour of greatest need, Juliet meets total rejection from both her parents.

When the Nurse, too, abandons her, Juliet is left in despair. Her last recourse is the Friar who performed the marriage ceremony. Before going to him, she makes a desperate vow: "If all else fail, myself have power to die." She has come to see suicide as her last means of asserting her will and remaining "a stainless wife" to Romeo. Rather than condemn this sui-cide wish as the ultimate sin, in accord with his vocation, the Friar com-mends her "strength of will" (IV.i.72). He proposes a course nearly as escapist and adolescent as Juliet's: that she take a potion that simulates death, awaken in the family vault, and run away with Romeo. He warns that the scheme requires enormous "valor" and that no "womanish fear" must deter her (ll. 119–20). Never does Friar Laurence consider going to her parents with the truth and making a plea for this compelling reason to end the feud. Perhaps he, like Juliet, fears Lord Capulet's probable fury, a qualm that is justified by the outburst that we have just witnessed.

Juliet's desperation makes her welcome the feigned death that Friar Laurence proposes. With a brief, fervent prayer, "Love give me strength," she accepts the vial he offers. Her last words to him are affectionate and grateful: "Farewell, dear father." Imbibing the soporific acts as a kind of rehearsal for her actual suicide and makes it easier for Juliet to carry out her fatal resolve. Unlike Romeo, who at least sends his father a final letter, she has no words of farewell for her actual father. Could Juliet have awakened as her parents discover her supposed corpse, she would no doubt have been amazed at the intensity of their grief.

Capulet, for his part, does not take his rejection of Juliet seriously, as Shakespeare signals when he shifts the action to the father's point of view. In spite of the quarrel's rancor, the old lord has gone on happily planning the wedding. The news that Juliet has gone to Laurence's cell, supposedly to confess her wrongs, makes him jubilant. "He may chance to do her good," Capulet says condescendingly, and describes Juliet in tones of grumbling affection: "A peevish self-willed harlotry it is" (IV.ii.14). His mood becomes positively buoyant when she returns "with merry look." His words to her are fond and teasing: "How now, my headstrong? Where have you been gadding?" On one level, he is proud of her show of temper, seeing in it a reflection of his own strong will. Juliet has learned the futility of revealing her true feelings. Instead, she assumes the persona of the Penitent Child, supposedly advocated by Friar Laurence. In her eagerness to try the Friar's dire remedy, she overplays the role. She will "fall prostrate," she says, and "beg [her father's] pardon." And she adds the cunning lie: "Henceforward, I am ever ruled by you" (ll. 20–22). Capulet is entirely fooled: "This is well.... This is as't should be" (ll. 28–29). He congratulates himself on his success as moral authority: "My heart is wondrous light, / Since this same wayward girl is so reclaimed" (ll. 46–47). In his delight, he moves the wedding a fatal day forward, careless of the sleepless night and hasty preparations that the change entails.

Why does Juliet die? In a nutshell, because her father's own concept of her future makes him oblivious to hers. Seen from Capulet's perspective, his plan is not only reasonable but generous. He has found an ideal suitor for her, accepted the young man's proposal, and arranged a gala celebration in the couple's honor. When the girl unexpectedly refuses, claiming to be too young and too shocked by her cousin's death, he dismisses those pleas as callow. When Juliet persists, he throws the sort of tantrum that has always before allowed him to prevail. We have seen a minor instance of Capulet's temper in his squelching of Tybalt's own tantrum at the feast: "Am I the master here or you?" the old lord demanded. Owner-ship is authority. The girl is naturally shocked by the suddenness of the match, he reasons, so she cries and whines, but he refrains from striking her and waits for her to see her duty. Juliet returns from confession appar-ently persuaded that he is right. Capulet, elated, is convinced both that father knows best and that he has won, for himself and for her.

Juliet's sudden "death" knocks flat the whole self-flattering facade. Lord Capulet's reaction is more complex than his wife's and the Nurse's hysteria. Stunned, he begins not by lamenting the fact of Juliet's death but by describing its effect on her body in terms of almost scientific objectiv-ity: "she's cold! / Her blood is settled, and her joints are stiff" (IV.v.25–26). Then, as the truth sinks in, Capulet goes through several stages of shock and grief. Juliet's beauty and youth come suddenly clear to him with a poignancy he never felt when he considered those qualities his to display. He is moved to mournful simile: "Death lies on her like an untimely frost / Upon the sweetest flower of all the field" (ll. 28–29).

For a few moments, he is too overcome to speak further: "Death … ties up [his] tongue" (IV.v.31–32). With the entrance of Paris and the Friar, his poetic sentiments take a grotesque turn. Death becomes personified as his "son-in-law" and "heir," "deflowerer" of Juliet, "Flower as she was." Abruptly, Capulet realizes that his loss is final and absolute: "I will die / And leave him all. Life, living, all is Death's" (ll. 39–40). He becomes more overwrought, first tenderly addressing the dead girl and then arriving at a more intimate understanding of the tragedy:

> O child, o child! my soul, and not my child!
> Dead art thou — alack my child is dead,
> And with my child my joys are buried [ll. 62–64].

He has come finally to a realization so simple that he has never before acknowledged it: Juliet was uniquely precious, his only child, the person whose "soul" most resembled his own. With her have died any possibil-ity of future encounters, any hope of replicating her features in a grand-child, any foreseeable happiness.

Capulet is moved not only to a full sense of his loss but, at last, to empathy for his daughter's anguish. The other mourners describe only the effects of the death on them, but he seems in addition to sense what Juliet suffered in her final hours, when she was "Despised, distressed, hated, martyred, killed." At the end, Paris still believes that Juliet died of "grief" over Tybalt's loss (V.iii.50–51). Only when she is actually dead will the Friar reveal the "true ground of all these piteous woes" (l. 180)— that Lord Capulet "would have married her perforce" (l. 238).

Juliet is not faultless. She marries without her parents' consent and then keeps the act a secret. She never confides in them the real explanation for her angst and so gives them no chance to react, either to manifest their opposition or to overcome it. On the other hand, every approach that she makes to such confiding, every plea for understanding, meets with rejection. Admittedly, this is art, not life: the pace and circumstances of the lovers' crisis are more extreme than they would likely be in actuality. Still, in stylized form, the ways that feelings lead to actions ring true. People in general and adolescents in particular often only hint at their deepest hopes and fears. Those who care about them must listen for what they mean as well as what they say. Denial and coercion breed deception: Capulet drives Juliet to show him the image of herself that he has demanded to see. He discovers her actual plight — and her worth — only when it is too late.

Capulet understands the effect of the feud in causing the scourge on the families. He tells Montague that the lovers are "poor sacrifices of our enmity" (l. 304). As in *The Tempest*, the old enemies are reconciled by their children's love, though by partaking not in "wedding cheer" but "sad burial feast" (IV.v.87). The bereaved fathers take refuge in the only consolation they can conceive: providing "statue[s] in pure gold" of their dead children. Capulet is oblivious to the irony that Juliet's "rate" is once again being expressed in material terms. How fully does he realize that even the "ancient grudge" would not have killed his daughter if he had listened with "patient ears" (first Chorus) to her soul's voice?

The Tempest

The Tempest is Miranda's coming of age ritual. It begins with the revelation of her true identity and ends with her betrothal. Every stage in this initiation process is overseen by her magician-father. Prospero is one of the earliest examples in literature of father as single parent. He protects Miranda, both from knowledge that would make her unhappy and from physical and emotional danger. He lavishes affection on her, never hesitating to say how and why he prizes her. At the same time, he respects her individuality. He has acted as Miranda's "schoolmaster," setting high standards and training her mind. Like a good teacher, he encourages her to express herself and to make her own choices, even to the extent of countermanding his orders about how she should behave. Although Prospero has pressing reasons for wishing her match with Ferdinand, the young prince whom his magic brings to the island — it is Miranda's and Prospero's one chance for future security — he will not force her to acquiesce. In fact, he does everything possible both to gauge her feelings and to test the young man's worth before giving his own consent. In this, he is strikingly different from Capulet who, in spite of Juliet's abundance of potential suitors, is grimly insistent on Paris. Finally, Prospero frees Miranda to leave the sanctuary he created for her and to enter the larger world.

A daughter raised in such hermetic circumstances could be helpless or rebellious — incapable of asserting herself, resentful of her father's authority. Instead, Miranda is self-assured, resourceful, and kind. She reciprocates Prospero's love and respect, but she does not feel constrained to limit her circle of affection to him. Despite her isolated childhood, she is quick and prescient in judging others, and she recognizes in Ferdinand her soulmate. Miranda shows the confidence of a child who can love and trust others because she has been loved and trusted herself.

For Prospero the quest for Miranda's happiness is fraught with difficulties. The young suitor he has provided could prove unworthy — Prospero has never met him, and, as the son of his enemy, he does not have a promising heritage. Even should Ferdinand fulfill Prospero's hopes, the magician must face an arduous confrontation with the men who betrayed him. If his plan succeeds, the price he must pay is the loss of his powers and a lonely old age. He must return to governing Milan, while Miranda will join her new husband in ruling the Kingdom of Naples. Yet for the sake of his daughter's well-being, Prospero is willing to sacrifice the chief consolation of his life, his delight in her company. The emotional motor of *The Tempest* is the bittersweet satisfaction parents feel when they let their children go.

As the play opens, Prospero senses that the moment has come for Miranda's emergence into womanhood. The rousing action of the storm is followed by a long tête-à-tête in which he recounts her past and hints at her future. Prospero knows that this is the turning point in Miranda's self-awareness: "naught knowing" (I.i.18) of his origins, she is "ignorant" of what she is. The child's status is derivative, dependent on the parent's titles and goods, which she stands to inherit. Always before, he has deflected her questions about her past. Now, he tells her, "'Tis time / I should inform thee further" (ll. 22–23).

Miranda, who was only three when they arrived on the island, has little memory of her early years. He begins with the most shocking fact:

> Twelve year since, Miranda, twelve year since,
> Thy father was the Duke of Milan and
> A prince of power [ll. 53–55].

The echoed words and the falling cadence resonate with *The Tempest*'s peculiar elegiac music. Prospero was subjected to exile by the perfidy of his younger brother Antonio, whom, he tells Miranda bitterly, "next thyself / Of all the world I loved" (I.ii.68–69). Prospero recognizes his own fault in "neglecting worldly ends" and giving Antonio "the manage of [his] state" while he himself was "rapt in secret studies" (l. 77). Antonio eventually joined in league with Alonso, the King of Naples, "an enemy ... inveterate" to Prospero. With Alonso's aid, Antonio drove the "right duke of Milan" out to sea in a "rotten" bark, its only passengers, he tells the girl, "me and thy crying self" (ll. 128–48).

Miranda wonders, wisely, if it was "foul play" or a "blessed event" that brought them to the island, and he responds, "Both, both, my girl!" (ll. 60–61). Their rescue came about not only by "providence divine" but human "charity" (ll. 159, 162)—that of the faithful old councilor Gonzalo. He furnished them with clothes and the "volumes" on magical lore which, Prospero asserts, "I prize above my dukedom" (l. 168). During the hard voyage, the child seemed to her father "a cherubim ... that did preserve [him]." His care for her and "a fortitude from heaven" gave him the will to endure.

Now it is Prospero who must play the role of divine protector for Miranda. The "god" of his island-kingdom, he presides over spirits evil and benevolent, directs the forces of nature, and influences the acts of mortals. But he is not omnipotent. Prospero can precipitate certain events, but he cannot guarantee their outcome; he must act swiftly, be ever vigilant, and hope for the best. He depends on Ariel, his "tricksy spirit" (I.ii.226), to carry out his plans. He must be on guard against Ariel's weariness with his duties and stanch his eagerness to be set free, in accord with Prospero's promise. The time for fulfilling that vow is almost upon them: as the play opens, it is within "two days" (I.ii.299). "Bountiful Fortune" (I.ii.178) has brought Prospero's enemies near; the tempest that he devised and Ariel wrought have driven them to the island. Now the dreamy scholar, the man who preferred his books to his dukedom, must act quickly and decisively. As he reveals to Miranda, both intuition and astrology, "prescience" and "a most auspicious star," assert that this is his one chance to right his life's wrongs (ll. 180–84).

What he does not tell the girl is that her fortunes, too, depend on his vigilance and agility. Should he fail, she would be left with an aging, Ariel-bereft father, in danger of some day facing the monster Caliban alone. A mark of Prospero's compassion is that he only hints at this dire future; he spares Miranda the anguish that full knowledge would entail. Like the sleep he casts over her while he and Ariel plot, the aim of his love is to protect and sustain. He strives not to bind his daughter to him but to free her, as he will his airy "son." But in Miranda's case he intends to make certain first that, vulnerable as she is, she is going to other loving arms and a safe haven.

It is clear that Miranda has inherited more than Prospero's rank. From him and, possibly, her late mother, "a piece of virtue" (I.ii.56), she has learned kindness and trust, and she treats her father with the love that he has shown her. She is a sympathetic listener to his story of betrayal, desperation, and rescue. "Your tale, sir, would cure deafness" (I.ii.106), she tells him, and sighs "Alack, for pity!" She senses the supernatural quality of his power: her first question is whether his "art" (I.ii.1) has created the tempest. She is sure, too, of his benevolence: her term of address is "dearest father." Miranda's concern is not her own safety but the fate of the "brave vessel" she has seen "dashed all to pieces" (l. 8). She exclaims: "O, I have suffered / With those that I saw suffer!" Prospero hastens to comfort her: "Tell your piteous heart / There's no harm done," "No harm" (ll. 14–15), he repeats soothingly. He assures her that he has "so safely ordered" things that all on the ship are protected. Thus, the play's main values— compassion, resourcefulness, loyalty—are all introduced by the end of Prospero's account, and father and daughter share them.

This ideal mentorship has not come easily. Prospero's previous efforts at nurture, first of his younger brother Antonio and then of the creature Caliban, have been bitter failures. As a brother, he was not, he admits, merely negligent but also naive. His "trust, / Like a good parent," "awoke" in Antonio "an evil nature" (ll. 93–94). The choice of metaphor is telling: Prospero feels a paternal sense of betrayal. But he did not, of course, raise Antonio, and he has taken great care with his actual child.

The chief threat to her well-being has come from the other object of Prospero's nurture, the "hag-born" (I.ii.283) monster, Caliban. Offspring of the witch Sycorax, he is a native of the island. Prospero virtually adopted the forlorn creature after the witch's death, treated him "with humane care" and "lodged" him in his "own cell" (ll. 346–47). But, he discovered to his fury, no "kindness" could alter the character of such a brute. The proof? When Miranda was only twelve, Caliban "did seek to violate [her] honor." The creature admits gleefully to this charge, boasting that if Prospero had not intervened, he "had peopled else / This isle with Calibans" (ll. 350–51).

For Prospero, the rape of a child is an unforgivable crime. He ceases all kindness to Caliban, makes him his "slave," and controls him with pinches, "cramps," "side-stitches," and threats of more such pains. The brute, unrepentant but wary of the magician's power, obeys and waits his chance for revenge. There has been a tendency lately to romanticize Caliban as a noble savage and to see the magician's habitation of the island as a metaphor for imperialism and his subjection of Caliban as tyranny over the native population. But such an interpretation ignores Caliban's malice and lack of remorse. In the play, the would-be child molester is literally a monster, his savagery softened by buffoonery but not, until he repents at the end, by sympathy. Shakespeare is on Prospero's side.

Caliban is easily cowed and Prospero despises him. Why then is the magician so disturbed at the creature's plot to overthrow him? In the midst of blessing Miranda's and Ferdinand's union, Prospero suddenly recalls Caliban's "foul conspiracy." He is "touched with anger so distempered" (IV.i.145) that he cuts short a magical dance he had commanded in the couple's honor. He is moved to make his great speech about the transience of earthly "revels," and then tells the lovers that he must walk "to still [his] beating mind." Ariel appears shortly afterward and assures him that the three plotters—Caliban, the drunken butler Stephano, and the clown Trinculo—have been led in "calf-like" subjection into a "filthy mantled pool" (l. 182): a fittingly comic fall for such incompetent villains. But Prospero remains grimly disillusioned by Caliban's latest betrayal, and denounces him as

> A devil, a born devil, on whose nature
> Nurture can never stick; on whom my pains,
> Humanely taken, all, all lost, quite lost! [ll. 188–90].

Prospero never shows such rage toward his more dangerous enemies. Nor is this, like Capulet's, a tantrum but a fixed rancor. Perhaps it conceals his fear, either that the daughter whose "nurture" he has overseen so lovingly might prove likewise false or, more probably, that, should his plan fail, she could be left at the mercy of this "devil."

The spirit Ariel, whom Prospero freed from a wicked spell, is his good stepson to Caliban's bad. In some ways, magician and servant are like two aspects—thought and action—of the same being. But Ariel is also a separate creature. Only Prospero can see and speak to him in his numinous form. Although he can delegate tasks of creating illusion and exerting control, he must constantly determine by anxious questioning if Ariel has carried them out: "Hast thou, spirit / Performed to point the tempest that I bade thee?" (I.ii.193–94). "But are they, Ariel, safe?" (l. 217). Prospero lavishes affection on him, calling him "my dainty Ariel" (V.i.95) and "chick" (l. 316). He responds to Ariel's child-like question about whether he loves him with the fond affirmative "dearly" (IV.i.49). But Ariel is not of his master's element and their natures cannot mix forever.

In his "prescience," Prospero has known all along that the foundering ship contains not only his enemies but his likely future son-in-law. They have never met. But, although Ferdinand is the son of Antonio's co-conspirator, the King of Naples, it is clear from his first appearance that he is worthy of Prospero's hopes. While the rest of the passengers and crew react to the tempest with curses and despair, the King and Prince of Naples are "at prayers" (I.i.50). After the ship splits asunder, Ariel lands Ferdinand alone, as Prospero instructs. Thinking the others drowned, the young man gives way to grief, sitting with "his arms in [a] sad knot" (I.ii.222–24) and "weeping again the King [his] father's wrack" (l. 437). Ferdinand is the good son of a bad father. That point should be qualified: the King, although a corrupt ruler, is a loving parent. As his despair over Ferdinand's supposed drowning shows, the affection between father and son is deep and mutual.

Ferdinand also proves a Romeo-like ideal lover, bold, ardent, and strikingly handsome — "a goodly person," in Prospero's measured description to Miranda, though "something stained with grief (that's beauty's canker)" (ll. 415–16). Miranda, who has seen no other man but her father, expresses no qualms about the young man's looks: "I might call him a thing divine, for nothing natural / I ever saw so noble." Though Ferdinand has known a number of other noblewomen, he is no less hyperbolic about Miranda's beauty. He thinks her "a goddess," and, before he discovers that she can speak his language, marvels: "O you wonder!" Prospero, watching this meeting, sees this mutual attraction as confirmation of his plan's rightness. He confides to Ariel in asides: "It goes on, I see, as my soul prompts it" (ll. 420–21). From the first, then, Prospero sees Ferdinand not as his rival but as his successor in Miranda's affections. He does not want to monopolize his daughter but to share her. As he later muses in soliloquy, he thinks of her as "his and mine loved darling" (III.iii.93).

Although his behavior may seem voyeuristic, Prospero is not observing the lovers for prurient ends. Miranda is utterly innocent and Ferdinand a still unproven entity. Prospero wants to be sure of the young man's mettle before he leaves his "loved darling" in his charge. All his magic would be mockery if the object of it were corrupt or weak. He puts Ferdinand to a number of tests, both to slow the hot pace of the courtship, "lest too light winning make the prize too light" (I.ii.452–53), and to gauge Ferdinand's worth. He accuses the prince of being a "spy" and a "traitor" (ll. 456, 461) who has come to usurp the island kingdom. When Ferdinand protests, Prospero devises cruel punishments: manacles, and a diet of sea water, mussels, and acorn husks— Prodigal Son fare. Ferdinand bravely draws his sword to defend himself but is "charmed from moving."

Such mistreatment spurs Miranda to action. Dismayed by Ferdinand's arrest, she "hang[s] on [her father's] garments" and cries, "Sir, have pity. / I'll be his surety." She is convinced of his goodness by his beauty: "so fair a house," she argues, could not contain an "ill spirit" (l. 459). In this idyllic world, Ferdinand proves worthy of Miranda's intuitive trust. Although he chafes at Prospero's harshness in sentencing him to menial labor, he gallantly refuses both her urging to disobey her father's orders and her offer of working in his stead. He lavishes praise on her, calling her "perfect" and "peerless," and begs to know her name, that he might include it in his prayers. When she reveals it, he relishes playing on its derivation: "Admired Miranda ... the top of admiration" (ll. 37–38).

Ferdinand's trials are also a test of Miranda's bond with her father. To her plea for her lover's release, Prospero barks: "What, I say, my foot my tutor?" (I.ii.469–70). When she continues to protest, he warns, "One word more / Shall make me chide thee, if not hate thee" (ll. 476–77). This is the only time in the play that Prospero expresses an unkind feeling toward his daughter. Although his anger is mild compared to Capulet's toward Juliet or his own toward Caliban, it could be disturbing. But Miranda seems to sense that it is feigned, or at least transient. Secure in a lifetime of devotion, she is unperturbed by his harsh words. As Ferdinand is led off to begin his sentence, she lingers to assure him:

> My father's of a better nature, sir,
> Than he appears by speech. This is unwonted
> Which now came from him [ll. 496–99].

Miranda is also undeterred by Prospero's "hests" about her behavior. He has told her *not* to reveal her name and not to "prattle" to Ferdinand of her love. He evidently wants her actions to be governed by "modesty" and her charms to retain an air of mystery. But Miranda ignores these directives. Juliet-like, she asks Ferdinand candidly: "Do you love me?" He responds ardently: "I / Beyond all limit of what else i' th'world / Do love, prize, honor you" (III.i.71–73). The declaration moves her to "weep" with happiness. Like Juliet, in spite or perhaps because of being a novice, she banishes "bashful cunning" and herself proposes marriage. She goes a step further and offers to "die [Ferdinand's] maid" if he refuses her and, in the meantime, to be his "servant." Miranda is taking a great chance on rejection, humiliation, even danger. But her instincts are sound. Though more idealistic than the father who has sheltered her from the world's wiles, she has his perspicacity.

Miranda has been right to feel no fear of Prospero's wrath. Unlike

Juliet, she has no soliloquies— no secrets from her father. One reason is that she is a simpler character, a sketch to Juliet's fully rounded young woman. But on the level of psychological realism, Miranda is so open because she is so secure. There is no need for guile with a father who senses her needs and puts her happiness before his own. In the idyllic world of *The Tempest*, the daughter's desired match is not only sanctioned but orchestrated by her father.

Prospero, who has entered "unseen," has been watching the proposal. But he is careful not to disturb the tête-à-tête: he arranges its circumstances, but he leaves the outcome to the lovers. Not only is he unperturbed by Miranda's disobedience, he expresses the utmost pleasure in this "Fair encounter / Of two most rare affections." He prays that the "grace" of the "heavens" will bless "that which breeds between 'em," (ll. 74–76), an allusion not only to their love but to the offspring that he hopes it will bring, the traditional fruits of a happy union.

Prospero later conveys his paternal blessing directly. He explains to Ferdinand that the "vexations" he has been made to suffer have been "but trials of thy love." Then he praises the suitor for having "strangely stood the test." His "compensation" is marriage to one who, her father boasts, "will outstrip all praise / And make it halt behind" (IV.i.10–11). Unlike Capulet, he does not hesitate to praise Miranda to her face and before her suitor. A last condition remains: the young man must not "break her virgin knot" before the wedding, on penalty of incurring a marriage marred by "barren hate, / Sour-eyed disdain, and discord" (ll. 19–20). Prospero is teaching him that care of Miranda is a sacred trust. Ferdinand is a willing disciple. He promises to eschew "lust" as he "hope[s] / For quiet days, fair issue, and long life" (ll. 23–24).

It takes more than words, however, to reinforce the lesson of chastity. When the magician goes off, the lovers quickly give way to "dalliance." Prospero returns and reproaches Ferdinand, warning him in Polonius-like terms against temptation: "the strongest oaths are straw / To the fire in the blood. Be more abstemious, / Or else good night your vow!" (ll. 51–54). He then creates a show of pagan goddesses. The avowed purpose is to entertain the betrothed couple. But the spectacle also serves as a reminder not only of Prospero's values but his powers: this is *not* a father-in-law whom Ferdinand would want to risk offending.

The theme of the show is stated by Iris, goddess of the rainbow: "A contract of true love to celebrate" (IV.i.84). Chastity is an important element of this concept: Venus and Cupid have been excluded, so that no "wanton claim" can entice the lovers into performing a "bed-right" before the wedding. Prospero will take no chance that Miranda be seduced and abandoned. As reward for abstinence, all the worldly blessings are promised the couple — in the words of Juno, queen of the gods: "Honor, riches, marriage blessing / Long continuance, and increasing" (ll. 106–07). As Prospero admits, he has summoned the spirits "to enact / [his] present fancies" (ll. 121–22): a fond father's fondest wishes. Ferdinand responds with awe and gratitude:

> So rare a wond'red father and a wise
> Makes this place a Paradise [ll. 123–24].

Gone is his previous resentment, his conviction that Prospero is "all harshness." Father and fiancé have become allies.

But Prospero knows too well that the couple cannot stay in this Eden. These are earthly blessings he is conferring, and for the lovers to receive them, he must engineer their return to the larger world. The conditions of that return are the defeat of his old enemies and the rescue of Ferdinand's father, King Alonso. The news of Caliban's "foul conspiracy" (IV.i.139) recalls Prospero to his duty and his pain. "My old brain is troubled," he confesses to the young people.

Prospero is right to be anxious. The two younger brothers, Antonio and Sebastian, are particularly corrupt: envious, cynical, murderous. When their fellow conspirator Alonso weakens, they turn against him. Deeply depressed by the supposed drowning of Ferdinand, he would be an easy prey to their assassination plot without Prospero's protection. His prayer before sinking into a heavy sleep — "Give us kind keepers, heavens!" — is heard by Ariel and granted by the man whose dukedom Alonso helped usurp.

Prospero knows the evildoers' hearts and is tempted to destroy them. In a subtle twist, he must be urged to empathy by Ariel, who imagines that his own "affections would become tender" if he were "human" (V.i.17–20). But it is Prospero's care for Miranda that chiefly restrains his fury. He chooses not the revenge that he would be justified in seeking but forgiveness and generosity. In return, he vows to ask only the villains' "penitence" (ll. 26–28). But when he confronts Antonio and Sebastian face to face, he admits that even that condition will go unfulfilled. His own brother is the worst of the lot. Grimly, Prospero says, "I do forgive thee, / Unnatural though thou art" (ll. 78–79). Antonio remains unmoved by this mercy. Except for a wisecrack about Caliban's marketability as a "plain fish," he says nothing during this trial. Ruthless and vindictive, he and his moral twin Sebastian represent the continuing presence of evil in the world. If *The Tempest* were a tragedy, their malice would predominate. In the romance, they are reduced to Iago-like spectators at the idyllic celebration.

In contrast, Alonso, Prospero's future in-law and Ferdinand's father, does undergo a change of heart. He admits his old "trespass" against Prospero, and blames that sin for Ferdinand's supposed death. When Prospero suddenly reappears in his ducal robes, Alonso repents spontaneously: "Thy dukedom I resign and do entreat / Thou pardon me my wrongs" (V.i.118–19). Prospero is not soft in his compassion. He "require[s]" that Antonio formally "restore" the title that Alonso has offered, and he torments the king a while longer with Ferdinand's loss. He will not, however, let his fellow ruler give way to remorse: "be cheerful," he counsels, "And think of each thing well" (ll. 250–51).

The main cheering element is the restoration of Ferdinand, and not Ferdinand alone but as half of a loving couple. Like his son, Alonso first mistakes Miranda for "a goddess," and he readily assents to the match. The prince asserts that she is his "by immortal providence"—whose agent we have seen is Prospero—and describes the magician affectionately as a "second father" (V.i.195). Even Caliban shares in the general reformation. A grotesque shadow of his master, he had been devising a twisted plan for Miranda's future: to match her with the sottish Stephano, the man he would have overthrow Prospero and rule the island. When Caliban sees the butler's greed and incompetence, he repents: "I'll be wise hereafter, and seek for grace" (V.i.295–96). It is a sentiment worthy at last of Prospero's nurture.

Miranda is enchanted by the "beauty" of the noble visitors from the "brave new world." Her father's response is wry: "'Tis new to thee" (V.i.184). Yet he is careful not to spoil the mood of celebration. He keeps silent about his inside knowledge of the evildoers, and he alludes only in a brief aside to the toll that parting from Miranda will take. For all his advice to Alonso about remaining cheerful, Prospero's own mood at the end of the "revels" he has devised is bleak. His one remaining wish is "to see the nuptial / Of these our dear-beloved solemnized" in Naples. Afterwards, he will "retire me to my Milan, where / Every third thought shall be my grave" (ll. 310–11). This line recalls his earlier description of Miranda to Ferdinand as "a third of mine own life / or that for which I live" (IV.i.3–4). Once he has carried out his vow to "abjure" his "rough magic," to "break [his] staff" and "drown [his] book," the old scholar will have only memories and his native "most faint" (Epilogue) strength to sustain him. But he shakes off his melancholy to perform a last benevolent act: he will use his magic to assure the travelers "calm seas" on their voyages home.

Prospero is in some ways the ultimate patriarch, protecting and guiding his child, engineering her future by means human and supernatural. But he embodies that figure in its most benevolent form. He accepts that the time has come for Miranda to pass from childhood into womanhood;

in Shakespeare's day the main rite of passage was marriage. The match that he arranges for Miranda is the one that she would — and does—choose for herself, and the union brings concord between nations and reunion between brothers. Miranda, with the confidence and resilience of the loved child, expresses no qualms about setting forth for the "brave new world." Her father approves, her husband-to-be is all she could wish, she is looking forward only to happiness. Prospero has not burdened her with his cares. His parting wishes to Ariel could as fittingly be addressed to her: "to the elements / Be free, and fare thou well!" (V.i.317–18). It is Prospero's willing sacrifice of his own well-being for the sake of his daughter's that gives the play its wistful, nostalgic tone. The "music of the island" is hauntingly sweet and sad. *The Tempest* is a fable of fatherly wish-fulfillment and ideal nurture.

By the time that Shakespeare wrote *The Tempest*, his own daughters were well past the vulnerable age of his heroine. According to Blakemore Evans' dating of the play in *The Riverside Shakespeare*, 1611, Susanna would have been twenty-eight and Judith twenty-six at the time of its composition. The older sister had married in 1607, at the reasonable age of twenty-four; Judith was to marry the year of her father's death, 1616, at the rather advanced age for those times of thirty-one. In 1596, the year most scholars estimate that Shakespeare wrote *Romeo and Juliet*, his elder daughter was about Juliet's age — thirteen — and he had just lost his only son. While no one would claim that Capulet is a stand-in for the playwright, it is possible that the intensity of the old man's grief has an autobiographical source.

Whether or not Shakespeare's relationship with his own daughters inspired *The Tempest*, the tone is one of nostalgic celebration, the main character a father devoted to a beloved child. This is not to suggest that Prospero is soft or self-effacing. He has an iron will, marked courage, and a temper every bit as fierce as Capulet's. He also has a comparable belief in his own authority. But he exercises those qualities not against but in sensitive concord with his daughter's feelings. His grief at his impending separation from Miranda is tempered by satisfaction that he has secured her happiness and by the prospect of future reunions. Capulet has no such consolations for his old age. By the final act, his oppression of Juliet has turned the wedding dance he anticipated into a dirge. In contrast, in *The Tempest*, under Prospero's guiding hand, the "music of the island" has come to soothe and bless all who have ears to hear it.

2

Daughters Who Rebel: Hermia (*A Midsummer Night's Dream*), Jessica (*The Merchant of Venice*), and Desdemona (*Othello*)

> There is more difference between thy flesh and hers than between jet and ivory, more between your bloods than there is between red wine and Rhenish.   *Merch*, III.i.41–43

In her rejection of the suitor her father favors, Juliet has many Shakespearean sisters. From Hermia in the early comedy *A Midsummer Night's Dream* to Jessica in the tragicomedy *The Merchant of Venice* to Desdemona in the tragedy *Othello*, young women in Shakespeare's plays insist on making their own choice of husband. Shakespeare pares the conflict to its simplest form: like Juliet, each of these daughters is an only child; like Prospero, each of the fathers is a widower. Juliet's rebellion is secret: Capulet does not discover the wayward course she has pursued until after her death. Jessica, too, conceals her defiance, though only until her elopement. Hermia and Desdemona take their independent stands openly. Each man prides himself on being the spokesman for family and communal values, but the common message in these plays is that father does not know best. His theatrical ancestor is a stock figure from Roman comedy, the blocking senex, the irascible old man, father or guardian, who tries to prevent the courtship. The darker the play's tone, the more beset is the daughter by her father's opposition and the more dire prove the consequences, for himself as well as for her.

In *A Midsummer Night's Dream*, Egeus believes in the paramount authority of the father and the duty of the daughter to unquestioning obedience. He is countermanded, however, by a higher power to which he holds fealty: that of the state, in the person of Duke Theseus. To emphasize the father's ineffectiveness, Shakespeare creates a second authority figure who also overrules Egeus, this one supernatural — Oberon, the king of the fairies. Both he and Theseus are themselves lovers, and both take the side of the rebellious daughter over that of the peevish old man. Hermia, in turn, is virtually unaffected by her father's decree, which she dismisses as preposterous and runs away to evade. Egeus's intransigence serves as little more than an unwitting catalyst to the love's fulfillment. From the lovers' irreverent stance to Egeus's utter defeat, this happy comedy ridicules even the possibility of an authoritarian father prevailing over a determined daughter. The lovers may make their famous lament: "The course of true love never did run smooth" (I.i.134). But Shakespeare leaves little doubt that, as the mischievous fairy Puck predicts,

> Jack shall have Jill
> Naught shall go ill,
> The man shall have his mare again, and all shall be well [III.i.461–63].

In *The Merchant of Venice*, Shylock advocates the supreme worth not only of paternal authority but of Judaism and of material wealth. Jessica pretends to embrace those values, but only long enough to defy her father by eloping with an impecunious Christian. In the process, she helps herself to a huge "dowry" from Shylock's horde of money and jewels. Her rebellion, like Hermia's, is sanctioned by the ruling Duke but for less benevolent reasons: he and the other Christians of Venice see Shylock as a usurer and an alien. They cheer Jessica's betrayal of all that her father stands for, and intensify Shylock's losses by forcing him to will his remaining fortune to the rebellious couple. Worse, they require that he convert to the religion he loathes.

On one level, this is a happy ending for Jessica, who attains financial security and marriage to the man of her choice. But the play gives several indications that that victory, devastating for her father, is not without cost to her. Although Shakespeare labeled the earliest edition of *The Merchant of Venice* a "comical history" (Pelican edition, 14) and most collections list it with the comedies, many commentators have argued that it should be called a tragedy. In part, the label depends on the character through whose eyes one views events. From the perspective of Portia, the wealthy heroine, it *is* a comedy (her story will be taken up in Chapter 5); for Jessica, who attains love and freedom at the cost of renouncing family and creed, it is still a comedy, but a dark one. From the point of view of Shylock, the play is a tragedy of the somberest shade.

In *Othello*, Brabantio appears only briefly, at the outset of the play. But his values and actions precipitate both Desdemona's tragedy and his own. Paternalistic and bigoted, he denigrates his new son-in-law's human worth and denies his daughter not only understanding but counsel and succor. Both the lovers seem, at first, to discount his contemptuous rejection. But once Iago, Othello's treacherous ensign, begins to echo Brabantio's demeaning views, Othello comes to credit them — to believe that his blackness and foreign birth repel Desdemona, and that she, like women in general, is fickle and deceitful. Desdemona, in contrast, is determined to take the opposite stance from her father: to deny Othello's external qualities and see him only as mind and spirit and to govern her own conduct by the highest standards of forbearance and integrity.

As in the *Dream*, the lovers plead their case before the ruling duke, and the higher authority overrules the father. In *Othello*, however, the duke's motive is not romantic sentiment but political expediency: he cannot afford to offend his leading general, whom he needs to lead the Venetian troops against the Turks. Outraged by the duke's judgment, Brabantio takes out his frustration on Desdemona. He accuses her of deceiving him, and he flings in the face of her new husband the warning that she will be equally devious toward him.

Furthermore, Brabantio refuses to let Desdemona reside with him while Othello is at war. Like Hermia and Jessica, she leaves the ordered place of her girlhood and goes off with her beloved to what she trusts will be a refuge. In keeping with the tragic tone of the play, however, it is not a greenwood inhabited by benevolent fairies nor an idyllic retreat but a fortified island unsettled by disrupted preparations for battle. With its army camp ambiance of bravado and bawdry, Cyprus could hardly be more alien to a refined and naive bride. There Desdemona is cut off from the forces of communal harmony that ordered her world in Venice. Her only female companion is her new waiting woman, Emilia, who also happens to be the wife of Iago, her secret enemy.

In the isolation of Cyprus, Brabantio's treatment contributes to a fatal pattern. After years of conforming to the role of dutiful daughter, Desdemona has transferred her allegiance to her husband. Deeply hurt by Brabantio's rejection, she lacks the confidence and experience to cope with the terrible changes that Othello is undergoing. Alone and distressed by his unfounded accusations and physical abuse, she first tries to rationalize his mistreatment, then to take the blame on herself, and at last to fantasize a conception of Othello that conforms to her earlier ideal. Desdemona has such a stake in proving her father wrong that she refuses to see any aspect of her husband but the "visage in his mind," the "honors" and "valiant parts" with which she fell in love. She tries to force the increasingly hostile Othello to fit this image by treating him as though he actually does. Her goals for her own behavior are equally fixed: to maintain the docile, modest decorum that Brabantio once praised in her and accused her of abandoning. Desdemona has not been taught to define herself apart from men or to defend herself against hostility.

A Midsummer Night's Dream

In *A Midsummer Night's Dream*, the father-daughter conflict is presented in its simplest terms. Old Egeus sounds his character note at his first appearance. He comes in "full of vexation ... with complaint / Against [his] child" (I.i.22–23). The reason is suggested in the cast list: Hermia is identified as "daughter to Egeus, in love with Lysander." The problem is that Egeus favors Demetrius, and has given him his consent. Lysander, Egeus claims, has "bewitched" Hermia, "filched [his] daughter's heart" with "rhymes," "love tokens," "verses of feigning love," "bracelets of his hair, rings, gauds, conceits, / Knacks, trifles, nosegays, sweetmeats" — in short, all the standard paraphernalia of courtship. The charge is made the more ludicrous by the list's detail. The real issue, as it was for Capulet, is the father's pride of possession. Lysander, Egeus charges, has "Turned her obedience, which is due to me, / To stubborn harshness" (ll. 27–38). For retribution, he appeals to the "ancient privilege" of Athenian law, and to its human representative, Duke Theseus: "As she is mine, I may dispose of her," he asserts, and he puts her choices in the harshest terms: either marriage to Demetrius or death.

This heavy sentence is not long allowed to overshadow the lovers' fate. Shakespeare gives several signs that the play will remain a comedy. The first is the arbitrariness of Egeus's preference: there is no extrinsic bar to Lysander's qualifications as suitor. Unlike Othello, whose future father-in-law also accuses him of seducing his daughter by means of witchcraft, Lysander is of the same race and social heritage as Hermia. Unlike Romeo, he does not hail from a rival family. As Lysander himself vouches, he is as "well derived as [Demetrius], as well possessed" (I.i.99–100). In fact, he is the worthier candidate, since Demetrius has jilted another young noblewoman, "Nedar's daughter, Helena," who nevertheless still "dotes" on "this spotted and inconstant man" (ll. 109–10). Both the unreasonableness of the father's edict and the accessibility of the rejected maiden signal that the means for a happy ending are at hand.

The other characters' reactions during the public hearing also suggest that the outcome will firmly favor the lovers. At Egeus's request, Theseus dutifully recites to Hermia the party line on filial obedience: her father "should be as a god" to her; having "composed [her] beauties," it is "within his power / To leave the figure or disfigure it" (I.i.47–51). Hermia is not daunted by this ugly threat. Not only does she defend her preference for Lysander, she appeals to the Duke to mitigate her possible punishment should she refuse to marry Demetrius. Although she makes a show of apology for this "boldness" in overstepping the bounds of "modesty," her request emphasizes that the Duke is a higher authority than Egeus. Like Desdemona, Hermia cunningly uses her father's faith in hierarchy against him.

Theseus, perhaps moved by Hermia's youth and beauty (he addresses her as "fair maid"), perhaps by the parallel with his own situation, tempers Egeus's black and white dictate. He proposes a third course of punishment, that Hermia "endure the livery of a nun" and "live a barren sister all [her] life" (I.i.70–72). This is slender mercy. Although it would spare her life, Theseus's very language — "endure," "barren" — suggests that "withering on the virgin thorn" holds few charms in this most earthly of paradises. Nevertheless, Hermia claims to prefer enforced chastity to bearing the "unwished yoke" of Demetrius's love. Lysander's response is a sarcastic retort to his rival:

> You have her father's love, Demetrius;
> Let me have Hermia's: do you marry him   [ll. 93–94].

He faces down his angry father-in-law with equal confidence: "I am beloved of beauteous Hermia. / Why should not I prosecute my right?"

Theseus, hearing this youthful defiance, restates the exigencies of the "law of Athens," backing the father's "will" against his daughter's "fancies," which, he claims, he "by no means ... may extenuate" (I.i.118–20). But then he draws away Egeus and Demetrius on "some business" about his own "nuptial." Is this accident, with Theseus so "over-full of self-affairs" (l. 113) that he does not think through his actions? Or has the tolerant older lover intentionally left the couple alone? In any case, they lose no time in devising a plot to defy their elders. Lysander takes the lead. After her public show of bravado, Hermia turns pale and threatens to cry, signs of emotion that, typically, Shakespeare describes in the dialogue. But her suitor waxes philosophical, first uttering the oft-quoted observation about the rough course of "true love," and then giving a series of similes for love's transience: "swift as a shadow, short as any dream"—"so quick bright things come to confusion" (ll. 144, 149). This nostalgia, we might suspect, derives less from the character than from the playwright looking, Theseus-like, with a fond eye at the young lovers.

Hermia's response is to preach "patience" in their "trial" (I.i.152). The bolder Lysander proposes a scheme to elude "the sharp Athenian law" by fleeing the city and taking refuge with his wealthy widowed aunt. Hermia must "steal forth [her] father's house" (ll. 162–64)—in other words, leave the confines of paternal authority and, in its extended form, the city walls and the Duke's edict. She agrees with no qualms except about the possible fragility of the proposed match, based as it is on "all the vows that ever men have broke" (l. 175). But she lightens this accusation by couching it in rhyme and agrees to meet Lysander that night.

The way to the dowager's house is through the woods, the usual setting in Shakespearean comedy of confusion, magic, and transformation—the world of dream alluded to in the title. There, the lovers' fidelity will be tested, and the forces that threaten to separate them will go beyond the external. Lysander passes the first test of his integrity, obeying the modest Hermia's request to "lie further off" when they lose their way and are forced to spend the night in the woods. Such a "separation," she says sententiously, "becomes a virtuous bachelor and a maid" (II.ii.57–59). The supernatural beings who rule this province have no such scruples. In fact, Puck, coming across the sleeping couple, is indignant at Lysander's supposed rejection of the "pretty soul" who "durst not lie" near "this lack-love" (ll. 76–77).

The fairies, led by their King, Oberon, and their Queen, Titania, are openly promiscuous. In fact, the royals are fighting a pitched battle over the jealousy caused by their various affairs. This permissiveness reaches a ludicrous extreme when Titania, drugged into amorousness by Oberon's magic flower, leads her latest lover, the "translated" Bottom, to her bower. She is delicate and lovely; he, in a metaphor made literal, is an ass. Her thoughts are of a situation opposite to her own, the horror of rape, with the moon and "every little flower, / Lamenting some enforced chastity" (III.i.184–85). The mortals follow Titania's words, not her actions, and uphold the usual strict standard of chastity that Shakespeare sets for his lovers. When Theseus and his hunting party discover all four sleeping—Demetrius has meanwhile been reconciled to Helena—he immediately puts an innocuous face on the situation: "No doubt they rose up early to observe / The rite of May" (IV.i.131–32). This placating excuse is directed particularly at the outraged Egeus. But Theseus teases the dazed couples in a way that shows he senses their actual motives: "Saint Valentine is past! / Begin these woodbirds but to couple now?" (ll. 138–39).

All four scramble to their knees and beg his pardon. After a night of confusion, discomfort, and barely averted battle, a farce directed by the mischievous Puck, the rivals are reconciled and the couples reunited. Hermia has proven her romantic heroine's credentials: she was bold in claiming her rights against her rival when Puck's error made Lysander abandon her for Helena, and steadfast in her concern for his safety even after he rejected her. Like Juliet and Desdemona, in a crisis she is resourceful and daring. But unlike those inhabitants of a tragic world, Hermia has not been forced to struggle alone. The wry Puck (whose watchword is "Lord, what fools these mortals be!" [III.ii.115]) is not the only guardian of their fates. Oberon, the fairy king, is there to assure that "all things shall be peace" (III.ii.377). "The pairs of faithful lovers" return to Athens to be "wedded with Theseus, all in jollity" (IV.i.91).

The difference in tone between the insouciant *Dream* and the later, more somber *Tempest* becomes evident if we compare the magical father-figures who determine the lovers' fates. Oberon, unlike Prospero, is immortal. He is also unrelated to the lovers and secure in his native element. Having bestowed his blessing on them and their posterity, he can return to the wood he rules, with Puck and the fairy band permanently in his service and the new reconciliation with Titania to cheer his nights. He need sacrifice none of his own well-being for the sake of a loved one.

The suffering falls to the mortal father, Egeus, who, when the lovers return, renews his complaint against Hermia and adds the plea that Lysander, too, suffer "the law upon his head." He tries to enlist Demetrius's support in punishing their slight to two bastions of male power: the father's "consent" and the suitor's contract of marriage. But Demetrius is no longer his ally, and Theseus steps easily into the breach to decree: "Egeus, I will overbear your will" (IV.i.178). Thus, the Duke, the human analogue to Oberon (their parts are often doubled on stage), assumes the paternal role. Egeus says nothing; his silence shows that he has been completely thwarted, and no harsh word breaks the joyous mood.

The play remains a "dream," with everyone except the irascible father given their fondest wish. Shakespeare acknowledges, through Theseus, the poet's role as dream-maker, giving to "airy nothing / A local habitation and a name" (V.i.16–17). He links him, with endearing self-mockery, not only with the "lover" but the "lunatic" as three beings comprised entirely of "imagination" (ll. 7–8). Shakespeare exercises that imagination once more in a last act that serves as an epilogue to the main action and provides further distance from Egeus's sour view.

The final act consists primarily of a play within the play that parodies the plot of the separated lovers. Some Athenian workmen present to the court their much toiled over "Pyramus and Thisby," "very tragical mirth," with "not one word apt, one player fitted" (V.i.57–65). Here it is an external barrier, and an animate one, that separates the lovers: a "vile wall" (l. 131). Coincidentally, the playlet also parodies *Romeo and Juliet*, written shortly afterwards, in Pyramus's erroneous assumption that his lady is dead, the setting of the deaths in a tomb, and Thisby's suicide with her lover's dagger. In this small comic masterpiece, Shakespeare boldly mocks not only his own material but the conventions of his stage: the absence of scenery, the jog-trot verse, and the boy actors cast in female roles. He mocks, too, theater as a medium and actors as a type — eager for applause, keen on playing all the roles, at the mercy of their audience's indulgence and the limitations of their own talents.

At the end of *A Midsummer Night's Dream*, however, solemnity and beauty return. Oberon, Titania, and their fairy train bestow on the newlyweds all the worldly blessings: "sweet peace," "safety," and "issue [that] ever shall be fortunate" (V.i.394–409). These wishes parallel those conveyed to Miranda and Ferdinand in Prospero's show of goddesses. Fittingly, in the simple comedy, the roles of father and supernatural overseer remain split: Oberon blesses the union while the irate Egeus remains conveniently off stage. Shakespeare's tenets for marital happiness remained remarkably constant from the beginning to the end of his career. The poet's alliance with the lover and with the father-figure who would promote wedded bliss, so early claimed, held firm.

The Merchant of Venice

The story of Jessica, the rebellious daughter in *Merchant*, also has the trappings of traditional romance. The woman, disguised "in the lovely garnish of a boy" (II.vi.45) evades her overbearing father and elopes with her true love. After honeymoon adventures — a gondola ride, a futile pursuit by an agent of her furious father, a prodigal spending spree — the lovers arrive at an idyllic setting where their union is sanctioned by a wealthy patron. In outline, this parallels Hermia's story, but only in outline. The differences, more significant than the similarities, give the later play its darker tone.

The contrast begins with the cast list, where Shylock is described not as "father to Jessica" or "a moneylender of Venice" but "a Jew" — not, in other words, in terms of his affiliation but of his alienation. Jews were a rarity in Shakespeare's England, the actual if not the designated setting of the play. They had few rights — could not, for example, own land, attend a university, or pursue most professions. The popular stereotype was that they were conspiratorial, greedy, and malevolent — the killers of Christ (the irony that Jesus was himself a Jew persecuted by the pagan Romans was lost on the Elizabethan populace). Their reputation was further sullied by the scandal of Dr. Rogerigo Lopez, a Portuguese Jew who was the revered Elizabeth I's personal physician. In 1594, a few years before the probable date of *The Merchant of Venice*, he was accused of attempting to poison the queen and executed for high treason. Whether or not the charge was true, the case prompted a resurgence of anti–Semitism in already xenophobic England.

The theater, most socially cognizant of the arts, reflected that bigotry. The most famous example is Christopher Marlowe's melodrama, *The Jew of Malta*. Marlowe, Shakespeare's chief theatrical rival before his early death in a tavern brawl, wrote the play in 1589. After the Lopez trial, it was revived in order to capitalize on the sensationalism of the case. (See Anne Barton's introduction to the play in the *Riverside Shakespeare*, p. 250.) The main character, Barabas, is a caricature of the inhumane, grasping Jew. When his daughter Abigail falls in love with a Christian, Barabas betroths her both to him and another powerful Christian and contrives to have them slay each other. Abigail takes refuge from his tyranny in a convent, whereupon Barabas poisons the entire sisterhood, including the offending daughter, with a gift of "a mess of rice-porridge." In the end, he is lured into the trap he has set for his chief enemy, Ferneze, Governor of Malta. Barabas perishes, cursing, in a giant cauldron of boiling oil, an apt demise for the satanic protagonist. Because his enemies are themselves so venial and unscrupulous and because Barabas has the Marlovian hero's daring and eloquence, he is the focal character.

Shakespeare was no doubt influenced by Marlowe's depiction when he created Shylock. Certainly, he adopts the stereotype in making his Jew, too, rich, miserly, and vindictive. Shylock also has a daughter who falls in love with a Christian. But Shakespeare's conception goes far beyond Marlowe's black humor caricature. Usury, one of the only means allowed Elizabethan Jews for earning a living, is more than simply a profession for Shylock. The financial success it affords him is inextricable from his identity as a Jew and even as a father. His first trustworthy — i.e., non-public — words to the audience on his "ancient grudge" against the merchant Antonio suggest his tangle of attitudes:

> I hate him for he is a Christian,
> But more for that in low simplicity
> He lends out money gratis and brings down
> The rate of usance here in Venice   [I.iii.38–41].

For the Christians, usury is not only unsavory but sinful—on the grounds, quaint to modern ears, that it is unnatural because it "breeds" money out of an inanimate substance. They see anyone, like Shylock, who dirties his hands in this unclean practice as a pariah, a "villain" and a "devil." In the apt malapropism of the clown Launcelot Gobbo, his master Shylock is "the very devil incarnation" (II.ii.24). The Christians conveniently ignore the fact that they have left him few other means of support and that, in any case, his religion automatically makes him an alien in their society.

The crucial point for the father-daughter issue is that Jessica does not elope with just any young man. She deliberately chooses a Christian, and one who is allied with the closest friends of Shylock's rival merchant, Antonio. In fact, she values Lorenzo not despite but because of his religious affiliation. She admits her "heinous sin" in being "ashamed to be [her] father's child." But she swears that, "blood" alliance aside, she is not "daughter ... to his manners" (II.iii.16–19). She is counting on Lorenzo to "keep promise" and elope with her. By that means, she vows: "I shall end this strife, / Become a Christian and [his] loving wife" (ll. 20–21). From the first then, Jessica links marriage with religious conversion and professes that her salvation, of soul and emotional well-being, lies in her suitor's good faith.

Unlike Hermia, Jessica has not picked a suitor who is a virtual clone of her father's favorite. Nor does she run away on impulse. The elopement is part of a precisely orchestrated scheme, devised by both lovers and carried out by means of secret messages, disguises, and careful timing. From the first, it is meant to include Jessica's theft of a great part of Shylock's wealth. We have Lorenzo's word to his friend Gratiano that the mastermind of the plan is Jessica herself:

> She hath directed
> How I shall take her from her father's house,
> What gold and jewels she is furnished with,
> What page's suit she hath in readiness...   [II.iv.30–33].

On the designated night, Jessica confesses to being "much ashamed"—but only of her male disguise, of being "transformed to a boy" (II.vi.35, 39) before her lover's eyes. The elopement and the burglary do not touch her conscience. From her window, she tosses Lorenzo a "casket" of jewels, commenting wryly, "it is worth the pains" (l. 33). The casket, long a symbol of female sexuality, is Jessica's self-bestowed dowry. Unlike Portia, Jessica is the one who chooses the "casket" for her suitor, though she, too, gives herself with her fortune. But, again in contrast to the heiress, Jessica steals the prerogative that she knows her father would never grant.

Far from feeling remorseful, Jessica is elated. She promises to join Lorenzo immediately, pausing only long enough to "gild [herself] / With some more ducats" (II.vi.49–50). The gild/guilt pun, to which she seems oblivious, resounds clearly in the audience's ears. Lorenzo, like Jessica, sees no perfidy in the theft. He praises it as his bride's means of "prov[ing] herself" "wise," "fair," and "true," deserving of placement in his "constant soul" (ll. 53–55). The religious allusion is a reminder that he, too, sees the marriage as the instrument of Jessica's salvation. In fact, he expresses the hyperbolic wish that her act might sanctify even her "faithless" father:

> If e'er the Jew her father come to heaven
> It will be for his gentle daughter's sake   [ll. 33–34].

The pun (gentle/gentile) again emphasizes that social status and religious affiliation are inseparable in Venice. It is worth noting, too, that Lorenzo's designation for Shylock is "the Jew." In his capacity as bereft parent, he has not roused the sympathy of either lover.

The reasons for Jessica's alienation from her father are not far to seek. He has not made her life pleasant or easy. She complains to Launcelot, her one companion, that her house is "hell," relieved of its tedium only by the clown himself, a "merry devil" (II.iii.2). Launcelot, however, is about to leave his post to serve the indulgent Christian gentleman Bassanio. Shylock is not sorry to see him go. He reproaches Launcelot, to his face and in soliloquy, with being "a huge feeder" whose only functions are to "sleep," "snore," and wear out his clothes (II.v.3–5). Shylock begrudges him, in other words, the commonest human needs. Although he grants privately that Launcelot is "kind enough" (l. 44), all his words to the servant consist of commands, insults, and threats.

With Jessica, too, Shylock's principles are thrift and duty, his tone stern and authoritarian. In their one tête-à-tête, his main concern is instructing her on how to protect his property: "Look to my house," he orders, "Lock up my doors" (II.v.16, 28). That guardianship extends to her: his longest speech is a warning not to look out the "casements … into the public street" during that night's music and masquerading. Scornfully, he adds that these "sounds of shallow foppery" will emanate from "Christian fools with varnished faces" (ll. 32–34). Her duty is to protect his "sober house" from such intrusion. He assumes, of course, that Jessica is his ally in this enterprise, as well as in his malice toward Christians. He confides that his motive for attending the supper to which his new client, Antonio, has invited him is rancor: "I'll go in hate to feed upon / The prodigal Christian" (ll. 14–15). Still, he says, he feels "loath to go." He senses "some ill a-brewing towards his rest." The bad omen is his recent dream of "money-bags," the comic symbol of his security and status. Shylock's solution is to lock up his treasures with extra care: "Fast bind, fast find" is his sententious last word to Jessica. What he does not take into account is that he cannot "fast bind" the human "treasure"— that he has more to fear from traitors within his house than from robbers.

Shylock has been so busy lecturing Jessica that he has taken no notice of her reactions. The sounds of music and partying are hardly repellent to her young ears. Nor has he uttered any word of affection or appreciation. She says almost nothing to her father during this scene, except to ask "What is your will?" and, later, to lie about what Launcelot has whispered to her — not "farewell" but details about the elopement. Shylock's opposition to revelry, music, and romance have made Jessica all the more determined to enjoy them. No sooner has the old man shut the door than she makes a grim vow to escape his oppression:

> Farewell; and if my future be not crost,
> I have a father, you a daughter lost   [II.v.54–55].

She expresses neither love nor remorse. Jessica has played the role that her father demanded of her: caretaker of his possessions, acquiescer in his prejudices— the self-effacing Good Girl. Like Lear (see Chapter 4), Shylock takes that guise at face value. As Launcelot wryly observes of his own parent: "It is a wise father that knows his own child" (II.ii.70–71).

Typically, Shakespeare has put this wisdom into the mouth of the clown. In context, it arises from a literal failure of recognition: all Shakespeare's clowns are adamantly literal-minded. Old Gobbo, nearly blind, is tricked by the fatuous Launcelot into believing that his son has died in Shylock's service. But the pronouncement echoes in the serious plot, as does the old father's reaction to the "death": "God forbid! The boy was the very staff of my age, my very prop" (II.ii.60–61). Shylock, in failing to see his daughter as she really is, suffers the devastating loss of his life's "very prop." By running off with Lorenzo, Jessica betrays her religion, her culture, and her one living parent. Her act makes her father an object of derision to his enemies and drives him to greater isolation, hatred, and despair. Before Jessica's elopement, the play is a comedy. We are on the side of the lovers, as usual, and against the killjoy father. But the conventional comic plot calls for a play to end in weddings, as does the *Dream*. When a marriage occurs earlier on, obstacles to the match become the focus and the tone darkens. Here, Shylock goes from dupe to would-be avenger to victim; moreover, Shakespeare implies, the union founded on the old man's misery is not entirely happy.

Shylock has nothing like simple old Gobbo's understanding of his love for his child. His first reaction to Jessica's flight is a howl of pain and fury that confounds all his forms of loss: "'My daughter! O my ducats! O my daughter! / Fled with a Christian! O my Christian ducats!'" (II.viii.15–16) This is the illogic of free association: the "very prop[s] of [his] age"—child, wealth, religion — have all been knocked out from under him. In his shock, Shylock cannot separate the perpetrator from the possessions, the sense of betrayal from the material loss.

His suffering is given a comic twist by being reported rather than staged — an "unscene," in Marjorie Garber's apt term. The witnesses are Antonio's obsequious cronies, Salerio and Solanio, for whom the moneylender's troubles mean only the latest item of gossip. They turn his outburst into an object of ribald humor: "'Justice! Find the girl!'" they quote Shylock mockingly. "'She hath the stones upon her, and the ducats!'" (II.viii.21–22). The word "stones" is Elizabethan slang for testicles; Solanio stresses Shylock's unwitting pun when he reports gleefully: "all the boys in Venice follow him, / Crying his stones, his daughter, and his ducats." Their ridicule has a grim underlying implication: Jessica has robbed her father of his manhood, and done so in a way that makes his humiliation public.

Later, when Shylock comes upon the gossiping toadies, his tone is somber and his words dignified. His opening remark is a sad accusation: "You knew, none so well, none so well as you, of my daughter's flight" (III.i.21–22). They are undeterred from their malicious ridicule, admitting not only their foreknowledge but their approval. When Shylock's despair drives him to exclaim "My own flesh and blood to rebel!", they react not with sympathy but with another lewd pun, and Salerio dismisses the old father's claim of kinship: "There is more difference ... between your bloods than there is between red wine and Rhenish" (ll. 34–36). Shylock has described Jessica as an extension of his body and his will; they deny that there is any connection at all. Shylock's isolation is made more poignant because Salerio and Solanio are such shallow fops. As with Rosencrantz and Guildenstern, the sycophants in *Hamlet*, Shakespeare has rendered them ridiculous by making them virtual twins. In fact, so indistinguishable are their characters that the playwright himself seemed to forget the similar Italianate names he gave them and in the quarto text several times calls "Salerio" "Salerino." Modern actors have echoed this mockery by nicknaming them "the Salads."

The contemptible clowns serve several dramatic purposes: to report to the audience Shylock's reaction to the elopement, to goad him into further response, and to spare the more important Venetians— Antonio, Bassanio, and Gratiano— the unsavory role of tormenting the old man when he is down. They are also the first to make the connection between Jessica's betrayal and Antonio's peril. Before Shylock appears, Solanio suddenly cuts off the banter with an ominous surmise: "Let good Antonio look he keep his day, / Or he shall pay for this" (II.viii.25–26). This is the first hint that ruthless materialism can be the means of solacing a bruised heart and restoring lost face.

Shylock himself makes this connection when he is talking to his one friend, his fellow Jew Tubal, who has come to report the futility of his search for Jessica, undertaken at Shylock's behest. Tubal has discovered a long trail of extravagant purchases and wild exploits—"A diamond gone cost ... 2,000 ducats in Frankford," the squandering of "fourscore ducats at a sitting" (III.i.74–75; 98). Shylock is appalled at the "loss upon loss," compounded by "what's spent in the search." But, as in his reported cry, he is incapable of articulating the real cause of his anguish: his daughter's betrayal of family loyalty and religious faith.

Shylock is not an introspective man. He never admits—probably never realizes—his own part in provoking Jessica's rebellion. Instead, he displaces love with wealth and grief with fury in a grotesque conflation: "I would my daughter were dead at my foot, and the jewels in her ear! Would she were hearsed at my foot, and the ducats in her coffin!" (III.i.78–80). This curse is too terrible for him to dwell on, and, in any case, the thief is out of his grasp. He is bemoaning that he can have "no satisfaction, no revenge" and, more broadly, that only *he* has "ill luck," when Tubal supplies a new target for Shylock's rage: Antonio. The merchant, too, has been unlucky: he has lost one of his cargo ships. Shylock shifts to this object with alacrity: "I thank God, I thank God! ... I am glad of it. I'll plague him; I'll torture him. I am glad of it" (ll. 91; 103–04). The repetition of words and syntax, typical of Shylock's diction whenever he is intent on a point, here suggests his rapacity and his eagerness to turn impotence into action.

There is no question that Shylock has been deeply hurt by Jessica's betrayal. He reveals to Tubal the emotional wounds that he conceals from his Christian enemies, who see him only as a "stony adversary" (IV.i.4). To his friend, Shylock confesses his "sighs" and "tears," and says with every new detail of the man's incoherent account, "Thou torturest me, Tubal" (III.i.106). The most painful news is that Jessica traded a ring for a monkey. This, Shylock cries, was his "turquoise," given him by "Leah when [he] was a bachelor." We do not know Leah's identity, but most critics have assumed that she is Jessica's long-dead mother. This interpretation is suggested by Shylock's comic/poignant protest: "I would not have given it for a wilderness of monkeys" (l. 108–09). It is the one point in the play where he chooses love over wealth. Immediately afterwards, he vows about Antonio: "I will have the heart of him if he forfeit." Shylock's own heart, Shakespeare implies, is gone — or, to use Antonio's metaphor, become so hard that neither pleas nor "prayers" can "soften" it (IV.i.77–80). Love, thwarted, has turned to hate.

In the 1970 film of the London stage production, Laurence Olivier, playing Shylock, implies that this is the point in the play when Shylock's "merry bond" turns grimly earnest. His main motive for revenge is not the religious cause that he professes at the outset —"I hate him for he is a Christian"— or the financial one that Antonio disingenuously offers— his own beneficent "delivery" of Shylock's debtors (III.iii.22–24). Olivier's production focuses on the searing pain caused by Jessica's elopement. The film is set in Edwardian times, and Olivier plays Shylock as a dignified businessman and lonely widower. When he mentions Leah, he turns to a framed portrait, holds it mournfully to his chest, and then dashes it to the floor. The scene ends with the old man donning a prayer shawl, bowing his head, and swaying back and forth as he chants the Hebrew prayer for the dead. For him, Olivier suggests, Jessica is lost in soul as well as body.

Although Olivier's gestures may be exaggerated and his interpretation of Shylock idealized, the motive for revenge rings true: Shylock blames the Christians for Jessica's betrayal and sees himself solely as the wronged party. In the trial scene, he demands "justice" and "the law" (IV.i.196, 204), and his answer to Portia's pivotal plea about his own "hope for mercy" is the uncompromising: "What judgment shall I dread, doing no wrong?" (l. 89). He maintains that no "mercy" has been shown him, either by his daughter or the enemies she has allied herself with, and he falls back on his old biases. The Christians condemn him as "an inhuman wretch, / Uncapable of pity, void and empty / From any dram of mercy" (ll. 4–6). They compare him to a natural force, cruel and unstoppable — a "flood," a "wolf," (ll. 72–73). Certainly Shylock's intention of cutting out Antonio's heart is nothing less than barbarous. At the same time, the mercy-preaching Christians are far from altruistic. *The Merchant of Venice* is a play whose interpretation has inevitably been affected by history, to the point that some have argued against the appropriateness of its being staged at all for post–Holocaust audiences. That stance ignores the considerable ambiguity that Shakespeare has written into the portrayal of the Christians.

Portia's sentence, backed by the Venetian court, is a series of hammer blows: not only must Shylock forfeit the bond, he must cede "half [his] wealth" to Antonio, his bitterest enemy. He makes an appalled protest: "You take my life / When you do take the means whereby I live" (IV.i.374–75). Having lost his family, he wants to retain his profession and economic status. But worse is coming. Antonio's "mercy"— Portia's term — is that Shylock be required to leave "all he dies possessed [of] / Unto his son Lorenzo and his daughter" (ll. 387–88). The filial designation sounds especially galling given Antonio's frank description, just a few lines earlier, of Lorenzo as "the gentleman / That lately stole his daughter." Finally, Shylock must "presently [i.e., immediately] become a Christian" (l. 385). The penalty for failing to comply is the Duke's retraction of the pardon he has just given the "alien."

Some critics have argued that this is "kind" treatment — the Christians' way of bringing Shylock into the mainstream of their society and of saving his soul. That is not the effect on stage. After the terms have been meted out, Portia demands, "Art thou contented, Jew? What dost thou say?" The familiar second person pronoun, used toward inferiors, the contemptuous reference to the religion he is being forced to forsake, and the repetition of the prompt to the response she expects— all indicate who has the upper hand. Shylock can manage only a faint echo of her words, "I am content," before Portia matter-of-factly completes the blank verse line: "Clerk, draw a deed of gift." Shylock's property will of course go to Jessica and Lorenzo: she has left him no choice. Saying, "I am not well," Shylock begs leave to depart, promising, however, that he will sign the deed. As usual, Shakespeare's text provides no stage directions for this crucial moment. Directors have chosen to signal Shylock's feelings in a variety of ways, depending on the degree of sympathy they want to convey. The choices have ranged from a lightly self-mocking acquiescence to a tremulous stammer to a near collapse to Olivier's famous off-stage howl in the wings of the Old Vic. No matter what reaction Shylock shows his enemies, it is clear that he has lost everything. The Christians stay behind to exult.

And what of the daughter who exposed her father to such treatment? Did she wish his downfall? Yes, in fact she joined in the scheme against him. At Belmont, before the trial, Salerio comes to report Antonio's arrest and to warn the company about Shylock. Jessica, now Portia's guest, adds confirming testimony, both of her father's malice and of his particular enmity to Antonio:

> When I was with him, I have heard him swear
> To Tubal and to Chus, his countrymen,
> That he would rather have Antonio's flesh
> Than twenty times the value of the sum
> That he did owe him   [III.ii.284–88].

This, her only speech in the scene, reads suspiciously like a newcomer's eagerness to ingratiate herself by playing informer.

But does Jessica secure a place in Christian society and in her new husband's heart? Shakespeare implies that the union is a tenuous one. Although Jessica expresses hope that she "shall be saved by [her] husband" through her conversion, Gratiano describes the couple approaching Belmont as "Lorenzo and his infidel" (III.ii.218). Granted that he is the play's crude prankster, the nobleman who expresses anti–Semitism in its rawest form; still, his fellow Christians display similar bigotry. In Portia's Belmont, Jessica seems very much the outsider. She speaks freely only to her former servant, Launcelot, who has come along in Bassanio's service, and to Lorenzo. When the other Venetians are present, she is largely silent. She praises her hostess in elaborate terms, claiming to like her "past all expressing" and to believe "the poor rude world / Hath not her fellow" (III.v.66, 75–76). Yet Portia says almost nothing to her — nearly all her lines, both before leaving for Venice and on her return, are addressed to Lorenzo.

At the end, Jessica discovers, along with everyone else, that her hostess is the brilliant lawyer who has defeated and humiliated her father. Lorenzo exults at the news of the "special deed of gift" from "the rich Jew": "Fair ladies, you drop manna in the way / Of starved people" (V.i.294–95). This is an insensitive allusion to Jessica's Old Testament roots, and a reminder that the ultimate source of her wealth will be the death of the father who accrued it. Jessica says nothing.

As fitting the play's comic ending, Shakespeare provides no subsequent confrontation between Jessica and Shylock. The last act, as in *Dream*, is largely an epilogue to the main plot. The resolution has come in Act IV, with Shylock's defeat. In this darker play, the irascible father has been not only silenced, like Egeus, but banished from the final idyll. It is Jessica who remains silent during the scene of Portia's triumphant return, and we can only guess at her feelings. The choices that a director makes about Jessica's gestures and movements can have a substantial effect on the play's tone. The comic/romantic choice requires that she engage in affectionate flirtation with Lorenzo and regard Portia with smiling awe. The 1987 Royal Shakespeare Company production took a strikingly different approach. Jessica was played as awkward and isolated, dressed in a colorful Old World costume, at odds with the fashionable Belmont crowd. At the end, the group, including Lorenzo, followed Portia and Nerissa off stage, eager to hear the details of the courtroom victory. Jessica was left alone with her father's enemy, Antonio. In the final moment, before the lights dimmed, he dangled a crucifix over her and she dropped to her knees, stricken.

Is there evidence in the text for this dark view of Jessica's marriage? Certainly there are hints that it is not perfect. The "monkey" for which she so willingly trades Leah's turquoise was for the Elizabethans a symbol of sexual license, and the play is full of references to lust as a threat to fidelity. Gratiano, the "all-licensed" advocate of the appetites, says that anticipation is ultimately more pleasurable than gratification: "All things that are / Are with more spirit chasèd than enjoyed" (II.v.12–13). In the spirit of the locker room bull session in which this remark is uttered, Salerio expresses doubt about Lorenzo's will to "keep obliged faith unforfeited"—i.e., be true to his marriage vows. "Love's bonds new-made," he says, are more appealing. Granted, these two wastrels are hardly the most reliable spokesmen on this subject, and Lorenzo does carry out his promise to marry Jessica. He does not simply seduce and abandon her. He also speaks some lovely poetry in her praise. Still, on their honeymoon at Portia's borrowed estate, they begin a contest in verse on lovers who also enjoyed such an idyllic night. Lorenzo's examples, Troilus and Dido, allude to affairs that ended in betrayal; Jessica's— Thisbe and Medea — to loves destroyed by death. All four of these stories are tragedies. Then Lorenzo shifts rather insensitively to the present, to the night when Jessica "Did steal from the wealthy Jew," and she counters by accusing him of "stealing her soul with many vows of faith, / And ne'er a true one" (V.i.19–20). Their tone is playful, the duel of wit a typical romantic device, Jessica a willing and equal participant. But the tenor of the allusions is ominous.

When Lorenzo changes the subject to rhapsodizing on "the touches of sweet harmony" in the air, Jessica responds moodily, "I am never merry when I hear sweet music" (V.i.69). He urges her to "mark the music," and warns against "the man that hath no music in himself" as "fit for treason, stratagems, and spoils," with "affections dark as Erebus" (ll. 83–85). Shylock, we are reminded, hated the sound of "the wry-necked fife" and warned Jessica against harkening to it. Is her gloominess the mark of a belated — and ineffable — twinge of conscience? Is it a sign, again in the words of the prescient clown Launcelot, that "the sins of the father are to be laid upon the children"? (III.v.1–2). Jessica's story ends before we see the course of her marriage. The larger play is, after all, a comedy, and it returns at the end to the main love plot between Portia and Bassanio. But Shakespeare implies that the happiness Jessica achieves at the cost of her father's pain does not go unscathed, that for all her defiance, she remains Shylock's "flesh and blood."

Othello

Like Jessica, Desdemona, the rebellious daughter in *Othello*, marries a man who is anathema to her father. In keeping with the tragic plot, the basis for the father's opposition to the match is not arbitrary and superficial, as in *A Midsummer Night's Dream*, but intrinsic. This time it is not the suitor's religion that is the issue, as in *The Merchant of Venice*, but his race: Othello, who has been a welcome guest at Brabantio's manor house in his capacity as legendary general, becomes a pariah as a husband for Desdemona. The senator, wealthy and privileged, is appalled at the idea of his daughter allying herself with a "stranger of here and everywhere," and, what is more shocking, "a Moor"— in Elizabethan parlance, a black man. Again, the timing of the marriage suggests the tone of the play: the wedding does not bring the action to a happy close, as in the comic *Dream*, or occur in mid-play, as in the tragicomic *Merchant*. Othello and Desdemona elope before the first scene begins; the rest of the play traces the results of that impulsive act. After a brief ascent, events move relentlessly toward their fatal conclusion. Usually, the blame for the love's failure has been laid on Iago, Othello's malevolent ensign. Certainly he is the instigator of Othello's violent jealousy. But it is Brabantio's jaundiced outlook that informs the play. Bigotry, chauvinism, the inferiority and deviousness of women: these are the values that the magnifico professes. Iago, master artificer that he is, merely spins his web of lies from this insidious matter.

Before Desdemona's elopement, Brabantio feels secure in his conception of both his rank and his daughter's nature. He is an established member of the ruling class, accustomed to ease and deference. Desdemona is his only child and heir, a "jewel" (I.iii.195) whose duty is to run his household smoothly until such time as he chooses a husband for her. All these complacent assumptions are apparent in the opening scene. Iago, with his usual eye for human foibles, predicts how the senator will react to the news of Desdemona's flight. He rouses Brabantio from sleep and "poison[s] his delight" (I.i.68) with a cry against "thieves": "Look to your house, your daughter, and your bags!" (ll. 79–80). The equation of family relationships and material possessions sounds like Shylock. But Iago immediately connects the "robbery" to greater loss: "Your heart is burst; you have lost half your soul."

As the dazed old man attempts to understand "the reason of this terrible summons," Iago, under cover of darkness, uses crude barnyard metaphors to describe the new marriage: "an old black ram / Is tupping your white ewe" (I.i.88–89). His taunts debase not only the marriage but its progeny: "You'll have your daughter covered with a Barbary horse; you'll have your nephews neigh to you" (ll. 110–12). Lest the father, or the audience, misunderstand, Iago's feckless sidekick, Roderigo, puts the message in more prosaic terms:

> Your daughter, if you have not given her leave,
> ...hath made a gross revolt,
> Tying her duty, beauty, wit, and fortunes
> In an extravagant and wheeling stranger
> Of here and everywhere   [ll. 132–36].

The implication is the familiar one that the daughter is the father's possession, to be bestowed on a husband he approves of. But Desdemona, Roderigo charges, is even at that moment in "the gross clasps of a lascivious Moor." The alliterated "s" turns the line into a hiss.

Brabantio condemns her act as "treason of the blood" (I.i.168), a betrayal not only of morality but of family alliance. Like Shylock, he sounds more like a cuckolded husband than a grief-stricken father: "O, she deceives me / Past thought!" he exclaims (ll. 164–65). Several commentators have labeled father-daughter relationships in the plays incestuous. Although such charges, taken literally, seem exaggerated, it is true that Shakespeare's most damaging fathers are also the most possessive.

Brabantio asserts that his only consolation would have been to act as the arbiter of Desdemona's choice. In an about-face so sudden that it is comic, he cries to Roderigo, "O, would you had had her!" (I.i.174). This to the drunken fop whom, moments earlier, he was reproaching for "haunt[ing] about [his] doors" after being told outright "My daughter is not for thee" (ll.96–98). Her act makes fatherhood itself seems worthless to him: "Who would be a father?" (l. 163) he demands melodramatically. But Brabantio will not give Desdemona up without a fight. He means to exercise all of his political and social influence to divorce the new couple. Armed and assisted by "special officers of night," he sets out to "apprehend the Moor" and arraign him before the Duke.

Iago, now playing the role of loyal officer, conveys Brabantio's invidious purposes to Othello: "He will divorce you," he warns, or at least use the "law" to exert "restraint and grievance" (I.ii.14–17) on the newlyweds. Under ordinary circumstances, Iago would be right, as we see when Brabantio pleads his case before the Duke and his council. The senator calls this marriage a "wrong" which, he asserts, "any of [his] brethren of the state" must feel "as 'twere their own" (ll. 95–97). Like Hermia's father, he assumes that only "witchcraft" or "drugs" and "minerals" could cause "nature so preposterously to err" (I.ii.74; I.iii.62–64). By "nature," he means *his* conception of Desdemona's character and predilections: "a maiden never bold; / Of spirit so still and quiet" that she "blush'd" at her own emotions (I.iii.94–96). She seemed entirely opposed to marriage, having "shunned / The wealthy curlèd darlings of [their] nation" (I.ii.67–68). How could such a paragon of modesty and chastity, he flings at Othello, have "run from her guardage to the sooty bosom / Of such a thing as thou — to fear, not to delight" (ll. 70–71). "Sooty" and "thing" reduce the noble commander to a soiled object. Such a choice, he adds cuttingly, could only "incur a general mock." To him, Othello's noble lineage means nothing. Although the general descends "from men of royal siege" [rank], and can claim "as proud a fortune" as that of his bride (ll. 21–24), the outraged father sees only his racial heritage and ranks him with "bondslaves and pagans" (l. 99).

This bigotry reflects the typical Venetian attitude, expressed in the slurs of Iago and Roderigo and in the Duke's initial reaction to Brabantio's charge. He first grants the magnifico absolute power over the man who has "beguiled" his daughter, promising that the father himself shall read "the bloody book of law" to the malefactor, even should he prove to be the Duke's "proper [own] son" (I.iii.65–70). But that is before he discovers that the groom is "valiant Othello," whom he has just summoned to lead the Venetian fleet "against the general enemy Ottoman" (l. 49). Two sources of power are in conflict here: social status and political expediency. In this instance, the general is a much more valuable ally to the Duke than the senator. Still, not wishing to affront Brabantio, he politically takes the middle course and grants the accused a hearing.

Othello calmly admits the factual charge: "That I have ta'en away this old man's daughter, / It is most true; true I have married her" (I.iii.78–79). But, he adds wryly, it was not a seduction brought about by "drugs" and "conjuration" but a mutual accord. He bids them "send for the lady," staking not only his "office" but his "life" on her confirmation (ll. 115–20). Meanwhile, he recounts the actual "process" of courting Desdemona, which consisted of telling her "the story of [his] life," with its "disastrous chances," "moving accidents," and "hairbreadth scapes" (ll. 129–36). The setting for this account was her own home, where, Othello recalls, Brabantio himself "oft invited me"; in this capacity as heroic adventurer, he recalls, "her father loved me." Desdemona listened to the tale with "a greedy ear" (l. 149) and reacted with tears, "a world of sighs," and exclamations of awe: "She swore, i' faith, 'twas strange, 'twas passing strange; / 'Twas pitiful, 'twas wondrous pitiful" (ll. 159–61). Othello's echo of his beloved's diction shows affection and pride. He recalls fondly her remark that if he could teach this story to "a friend," it alone "would woo her." Othello heard this as the indirect proposal that it was, and declares, "Upon this hint I spake" (l. 166). The impetus for the love, then, is the sheltered woman's admiration for the man's prowess and stoic suffering, her "pity" for "the dangers [he] had passed," and his gratification at her sympathy: the classic warrior/maiden bond.

The Duke is charmed: "I think this tale would win my daughter, too," he murmurs indulgently. But Brabantio is counting on a last chance to prove his fixed conception of his daughter. When Desdemona enters, he leads with what he thinks is his strongest card: he asks the young woman who has hitherto been all compliance to state "Where most you owe obedience" (I.iii.181). She responds with an eloquent statement on the "divided duty" she perceives: "respect" for the father who has given her "life and education," but a more compelling devotion to her new husband. She cites as precedent her own mother's "duty" to Brabantio, "preferring you before her father" (ll. 186–89).

Brabantio had chosen this public forum as a means of pressuring Desdemona to resume her former role. But with great poise and dignity she has stood her ground, and his ploy backfires: not only his political allies but the child of his loins have denied him, and the hearing becomes the scene not of her but of his humiliation. Brabantio is stung into vindictiveness. First, he denigrates the family bond: "I had rather to adopt a child than get it." Then he imagines vicarious vengeance on other daughters if he had them, for Desdemona's "escape" would "teach [him] tyranny"— to keep them in manacles (ll. 191–98). He again insults his new son-in-law, addressing Othello by his racial designation, "Moor," and telling him that, had he not won Desdemona already, Brabantio would "with all [his] heart … keep [her] from thee" (ll. 192–95). The intimate pronoun signals not affection but contempt.

The Duke tries to intervene in this painful public quarrel and "help" the lovers back into the father's graces. But Brabantio turns aside his consoling aphorisms with cutting sarcasm and shifts the focus to the military crisis. Othello agrees to lead the campaign against the Turks, asking only "fit" accommodation for his bride while he is away. The Duke responds, "If you please, be't at her father's" (ll. 239–40), the usual abode for a wife whose husband was absent. But Brabantio cuts him off, completing his blank verse line with the curt "I will not have it so." The negation is immediately echoed by both Othello and Desdemona. She elaborates: "I would not there reside / To put my father in impatient thoughts" (ll. 241–42)— tactfully avoiding accusation and focusing instead on the issue of his undisturbed tranquility.

Out of this stalemate arises Desdemona's impulsive request to accompany her husband to the scene of battle. She couches her plea in the most idealistic terms: She has "consecrate[d]" not only her "fortunes" but her "soul" to Othello's "honors and his valiant parts" (ll. 253–54). The religious allusions suggest the fervor of the young bride's commitment. She professes to the assembled company her devotion to "the very quality of

[her] lord," and adds, "I saw Othello's visage in his mind" (ll. 251–52). This platonic conception of the essential Othello directly counters her father's disparaging view of his mere outside. It is an ideal that Desdemona will persist in maintaining against all evidence of the actual man's fearful decline.

For the moment, however, Othello's idealism equals his bride's. He asserts that he wants her to accompany him not to "please the palate of [his] appetite"—for physical gratification—"but to be free and bounteous to her mind" (I.iii.262–65). The Duke, pragmatist that he is, leaves the decision to the newlyweds, "either for her stay or going," demanding only "haste in the preparations." He makes one last attempt to ingratiate Othello with Brabantio: "noble signior / If virtue no delighted beauty lack, / Your son-in-law is far more fair than black" (ll. 288–90). The light rhyme suggests his own ingrained bigotry. Brabantio's response is to bestow not a parting blessing but a curse:

> Look to her, Moor, if thou hast eyes to see:
> She has deceived her father, and may thee   [ll. 292–93].

His words reflect his adamant belief in male authority. For the moment, Othello seems above such bias. He defends Desdemona nobly: "My life upon her faith." But his father-in-law's warning will return to haunt him when he has lost faith in himself. The agent of that loss is at hand: Othello sends Desdemona off in the care of "honest Iago," the very man bent on destroying the new marriage.

But Iago alone could not undermine so seemingly perfect a union. What causes the love to deteriorate horrifically into murder and suicide? For one thing, the lovers do not know each other very well: the courtship has been brief and superficial. Also, the couple relocates to an unfamiliar place that is hostile to romance and to women. But the most important factor is Brabantio's unyielding rejection. When Brabantio first lodged his complaint, the Duke questioned him about the cause of his laments for his daughter: "Dead?" The father responded, "Ay, to me" (I.iii.59). The rest of the play shows the effect of that cruel decree.

Desdemona has been charged with weakness and gullibility in the face of Othello's increasing rage. But if she is merely a fool and Othello a brute, the play is reduced to a farce in which we lose sympathy for the lovers and simply relish Iago's machinations. In fact, Desdemona does not lack courage or wit: She has been bold and eloquent in defense of her love, even before an assembly of the most powerful men in the state. But because her devotion to Othello has cost her so much—father, society, home—she clings to her absolute concept of his worth. Without Brabantio's paternal protection and advice, Desdemona has no one to shield her from Iago's schemes. Brabantio has provided his daughter neither the emotional means to independence nor the continued shelter that her naiveté requires. She has dared to defy his will, and, feeling abandoned, he abandons her, concealing his hurt with anger. Brabantio does not witness the dire results of his rejection: he makes no further appearances in the play. But, as we discover in the end, the sentence that he passes on her — isolation and death — will fall on him as well.

Desdemona suffers this fate partly because she is what she seems, the "jewel" of "perfection" that both her father and her husband conceive her to be: in Othello's words, an "entire and perfect chrysolite" (V.ii.146). But the metaphor has an ominous ring: a woman should not be seen as a possession, whose beauty and purity reflect well on its owner. The concept of ideal femininity that the play presents literally, rather than metaphorically, is equally troubling. Fittingly, it is offered by the villain.

Iago has conducted Desdemona safely to Cyprus and they are waiting through a terrible storm for the arrival of Othello's ship. With noble self-possession, she tries to "beguile" her anxiety by engaging the ensign in repartee. Since he has insulted his wife Emilia and women in general, the new bride demands archly: "How wouldst thou praise me?" (II.i.124). Instead of addressing her, he continues to mock the whole female sex until she demands that he describe "a deserving woman indeed" — someone that even "malice itself" must revere. Iago complies with a description that in fact fits the character of his interlocutor: "ever fair, and never proud," "ha[s] tongue at will and yet [is] never loud," "being angered, her revenge being nigh / [Bids] her wrong stay, and her displeasure fly"; "Sees suitors following, and not look[s] behind" (ll. 148–56). In short, beautiful, articulate, modest, poised, faithful — and conveniently subservient to masculine authority: Brabantio's very ideal. Typically, Iago gives it a misogynistic twist: Even if such a paragon existed, he concludes, her only functions would be "to suckle fools and chronicle small beer" — produce worthless offspring and tend petty household accounts. Desdemona denounces this "lame and impotent conclusion" and calls Iago a "profane and liberal counsellor" (ll. 160–63). But she misses the genuine spite underlying his wit. In turning to "malice itself" for praise, she has once again trusted in those incapable of cherishing her intrinsic value.

Iago has maintained to Roderigo that this marriage consists merely of "sanctimony and a frail vow between an erring barbarian and a supersubtle Venetian" (I.iii.352–53). In fact, he does not think that Desdemona is promiscuous or hypocritical — that she could be anything but sincere and steadfast. He believes something more dangerous: that her essential goodness is a weakness, out of which he can "make the net / That shall enmesh them all" (II.iii.343–45).

Iago begins by reinforcing the stereotype of the young wife wearying of an old husband, practicing first on the gullible Roderigo. "She must change for youth," he tells the smitten suitor, "when she is sated with his body, she will find the error of her choice" (I.iii.347–48). After he and Roderigo have watched the passionate reunion at the harbor, he comments scornfully: "Her eye must be fed; and what delight shall she have to look upon the devil?" (II.i.223–24). Elizabethans thought of the devil as black, so the allusion is a slur on both Othello's spirituality and his race. "To give satiety a fresh appetite," Iago continues, warming to his subject, Desdemona would require "loveliness in favor, sympathy in years, manners and beauties; all of which the Moor is defective in." Inevitably, he predicts, she will "begin to heave the gorge" (ll. 226–30) — sicken of that diet and vomit. Again, this is an exaggerated version of Brabantio's bigotry and chauvinism.

The villain uses these same ideas, put in less crude terms, to persuade Othello that Desdemona could not possibly love him. Pretending to be a sympathetic confidante, he says that he wishes to protect Othello's "free and noble nature" from becoming the means to his abuse. In fact, that is exactly the ploy that Iago is in the process of using. At first, Othello resists the terrible suggestion by means of logic:

> 'Tis not to make me jealous
> To say my wife is fair, feeds well, loves company,
> Is free of speech, sings, plays, and dances;
> Where virtue is, these are more virtuous   [III.iii.183–86].

Besides, he reasons, "she had eyes, and chose me." But soon Iago is posing as the expert on Venetian sexual norms: "I know our country disposition well," he claims (l. 201). As such, he sees in Desdemona's attraction to a Moor "a will most rank" and "thoughts unnatural." Taking his cue from Brabantio, he ignores Desdemona's preferences and presents himself as the definer of the "natural." A desirable husband, he asserts, must be "Of her own clime, complexion, and degree" (ll. 229–33).

Iago alludes more directly to Brabantio's views by echoing the old man's parting warning:

> She did deceive her father, marrying you;
> …She that, so young, could give out such a seeming
> To seel her father's eyes up close as oak —
> He thought 'twas witchcraft   [III.iii.206; 209–11].

Iago exaggerates this charge, using the oak simile to depict Desdemona as preternaturally manipulative. His specialty is the graphic word picture that burns itself into the listener's imagination. He uses the same technique to demean the courtship and to slip in another insult to Othello's appearance: "when she seemed to shake and fear your looks, / She loved them most" (ll. 207–08). As with Brabantio, Desdemona's devotion to Othello is made to look like treachery.

Othello, who only moments before had been defending his wife, starts to accept this reading of his own worth and hers. Perhaps, he reasons, because he is "black," lacks the courtier's "soft parts of conversation," and is "declined / Into the vale of years" (III.iii.263–66), Desdemona has deserted him for the handsome young Florentine, Cassio. He has already begun to think of her as less than human — a "haggard" (wild hawk) — and to call love "appetite" (ll. 260, 270).

Desdemona is not blind to the change in Othello's mood, but she sees it only in terms of his comfort. Ever solicitous, she asks: "Are you not well?" (III.iii.283). He replies that he has a headache — traditional complaint of the cuckold, whose pain is caused by his sprouting horns. She takes him literally and attempts to apply the folk remedy of binding his forehead with her handkerchief. Othello knocks it aside with a curt dismissal: "Your napkin is too little" (l. 287). In her concern for his affliction, she lets it drop unnoticed. It is the symbolic climax of their relationship. The handkerchief, a courtship gift that Desdemona treasured, will become the circumstantial evidence that convicts her of adultery in Othello's eyes. But those eyes have already been tainted by Brabantio's imputation, distorted into guilt by Iago. The handkerchief is "too little" to encompass Othello's jealousy. Nothing that Desdemona thinks to do from this point on can compensate her husband for his supposed loss. Long before the phrase spousal abuse came into popular usage, Shakespeare understood its nature. The wife who ignores the hostile signs or assumes that faults in herself cause her husband's rage only puts herself in greater peril.

Desdemona's situation is complicated by the military setting. After Iago has engineered Cassio's dismissal for dereliction of duty, the disgraced lieutenant asks her to plead his case to Othello. He is acting on the advice of Iago, who has praised her "free," "kind," "blessed disposition," and sworn that the infatuated Othello would do anything she asked (II.iii.305–06).

Desdemona reacts to Cassio's plea exactly as Iago predicted. She assures him: "I will do all my abilities in your behalf" (II.iii.1–2). That includes, she says, petitioning Othello to restore Cassio's lieutenancy to the point that "his bed shall seem a school, his board a shrift" (l. 24). She takes up his cause for disinterested motives. She judges Cassio, rightly, as "one that truly loves" Othello, and that "err[ed] in ignorance, not in cunning" (ll. 48–49). She goes so far as to excuse his "trespass" as so petty that it would scarcely merit "a private check" (ll. 64,67), rather than the public shame and loss of rank that Cassio has in fact suffered. But this reaction reveals the other side of Desdemona's pure nature: she is too compassionate and unworldly to function in a military realm. A ruling general cannot be so lenient toward an officer who has failed in his duty and endangered the post he was assigned to guard. Worse, she seems oblivious to the suspicious appearance of the situation: a beautiful bride fervently defending a charming courtier.

The shades that Desdemona does not see with her innocent eyes Iago is quick to perceive with his cynical ones. Soon he is providing Othello with the "ocular proof" (III.iii.360) — the appearance of guilt — that the general demands. First, Othello accepts that Cassio's hasty exit is evidence of a liaison between the courtier and the bride, rather than what it is: shame before the revered officer whom he has failed. A corrosive tissue, woven of such circumstantial evidence, innuendoes, and outright lies, torments Othello until he is entirely persuaded of Iago's twisted views:

> Her name, that was as fresh
> As Dian's visage, is now begrimed and black
> As mine own face   [ll. 386–88].

He cannot see that he is basing his judgment solely on externals — Desdemona's supposed reputation and his own supposedly repellent appearance, offered by a supposedly authoritative male comrade — exactly Brabantio's reductive credo.

By the time Iago has convinced Othello that he saw Cassio "wipe his beard" with the handkerchief — a singularly contemptuous and suggestive act — the once supremely poised general is "eaten up with passion" (III.iii.391). He cries, "I'll tear her all to pieces!" (l. 431). Othello regains only enough control to put a ceremonial face on his rage. Kneeling, he pledges vengeance "in the due reverence of a sacred vow" (l. 461) — this from a man who only a short time before made a similarly fervent vow to his new wife. To underline that blasphemy, Shakespeare has Iago kneel beside him and pledge his "wit, hands, heart" (l. 466) to Othello. This is a perverse echo of the marriage ceremony, and at the same time a satanic rite. Convinced that Desdemona is a "fair devil" (l. 479), Othello gives his soul to the real demon. The act ends with Iago's chilling seal on that pact: "I am your own for ever."

At first Desdemona refuses even to acknowledge the dire change in her husband. Fretting over the missing handkerchief, she professes herself relieved that Othello is not the sort of man to be made suspicious by the loss of his special gift. She assures Emilia:

> my noble Moor
> Is true of mind, and made of no such baseness
> As jealous creatures are...   [III.iv.26–28].

The worldly maidservant questions this callow assertion: "Is he not jealous?" But Desdemona remains determinedly optimistic. When Othello observes that her hand is "moist," she responds cheerfully, "It hath yet felt no age nor known no sorrow" (l. 37). She ignores— or misses— his implication: according to Elizabethan physiology, a moist palm is a sign of lasciviousness. When his accusation becomes more explicit and his tone threatening, she is stunned: "Why do you speak so startlingly and rash?" (l. 79). The question has a childlike directness. She admits that he has changed only when his once-eloquent diction is reduced to curses and obsessive demands for "The handkerchief!" Watching him stalk off, she expresses amazement: "My lord is not my lord; nor should I know him, / Were he in favor as in humor altered" (ll. 124–25). But it is telling — and ominous— that she sees the alteration as superficial, a question of mood ("humor"). She will not relinquish her image of his essential nobility.

Desdemona applies the same high standards of integrity to her own conduct. Generously, she assures the despairing Cassio that she will continue to petition for his reinstatement: "What I can do I will; and more I will / Than for myself I dare" (III.iv.130–31). She tries to convince herself that political troubles, originating either in Venice or in Cyprus, have "puddled [Othello's] clear spirit" (105). Again, she insists on seeing this spirituality as his fundamental nature. When Emilia at last convinces her that he is jealous, Desdemona protests, "Alas the day! I never gave him cause" (l. 158). Emilia rejects the naive assumption: "Jealousy," she says, is a solipsistic "monster," "begot upon itself, born of itself." Desdemona's response is to pray that "heaven" will "keep that monster from Othello's mind" (ll. 161–63). She is still speaking in the future tense. It takes public humiliation at Othello's hands to convince her that the monster has struck.

By this point, Othello has completely succumbed to Iago's falsehoods. He ignores his instinctive approbation of Desdemona: "A fine woman! a fair woman! a sweet woman!"— a talented musician, a beauty, a speaker of "high and plenteous wit" (IV.i.174–75; 186–87). Those gifts can only rankle if she is lavishing them on his junior officer. He can cope with his hurt only by turning it to fury, by converting painful feelings to brutal actions. "My heart is turned to stone," he tells Iago. "I strike it, and it hurts my hand" (ll. 179–80). In this dangerous mood, he is both self-destructive and sadistic. Consummate soldier that he is, Othello sees cleansing violence as the readiest remedy. He vows to murder his supposed betrayer "this night." His satanic confidante is ready with the means: to "strangle her in her bed, even the bed she hath contaminated" (ll. 202–03). Othello professes himself "pleased" by the "justice" of the scheme.

Into this explosive situation walks Lodovico, the ambassador from Venice, come to greet the "worthy general" and his fair cousin. The unsuspecting Desdemona appeals to this new party to mend the "unkind breach" (IV.i.219) between Othello and Cassio. The recurrence to that sore topic sets Othello frowning and mumbling ominous asides as he pores over the dispatch from Venice. Desdemona is puzzled by his mood: "What, is he angry?" (l. 228) she asks naively. When she attempts to comfort him with affectionate words—"Why, sweet Othello"—he shouts "Devil!" and strikes her. Her reaction is dignified and respectful of his authority: "I have not deserved this" (l. 235). It is left to Lodovico to express shock and to defend her. Othello, beside himself, commands: "Out of my sight!" (l. 240). Her dutiful response, "I will not stay to offend you," recalls her comment on her father's objection to her remaining in his house: An angry man must be spared the sight of a woman who has provoked him. The credo of the abused wife was taught Desdemona at home.

Othello is not through humiliating her, however. He calls Desdemona back, mocks her compliance as evidence of concupiscence—"Sir, she can turn, and turn, and yet go on / And turn again" (to various partners)—and her tears as feigned: "O well-painted passion!" (IV.i.246–50). With a final "Hence, avaunt!"—the command used to exorcise devils—he dismisses Desdemona from their presence. Lodovico, who has not seen the couple since their loving declaration before the senate, is astonished by the terrible change in Othello.

Yet even this public shaming does not teach the young wife sufficient fear of her own danger. When next she sees Othello, he has summoned her for private questioning. Only then, after all his conference with Iago and the excruciating public quarrel does he state his suspicions explicitly. His purpose is not to give her a fair hearing. We have seen from his preceding inquisition of Emilia that he is convinced that Desdemona is "a subtle whore" (IV.ii.21). He dismisses the maid's staunch defense of her mistress as a mass of lies and Desdemona's frequent recourse to prayer as hypocrisy. The form of his dismissal to Emilia reflects his cynicism: "Leave procreants alone and shut the door; / Cough or cry hem if anybody come" (ll. 28–29). The man who a short time earlier swore that his love for his wife was entirely spiritual is now treating her as though she is a prostitute and her servant the madam of a brothel. In happier times, Desdemona responded indulgently to Othello's whims: "Be as your fancies teach you; / Whate'er you be, I am obedient" (III.iii.88–89). Now in these dire circumstances, she maintains her former graciousness. Her greeting to the man who has just struck her in public is "My lord, what is your will? ... What is your pleasure?" (IV.ii.24–25).

When he begins abusing her anew, Desdemona senses his mood but not his purpose: "I understand the fury in your words, / But not the words" (IV.ii.33–34). Even when he calls her "false as hell," she is baffled: "To whom, my lord? With whom? How am I false?" She assures him that "heaven" is her witness to what she is: "your wife ... your true and loyal wife." Desdemona retains the naive conviction that guiltlessness will save her. She still cannot take in the full import of Othello's accusation. She poses the unlikely theory that he is angry because he believes that her father has caused him to be recalled to Venice. She is eager to exonerate herself and to share his pain: "Lay not your blame on me. If you have lost him, / Why I have lost him, too" (ll. 46–47). This is the one time that Desdemona expresses her hurt at her father's rejection and suggests the price she has paid to leave his sheltered home.

It takes Othello's explosion of Job-like self-pity for Desdemona to admit, still tentatively, the cause for his fury: "I hope my noble lord esteems me honest" (i.e., chaste) (IV.ii.65). His response is to slander her outright in a crescendo of lewd epithets: "whore," "public commoner," "impudent strumpet!" Finally stung to indignation, she takes a stand, denying his accusations with the strongest oaths she knows: "By heaven, you do me wrong!" "No, as I am a Christian!" "No, as I shall be saved!" (ll. 82–87). He is too far gone to credit her piety. Calling Emilia back, he offers her money and asks her to keep customers' "counsel." Then he stalks off.

Alone with the older woman, Desdemona says that she is "half asleep" (IV.ii.97)—too shocked even to weep. When Emilia asks what is wrong with her "lord," Desdemona replies, "I have none" (l. 102). Othello has deteriorated to the point that she no longer recognizes him. But her own identity is also in flux. For counsel, she turns to her worst enemy: "Am I that name, Iago?" she asks pathetically. She cannot bring herself even to pronounce the vile word.

When Emilia, vulgar and candid, speaks for her, saying Othello "bewhored her," Desdemona confirms the term with another circumpraxis: "such as she said my lord did say I was" (ll. 116–19). Othello's fury has overwhelmed her. She is, she tells them, "a child to chiding"; the mild verb again puts her husband's abuse in euphemistic terms. Again, it is Emilia who expresses the indignation that is called for: this slander is an ironic reward for all that Desdemona has "forsaken" in the name of this marriage: "many noble matches, / Her father, her country, and her friends" (ll. 125–26). Desdemona herself is stoic and self-effacing, accepting the abuse as her "wretched fortune" and vowing to continue to "love [Othello] dearly" even if he should subject her to "beggarly divorcement" (ll. 157–58). She senses that he may have a worse fate in store for her: "his unkindness may defeat my life," she says, "But never taint my love" (ll. 161–62). This sounds like a description of pining away from unrequited love. But there are also hints that she fears a more violent demise.

Desdemona tells Emilia to obey Othello's orders that her wedding sheets be laid on their bed and the serving woman be dismissed for the night. "We must not now displease him" (IV.iii.16), she counsels, and says that she loves him so devotedly "that even his stubbornness, his checks, his frowns ... have grace and favor in them" (ll. 19–20). We have seen enough of Brabantio's temper to guess that she is accustomed to such expressions of male authority. Yet Desdemona understands something of the risk she is taking. Her mood as she undresses is melancholy. She asks Emilia to promise that, should she die first, the maid will use one of the wedding sheets as her shroud. And she is haunted by a song once sung by her mother's maid Barbary. The associations are ominous: "She was in love; and he she loved proved mad / And did forsake her" (ll. 26–27). The song "expressed her fortune / And she died singing it." Now Desdemona cannot resist singing it herself. The most prescient line is "Let nobody blame him; his scorn I approve" (l. 50). Barbary, too, was passive and forgiving. Emilia is their temperamental opposite. Her long speech blaming wives' "frailty" on men's mistreatment concludes with an injunction to revenge: "Then let them use us well; else let them know, / The ills we do, their ills instruct us so" (ll. 101–02). Desdemona counters by advocating not that women best a bad example but turn the other cheek, remain paragons and so set a standard that will "mend" the "bad." It is her old credo, which she will follow to the death.

Othello returns, obsessed with the self-glorifying concept that he is bearing the "sword" of "Justice" (V.ii.17) and that Desdemona must be the "sacrifice" (l. 65) on that cold altar. Only when he tells her to confess herself because he "would not kill her soul" does she fully realize her peril. "I hope you will not kill me," she gasps. She admits her own "fear," but she still makes the naive error of connecting suffering with guilt: "Why I should fear I know not, / Since guiltiness I know not; but yet I fear" (ll. 35, 38–39).

Desdemona's senses are painfully alert. She sees Othello's restless gestures with a child's awe of her chastiser, and she accepts his command to "be still!" (V.ii.46). But when he accuses her of taking Cassio as her lover, she is staunch in defense of her innocence. "I never...," she swears, denying in turn each article of Othello's accusations. The news that Cassio has been murdered causes her to break down, weeping equally at his betrayal and her own terror. Othello takes the tears as confirmation of adultery, and he moves in for the kill. Her pleas become more desperate as she bargains for time — "tomorrow," "but half an hour," "but while I say one prayer!" (l. 83). In these last moments, she fights him with all her strength: on stage, this can be a horrifyingly protracted struggle. Othello is inexorable; he smothers her as she cries once more to heaven: "O Lord, Lord, Lord!"

That cry could be Desdemona's last word, but Shakespeare gives her a more eloquent end. She revives to profess her innocence once more — "A guiltless death I die" (V.ii.123), and to spend her last breath in service to Othello. Emilia, who has burst in, demands to know who has attacked her mistress. Desdemona, who had managed to say that she has been "falsely murdered," now utters that the killer is "Nobody — I myself" (ll. 118, 125). Her last request is a final assertion of Othello's noble nature: "Commend me to my kind lord" (l. 126). By telling a lie on her death bed, Desdemona, a devout Christian, has willfully committed a mortal sin. Othello, who has shown grace only in the wish to spare her soul, now cries wildly, "She's like a liar gone to burning hell! / 'Twas I that killed her." Emilia immediately perceives the charity in Desdemona's act and pronounces her an "angel" for this self-sacrifice and Othello "the blacker devil" (ll. 130–32).

Although he is heartbroken at the loss of Desdemona, Othello still believes her guilty. The combined testimonies of Emilia, Roderigo, and the revived Cassio convince him that she was indeed the "entire and perfect chrysolite" she seemed, loyal and chaste. Her pure example sparks a restoration of his noble demeanor, and in his last moments, Othello regains both the idealism and the valor that Desdemona insisted were his essential nature. He calls his acts "unlucky" and himself "one that loved not wisely but too well" (ll. 341–44). "Nought did I in hate," he insists, "but all in honor" (l. 295).

But for all the sincerity of his suffering, in most ways Othello has learned nothing. These final claims, while noble sounding, are self-exculpating rationalizations. He never regrets his failure to heed his wife's word nor to treat her as a person with an independent will. He still sees Desdemona as a priceless object — a "pearl" — and himself as a despicable alien — "the base Judean" who cast it away (V.ii.347). And he again turns to violent action to resolve an emotional crisis. His military creed demands revenge — but the guilty party is Othello himself. He recalls a moment of past glory, when he slew "a malignant and a turbaned Turk" who had "beat a Venetian and traduced the state" (ll. 353–54). Casting himself as both loyal subject and loathsome foreigner — ironically, his own and Brabantio's initial opposing conceptions— he reenacts the execution. In the end, Othello shows no more mercy and little more understanding for himself than he did for Desdemona.

Not only Othello's tragedy but that of the father-in-law who rejected him is solipsistic. Both the husband's metaphors, of jewels and of military prowess, echo those of Brabantio at the beginning of the play. The ultimate irony is that although husband and father may seem at first to be diametrical opposites, they misjudge and mistreat Desdemona in remarkably similar ways. It is no accident that the couple whose union Brabantio refused to bless end by confirming his most dire misgivings. And the old father himself? Gratiano, another emissary from Venice, reports Brabantio's fate as he stares down at Desdemona's corpse:

> I am glad thy father's dead.
> Thy match was mortal to him; and pure grief
> Shore his old thread in twain. Did he live now,
> This sight would make him do a desperate turn   [V.ii.205–08].

Fittingly, Brabantio has died off-stage. The focus of the play has been on the daughter, not the father. But it is clear that he has borne the self-imposed sentence that he passed at the first news of Desdemona's elopement: the rest of his life was "a despised time" filled with "naught but bitterness" (I.i.160–61). Not Iago's malice but Brabantio's invidious credo creates the net that enmeshes them all.

In these three plays, then, the more tragic the tone, the more deeply are father and daughter locked in a struggle over the worthiness of her suitor. In the comedy, Hermia pays little attention to Egeus's objections to Lysander, and emerges with her choice secure and her father silenced by higher authority. Egeus's own suffering is limited to anger and frustration. In the tragicomedy, Jessica not only ignores her father's directives but robs him to attain marriage to the man she loves. There are hints, though, that the union is strained and that the daughter feels the burden of betraying her heritage. Shylock, like Egeus, is silenced by higher political authority — more than silenced, punished. Although he is still alive at the end of the play, he has suffered grave social and emotional harm. In the tragedy, Desdemona has eloped with the man she loves even before the play begins.

She must still face her father's bitter disapproval, however. She is so intent on proving Brabantio's rejection of Othello unjust that she accompanies her husband to a hostile place and closes her eyes to his faults. Brabantio's early overprotection and subsequent disownment of Desdemona combine to leave her virtually defenseless, and she falls prey to both her father's and her husband's abuse. The main catalyst to the tragedy is Brabantio's rigid conception of the father-daughter bond. Like Juliet, Desdemona attains freedom of will only at the cost of self-destruction.

3

Daughters Who Acquiesce: Hero (*Much Ado About Nothing*), Lavinia (*Titus Andronicus*), and Ophelia (*Hamlet*)

> "Green girls ... unsifted in perilous circumstance."
> *Hamlet*, I.iii.101–02

Not all of Shakespeare's daughters are rebels. Some are docile, eager-to-please young women — classic Good Girls. Their fathers view them as ideal children whose beauty and accomplishments reflect well on their families and whose conduct presents no threat to authority. Each young woman accepts the suitor of her father's choice and takes pains to make herself presentable and agreeable. The plays begin as that tranquil stasis is about to be disrupted. In the crisis that comes with the daughter's maturity, these fathers are convinced that they know what is best, and they feel no qualms about imposing their wills. These daughters, unlike their rebellious counterparts, do not question their fathers' views nor complain about the effects of their commands. Lest we credit this submissive stance as Shakespeare's ideal, or as the feminine norm for that period, we have only to look at the blight that it creates.

In the comic version of this plot, *Much Ado About Nothing*, Hero is rescued by external forces, and her reputation and happiness, so far as we can judge, are restored. In the tragic versions, the story of Lavinia in *Titus Andronicus* and Ophelia in *Hamlet*, the young women suffer isolation, abuse, and death. The gauge of each play's tone is the extent to which the damage caused by unquestioning obedience is made permanent and irreparable. Another indication of the skeptical eye that Shakespeare casts on the conventional model of daughterly subservience is the feigned version that he creates in other plays. Bianca, the supposed Good Girl in *The Taming of the Shrew*, is revealed to be a sly manipulator of both father and suitor. Goneril and Regan, the wily flatterers in *King Lear*, emerge as ruthless power-mongers and patricides. (They will be discussed in Chapter 4.) In no case does Shakespeare present the domineering father as the standard of justice and wisdom.

Much Ado About Nothing

Hero's story is in many ways the comic version of Desdemona's. She, too, is falsely accused of sexual license by an unscrupulous villain and publicly humiliated by the suitor he has duped. She, too, is rejected by a father who doubts her intrinsic worth and pronounces her better unborn than disobedient. Her groom is also a brave and accomplished soldier, just returned from a successful military campaign and eager for celebration and love. The setting is also analogous: Italy — Messina in this case rather than Venice — land of hot days and strong passions. The main characters are again aristocrats, well spoken, privileged, and idle. Hero, like Desdemona, has a woman friend who believes in her innocence and defies her male accusers in a passionate defense of her honor. The differences between the women's situations, however, are crucial in assuring that both the development and the outcome of Hero's story remain comic.

Rather than being exiled from her native city, relegated as Desdemona is to a fortified island, Hero remains ensconced in her native social element. The forces of religion, family, and friendship act in concert to rescue the wronged maiden. This time her female ally is not the recently met and socially inferior Emilia, but a cousin of her own class. Beatrice's defense of Hero, based as it is on both empathy and lifelong friendship, is infectious. It inspires first the Friar who conducts the disrupted wedding, then the groom's bosom friend, and finally the rejecting father to recognize her innocence. Unlike Othello, the lover is not a battle-hardened general but an impulsive junior officer, readily influenced by the mentors he reveres. The villain, the malcontent Don John, is much less cunning than the master hypocrite, Iago. It takes no great leap of imagination for the play's protagonists, Beatrice and Benedick, to see him for the "bastard" that he is by birth and nature. Don John is incompetent, his schemes transparent, his henchmen bumbling. It takes only coincidence and eavesdropping — the devices of comedy — to expose his thin stratagems.

Even the setting in time and place reinforces the comic tone. The military battle has just been won, not averted by chance. Instead of the barely contained frustration of the garrisoned island in *Othello*, the mood of triumphant Messina is celebratory. The scene is ripe not for scheming and bloodshed but for dancing and romance. Exoneration and expiation are possible, and the play ends not in murder but in marriage.

Just under the laughter and the pipers' melodies, though, resound more ominous notes. Hero is betrayed by both father and suitor. Her "happy" marriage is achieved at the cost of silent acquiescence, first in the men's rejection, then in their refusal to see their mistreatment for what it is. All the protest, like all the defense, of Hero is left to her rescuer, Beatrice. One of her functions in the play is to make us see her cousin's happiness for the tenuous and compromised thing that it is.

Claudio, like the rest of Messina, knows Don John to be a cynic and a malcontent. His moroseness is so at odds with the festive temperament of the other nobles that Beatrice comments after their first encounter on "how tartly" he looks, adding wryly that his every appearance leaves her "heartburned an hour after" (II.i.4). Even the mild-mannered Hero notes that he has "a very melancholy disposition." That Don John is not only sad but malicious is also clear to all: his own henchman, Conrade, reminds him that he has been at odds with his brother and should be conciliatory since he is only "newly" restored to "his grace" (I.iii.20). Don John growls back that he prefers to be "disdained by all" for the "plain-dealing villain" that he is. His flimsy plan for sullying Hero's reputation depends on his questionable claim that "the lady is disloyal" (III.ii.89–90). The evidence is circumstantial: his supposed witnessing of the young woman's assignation with another lover at "her chamber window ... even the night before her wedding day" (98–99). Yet it is enough to cause Claudio and his patron, Don Pedro, to denounce the modest young woman. Benedick, after a moment's reflection, divines the true source of the evil: "John the bastard, / Whose spirits toil in frame of villainies" (IV.i.186–87). Why then does Claudio so readily credit the vicious lies about the woman he professes to love? The short answer is that the groom scarcely knows his bride.

The reasons are partly situational. Claudio is a newcomer to Messina, a "Florentine," in the company of the Prince of Aragon, Don Pedro, who has just "bestowed much honor" on him for brave military feats. Claudio is very young — resembling more a "lamb" than the soldierly "lion" one might expect and eagerly following after his "new sworn brother," the cosmopolitan Benedick. He has "noted" (I.i.145) Hero at an earlier time, he admits, using the word that echoes through the play from title to climactic scene. In Shakespeare's day "nothing" and "noting" were pronounced alike; the pun becomes an extended metaphor on the superficiality of appearances. Before, Claudio says, he "looked upon [Hero] with a soldier's eye"—attracted but intent on his "rougher task." Now that he has returned victorious, "war thoughts" have been replaced by "soft and delicate desires" (ll. 269–71). We should note — pun intended — that Claudio is describing a fantasy, not an individual woman. He confesses to Benedick, "In mine *eye*, she is the sweetest lady that ever I *looked* on" (ll. 166–67, italics mine). The jaded Benedick parries his sentimental outlook: "I can see without spectacles, and I see no such matter." For him, Hero is merely "Leonato's short daughter (ll. 189–90). He demands wryly, "Would you buy her, that you inquire after her?" The enamored young courtier responds, "Can the world buy such a jewel?" The pretty sentiment sugarcoats the ugly implication: the woman is an object whose value lies in her looks. Again the worldly Benedick undercuts the romanticism: "Yea, and a case to put it into."

Claudio is undeterred. When Don Pedro enters, he confesses to his other mentor in turn: "That I love her, I feel." The Prince responds: "That she is worthy, I know" (I.i.203–04). The stichomythia suggests their complacency. But what is the test of this worth? Claudio's only question to Don Pedro is an indirect inquiry about Hero's dowry: "Hath Leonato any son, my lord?" Don Pedro, instantly understanding the implication, assures him: "No child but Hero; she's his only heir" (l. 263). In their minds, the issue is settled: it remains only for Claudio to get her father's permission for the match and then, Don Pedro avers, "Thou shalt have her" (l. 278). Although the young woman will be informed, she will have no choice: she will be matched for life to this man who has been pleased enough by her "modest" looks to claim her.

Leonato is in perfect accord with this patriarchal system. In fact, for him the eligible suitors are interchangeable. When he is mistakenly informed that Don Pedro is the one seeking Hero's hand, he sends his brother to order her to accept. The uncle, old Antonio, expresses the conventional view: "Well, niece, I trust you will be ruled by your father" (II.i.43–44). But Hero, like Claudio, has a more worldly ally; her witty cousin Beatrice answers for her:

> Yes, faith. It is my cousin's duty to make curtsy and say, "Father, as it please you." But yet for all that, cousin, let him be a handsome fellow, or else make another curtsy and say, "Father, as it please me" [ll. 45–48].

Since this is a comedy, Hero suffers none of Juliet's angst at being betrothed to the wrong man. The misunderstanding about Don Pedro is easily resolved, and the attraction between her and Claudio is acknowledged to be mutual. At Beatrice's amused prompting, Hero shyly "tells him in his ear that he is in her heart" (II.i.282–83). So the match is made without the couple's having exchanged a single word. All the ado has been over "noting" (observing surface appearances): no wonder that the undoing will occur over "nothing."

The superficiality of Claudio's attachment is evident from his courtship: not he but Don Pedro is the spokesman. The prince sums up that process to his protégé: "I have wooed in thy name, and fair Hero is won. I have broke with her father, and his good will obtained" (II.i.267–68). Till this point, Claudio had been ready to believe Don John's lie, conveyed under cover of masks and disingenuousness, that his patron was trying to steal his lady. Disabused, he is nonetheless easily persuaded of his more vicious lie about Hero's promiscuity. "If you will follow me, I will *show* you enough" (III.ii.105, my italics), the villain promises. He adds, "think you of a worse title [than "disloyal"] and I will fit her to it" (ll. 96–97). On the surface, this sounds like tact: Don John does not wish to utter the full extent of Hero's lewdness. But the double entendre is a sly boast: anything that Claudio and Don Pedro can accuse Hero of, the schemer can make them believe.

Claudio's most damning fault, however, is not gullibility but malice. He vows not only to reject Hero but to "shame her" before the entire "congregation" assembled for their wedding. Her humiliation, in other words, must be made greater than his: the total ruin of her reputation. Don Pedro instantly allies with his protégé "to disgrace her" (III.ii.112). Neither considers taking the more direct and kindly approach: simply asking Hero herself to answer these incredible charges.

The ruined wedding, too, reflects the shallow nature of Claudio's love. Shakespeare builds suspense as the groom pretends at first to go through with the ceremony. He calls Hero a "rich and precious gift" whose worth he cannot "counterpoise"— innuendoes that suggest again the quantitative way that he measures her value. "Nothing," his mentor and co-conspirator adds, can equal such a prize "unless you render her again" (IV.i.27). This paradox is precisely the resolution that the comedy will offer: once Claudio has been taught to regret his haste and to pity Hero, his supposedly dead bride will be replaced by her newly exonerated self.

Several of Shakespeare's plays present a situation in which a woman is falsely accused of sexual license: besides *Othello*, *Measure for Measure*, *The Winter's Tale*, and *Cymbeline*, for example. In all, the mood turns ugly at the advent of this most difficult to refute charge. The enormous value accorded to chastity becomes clear if we look at the case of Lavinia in the early tragedy *Titus Andronicus*. Daughter of a Roman general, and newly married, Lavinia is set upon in a dark wood and raped by the two sons of her father's enemy. They compound her suffering by murdering her beloved husband and mutilating her, cutting off her hands and tongue so that she cannot name her attackers. Lavinia does succeed in identifying them, however, writing their names in the dirt by the torturous means of holding a *"staff in her mouth and guid[ing] it with her stumps"* (stage direction, IV.i.76). Once her father Titus has learned the rapists' identity, all his efforts are bent on exacting the cruelest possible revenge. He lures the miscreants to his quarters and slits their throats, with Lavinia aiding him by using her mutilated arms to "hold / The basin that receives their guilty blood" (V.ii.182–83). But Titus is not satisfied with mere murder. He must torment their mother, Tamora, Queen of the Goths, who had urged her sons to the rape as the greatest means of afflicting Titus.

The grisly revenge goes on. Titus next "grind[s] their bones to powder small," "temper[s] … the paste" with the blood he has drawn, and "in that paste let[s] their vile heads be baked" (V.ii.198–200). A fairy tale ghoul, he relishes his morbid role: "I'll play the cook" (l. 204), he exults. He serves Tamora the dish, tells her that she has been the unwitting cannibal of her own children, and then kills her in the horror of that new knowledge. But the striking point for our purposes is that Titus also kills Lavinia.

The death is not accidental; in fact, it is one in which the young woman acquiesces. She enters the banquet like a sacrificial victim, *"with a veil over her face"* (stage direction, V.iii.25). Titus asks his guests-enemies whether the legendary Virginius was right "To slay his daughter with his own right hand, / Because she was enforc'd, stain'd, and deflow'r'd" (ll. 37–38). Saturninus, the corrupt emperor, commends Virginius, "because the girl should not survive her shame, / And by her presence still renew *his sorrows*" (ll. 41–42, my italics). This is the height of male arrogance and kill-the-messenger female subjugation. It is especially ironic when we recall that Lavinia was married, and so presumably not a virgin, and was also the innocent victim of her father's wars. Yet she remains still and acquiescent: neither then nor earlier does she oppose her male kinsmen's (uncle, brother, and nephew, as well as father) conviction that she is ruined beyond hope. Never does she make any attempt to save herself. Lavinia is simply the object of the men's pity and the spur to their revenge. Titus kills her swiftly, echoing Virginius's supposed motives: "Die, die, Lavinia, and thy shame with thee, / And with thy shame thy father's sorrow die!" (ll. 46–47). The ruthless Tamora is shocked: "Why hast thou slain thine only daughter thus?" Even she would not murder her own offspring. But Titus is impervious to guilt:

Not I ... 'twas Chiron and Demetrius.
They ravished her, and cut away her tongue,
And they, 'twas they, that did her all this wrong   [ll. 56–58].

Granted that this, Shakespeare's earliest tragedy, is crude in plot and thin in characterization—closer to farce and melodrama than to high tragedy. Granted, too, that by this point Titus is nearly mad with grief and rage. After all, he has also murdered two of his own sons, whom he accused of dishonoring him by betraying his cause. Nevertheless, the issue of his daughter's honor has different grounds. Lavinia is a passive, not an active, agent in her father's dishonor. She "stains" his reputation not because of something that she does against him but because of something that is done to her. He does not kill her to spare her further suffering but to destroy the living embodiment of his "shame." Chastity, in which is included marital fidelity, is an absolute, valued more highly than life. No wonder then that Claudio's denouncement of Hero is so devastating.

The shift in tone in the wedding scene occurs when Claudio subjects his bride to an excruciating public castigation. Changing the terms of his marriage mart metaphor, he demands of his intended father-in-law: "Give not this rotten orange to your friend." Hero's blushes— she is shocked into speechlessness at first — show "guiltiness, not modesty" (IV.i.40), he claims. He overwhelms her with oxymorons: she is "most foul, most fair," an exemplar of "pure impiety and impious purity" (ll. 101–02). Although Hero still looks to him like "Dian in her orb / As chaste as is the wind ere it be blown" (ll. 55–56), he will not trust the testimony of his own instincts. Instead, Claudio credits what the bastard Don John has told him he has seen. "Are not our eyes our own?" he demands with unwitting irony. Claudio also accepts the word of the "ruffian" Borachio, who "hath / Confessed the vile encounters" he has had with Hero "a thousand times in secret." (ll. 91–92) This hyperbolic number recalls the "thousand ducats" (III.iii.101) that Borachio boasts of receiving from Don John for staging the tryst, with Margaret disguised as Hero.

Claudio is questioning the worth of Hero's "name," which he, ironically, is even then sullying. She is so shocked that she too questions her identity. "Is it not Hero?" she responds pathetically, "Who can blot that name / With any just reproach?" (IV.i.78–79) No one can: but reputation, not justice, is the issue here.

If this were the only plot, Hero's young life would be blighted beyond rescue, and *Much Ado About Nothing* would be a tragedy. In the outraged words of Beatrice, Hero has suffered "public accusation, uncovered slander, unmitigated rancor," and has been "wronged," "slandered," and "undone" (IV.i.298–301). The accuracy of this counter-charge is proven by the aftermath of Claudio's denouncement. Hero faints dead away, the accusers make a hasty retreat, and the wronged maid revives only to face the recrimination of the man who should be her protector: her father. He demands a "dagger's point" for himself and wishes for her "death" as "the fairest cover for her shame" (ll. 107, 114). Worse, he urges the reviving girl: "do not live, Hero; do not ope thine eyes" and goes so far as to threaten to "strike at [her] life" (ll. 121, 125). Leonato curses his only child with the bitterest wish a parent can express: that she had never been born.

In exact parallel to Claudio, his accusation is based entirely on appearances: "Why wast thou ever lovely in my eyes?" he demands of the forlorn young woman, and claims: "she is fall'n / Into a pot of ink, that the wide sun / Hath drops too few to wash her clean again" (IV.i.137–39). This sounds like a schoolroom version of Macbeth's bloody metaphor. Leonato's evidence is based on hearsay and the testimony of witnesses he never thinks to question: "Would the two princes lie," he demands, and "Claudio lie," who wept, he recalls, as he made the charges. Instantly, he has taken the men's word, including that of the malcontent Don John, dignified in his description as a "prince." It never occurs to Leonato to ask his daughter for her version of events. Even after her fervent denials, he wants blood — theirs or hers. "If they speak but truth of her," he growls, "These hands shall tear her" (ll. 188–89). Throughout this painful confrontation, he does not comfort his daughter or even talk to her. Fortunately, in the other witnesses to her slander, Hero has powerful champions.

The first of these is her best friend and nightly bedfellow, Beatrice. The cousins share deep sympathies, especially about one another's love interests. In the opening scene, the quiet Hero's only line is her gloss of Beatrice's witty inquiry after "Signior Mountanto": "My cousin means Signior Benedick of Padua" (I.i.32). Under Beatrice's sarcastic show of indifference, Hero knows, is a sincere anxiety about the soldier's safety. Later, Hero is the instigator of the scheme to make Beatrice admit her love for the only man who is her mental match. Hero knows her cousin's faults, and she knows, too, how to exaggerate them so that Beatrice will take the "false sweet bait" wrought by "little Cupid's crafty arrow" (III.i.33, 22). "Disdain and scorn ride sparkling in her eyes," she tells her waiting gentlewoman and the eavesdropping Beatrice. "Her wit / Values itself [too] highly." And she adds the final jab: "She cannot love ... she is so self-endeared" (ll. 51–56). In the company of other women, Hero is bright and open, a shrewd judge of character and an eager partaker in the mischievous plot.

Hero is also the soul of honor. She agrees to aid Claudio and Don

Pedro in this matchmaking scheme with a statement that might be her byword: "I will do any *modest* office ... to help my cousin to a *good* husband" (II.i.333–34, my italics). In a play replete with cuckold jokes—the first is Benedick's response to the love-struck Claudio's announcement that he intends to marry (I.i.175–76), the last Claudio's own remark just before the wedding that as a husband Benedick is sure to become a "double dealer"—Hero keeps a staunchly clean tongue in her mouth. As she is dressing for her wedding, the loose-tongued Margaret offends her with some bawdy jests, and Hero snaps, "Fie upon thee! Art not ashamed?" (III.iv.25). Even in the duping scene, pretending to castigate Beatrice, she credits her with the values that both cousins, in fact, embrace: "truth and virtue," "simpleness and merit" (III.i.69, 70). So by the time of Claudio's accusation, the audience has had ample evidence that Hero is a paragon of modesty and sincerity.

We have seen, too, that Beatrice would be a formidable defender. As the overwhelmed messenger says after her invective about the absent Benedick: "I will hold friends with you, lady" (I.i.80), and Leonato concedes to his niece, "Cousin, you apprehend passing shrewdly" (II.i.70). What Beatrice "apprehends," she must express. While the men, including the usually poised Benedick, remain nonplussed by Claudio's denouncement, not "know[ing] what to say," Beatrice knows exactly how to answer the charges: "on my soul, my cousin is belied!" (IV.i.144). She dismisses Claudio as "Count Comfect"—no gallant but a sugar-coated flatterer and slanderer. "It is a man's office," she tells Benedick to "right" Hero. And the means? "Kill Claudio" (ll. 262, 284). The short, grim command fills Benedick—and us—with horror. It disrupts the comic tone and would, if carried out, turn the play blackly tragic. Shakespeare must pull out all his comic tools to patch together a happy resolution.

The simplest of these devices is dramatic irony: the Watch—and the audience—know the truth. The guards have overheard Borachio's account to Conrade of the conspiracy, and they take the "arrant knaves" (III.v.30) into custody. However incompetent they prove as witnesses—Dogberry fails to stop the doomed wedding because he is "too cunning to be understood" (V.i.217–18)—they have assured that the truth is there to be discovered. As the sardonic Borachio observes to the nobles: "What your wisdoms could not discover, these shallow fools have brought to light." To corroborate the bumblers' testimony, the henchman is moved to a remorseful confession, and the chief conspirator, Don John, confirms his own guilt by "secretly [stealing] away" (IV.ii.56). He, too, is caught and, safely off-stage, "brought with armed men back to Messina" (V.iv.123). So Shakespeare puts the plot structure in place for proving Hero's innocence.

On the deeper level of character development, Beatrice is not made Hero's only champion. The Friar who performed the wedding ceremony proves a thoroughly sympathetic witness. Simply on the evidence of his instincts and experience, "by noting of the lady," he stakes his "age," "reverence," "calling," and "divinity" on her being "guiltless" (IV.i.156; 165–66). This stranger's perception of Hero's blushes and protests is considerably more sensitive than that of the two men who claim to love her, her father and her fiancé.

The Friar's scheme for "righting" Hero depends not on violent action but on pathetic forbearance. He urges Leonato to publish the claim that her swoon was fatal, so that thereby the "dead" lady "Shall be lamented, pitied, and excused / Of every hearer" (IV.i.214–15). Claudio, the Friar predicts, will soon miss and value her anew: "Th' idea of her will sweetly creep / Into his study of imagination" and "every lovely organ of her life" be enhanced by "the eye and prospect of his soul" (ll. 222–27). This is an ironically fitting method to restore so superficial a love: to replace the suitor's tainted image of Hero with a newly shining version. Should this plan fail, the Friar offers an alternate possibility: concealment "in some reclusive and religious life"—the nunnery of Hamlet's bitter command to Ophelia—"as best befits her wounded reputation." In other words, Claudio's false accusation has ruined any chance for Hero to marry another. The best hope that the Friar can offer is "This wedding day / Perhaps is but prolonged" (ll. 251–52). He urges on her the passive course: "Have patience and endure." The dazed Hero remains silent.

Better Beatrice's violent response, most modern young women might think. But do suitor and father ever acknowledge how much they have abused the innocent Hero? No: they are agreed both on the limited extent of Claudio's guilt and on the superficial means of expiating it. After the Friar and Beatrice have persuaded Leonato to pretend that Hero is dead, he at last challenges Claudio: "I say thou hast belied mine innocent child" (V.i.67). But his chief concern is with defending his own "honor" and that of his "ancestors" and with lauding himself as a paragon of fatherly devotion. There can be, he claims, no other "father that so loved his child / Whose joy of her is overwhelmed like mine" (ll. 8–9). Admittedly, he is feigning grief in order to spread the rumor that Hero is dead. In a comic twist, his credulous old brother is so moved that he challenges the young gallant to a duel, and Leonato must restrain him. Still, Leonato prides himself on the depth of his own "bereavement"—in the form not only of mourning but of bitter disappointment. Like Brabantio in his appeal to the Duke of Venice, he will not agree to "patch grief with proverbs," and claims proudly:

> I will be flesh and blood
> For there was never yet philosopher
> That could endure the toothache patiently   [ll. 34–36].

Hero, of course, is expected to practice just such stoicism under much greater suffering. Nor does Leonato accuse Claudio of willful malice. Later he will call both him and Don Pedro "innocent," agreeing that they accused Hero only "in error."

Claudio's view of his actions exactly reflects Leonato's values. Having lost Hero, he misses his "image" of her, which appears to his fancy, he says, "in the rare semblance that I loved it" (V.i.238–39). Her posthumous reward for all the "shame" he has brought upon her, he claims, is "glorious fame"— the exculpation of the blot on her ancestral "honor" that preoccupies Leonato. The suitor, too, sees his only fault as gullibility: "Yet sinned I not / But in mistaking" (ll. 261–62). Nevertheless, his guilt at the offense to her reputation shows in his eagerness to return to his would-be father-in-law's graces. Between them, the men devise the perfect superficial expiation.

"I cannot bid you bid my daughter live," Leonato begins, lying slyly, "That were impossible" (V.i.266). He posits the ultimate substitute, his brother's daughter, "Almost the copy of my child that's dead," whom he decrees that Claudio must marry. It is *The Winter's Tale* resolution, telescoped in time and minus the husband's angst. At the ceremony, Claudio vows, "I'll hold my mind, were she an Ethiope" (V.iv.38). His major criterion for love — beauty, and socially acceptable beauty at that — remains unchanged. When the bride enters masked, his first request is to see her face. The mask lifted, he exclaims, "Another Hero!" (l. 62). She concurs: the first "died defiled"; she has been reborn "a maid"— virginal in fact and report. Leonato underlines the point: "She died, my lord, but while her slander lived" (l. 66). As in *Titus Andronicus*, the daughter's reputation is valued more highly than her life. Witnessing this resolution, old Antonio says complacently, "Well, I am glad that all things sort so well." No blame is attached to Claudio, no accusation of insensitivity or irresponsibility. No one speculates on the future of the match between this egotistical young man and self-effacing young woman.

Lest we think that this is the whole picture of romantic love, Shakespeare places it against the backdrop of Beatrice and Benedick's more open, more solidly based relationship. "I was not born under a rhyming planet," Benedick thinks aloud when he realizes that he is in love with his long-time sparring partner, "nor I cannot woo in festival terms" (V.ii.38). Practical and frank, the two set to wrangling for the upper hand even on the brink of their wedding. He comments wryly to his beloved, "Thou and I are too wise to woo peaceably" (1. 64). At the end of *Much Ado*, though, rhyme, festival terms, and harmony prevail. The villain and the threats to marital concord, suggested in Claudio's final jokes about cuckoldry, are matter for "tomorrow." The last word is Benedick's command to ignore all such dark thoughts and begin the wedding dance: "Strike up, pipers!"

Hamlet

The figurative fate of Hero, the dutiful daughter in a comic world, is to be duplicated, her shallow bridegroom pronouncing her "copy" as desirable as the original. In contrast, the metaphorical lot of Ophelia, her tragic counterpart, is to be cleaved in half, "divided from herself and her fair judgment." Even more readily than Hero, Ophelia hearkens to her father's every word. Her bywords are established in her first appearance: "I do not know, my lord, what I should think" and "I will obey, my lord." Lest we think that Shakespeare is portraying in Ophelia the ideal of Elizabethan daughterhood, he makes clear that the father whom she reveres is a hypocrite, a busybody, and a fool, and that Ophelia's rewards for subservience are humiliation, madness, and death.

Hero has no need to explain her dismay and mortification. She swoons, and her best friend speaks for her. Ophelia has no woman friend to confide in. The men who do put words in her mouth have little understanding of her feelings and needs. They give her orders, dismiss her protests, insult or condescend. Each attempts to make her conform to some feminine stereotype that reflects well on his "honor." Each betrays her.

Polonius and his son Laertes treat Ophelia like a child and picture her as a "chaste treasure" to be hoarded and guarded, even from the prince. It is *their* reputation that chiefly concerns them, as suggested by father and son's other favorite metaphor: they picture her virginity as a delicate "flower" that might fall prey to the "canker" of pregnancy and consequent public shame. Ophelia is caught in the middle: loyalty to her father and brother means betrayal of her lover. When she carries out the rejection that Polonius has commanded, her obedience, ironically, subjects her to the public humiliation they would avoid at all costs: Hamlet, stung by her sudden coldness, treats her like the loose woman of their deepest fears. When her lover murders her father, Ophelia breaks down. Only in her mad songs does she find a voice for her grief, her sexual longings, and her bitterness. Even that small rebellion against the men's expectations is short-lived. Treated like a flower, expected to look sweet and fragile, "pretty

Ophelia" reverts in her desolation to that sanctioned image. In her horrified brother's words, bawdry, insanity, "hell itself" she "turns to favor and prettiness." Polonius is no longer alive to witness the pitiful wreck that his daughter's life has become.

The vain old counselor of the opening acts could never have predicted such an end — or the destructive effect that he also has on his son. Shakespeare makes clear the bases for the father's treatment. A profligate in his own youth, Polonius expects all young men to follow that course. He guards his daughter against such supposedly universal license and sanctions it in his son. Intent on control, he wants to know the most intimate details of his children's private lives. Polonius's attitude toward Laertes comes through clearly in his tête-à-tête with his servant Reynaldo. Laertes has just returned to the pleasures of life in France, and the lord chamberlain is dispatching his man to take him "money" and "notes." The other purpose of this visit, though, is for Reynaldo "to make inquire / Of his behavior" (II.i.4–5). Polonius gives elaborate instructions for spying on his son. He even urges Reynaldo to spread lies that Laertes is "very wild, / Addicted so and so" (ll. 18–19), as a way of eliciting information, though "none so rank / As may dishonor him."

"Honor" — that is, reputation — is Polonius's chief preoccupation, as his earlier dicta to Laertes about dressing, quarreling, and borrowing suggested. Now he means, he explains to Reynaldo, the "usual slips ... most common / To youth and liberty" — gambling, drinking, and even "drabbing" — whoring. Reynaldo objects to the last rumor as a source of "dishonor." Polonius disagrees: he does not mean "incontinency," but only such passion as shows "The flash and outbreak of a fiery mind" (II.i.25–33) — manliness, in short. Whether or not Laertes is guilty of such "slips," Reynaldo is to discover through gossip. Thus, Polonius concludes complacently, "Your bait of falsehood takes your carp of truth" (l. 63). The sententiousness, the circumlocution, and the prying are all typical of him. He stresses that he has no wish to circumscribe his son's sensual pleasures. His last directive to the servant is the ambiguous "Let him ply his music" — perhaps, "practice his instrument" but, more likely, "indulge his vices." Towards his daughter, Polonius shows no such forbearance.

Laertes is his father's son. The first time that we see him, he is warning his sister about the very propensities in young men that Polonius believes are universal. Laertes also echoes his father's authoritarian tone and favorite metaphors. The subject he takes up is clearly one that he and Ophelia have discussed before. "For Hamlet and the trifling of his favor," he begins, that is only "a violet" of youthful impulse, "sweet, not lasting" (I.iii.5–8). He paints Ophelia as a tender bud, a "button of the spring" that might be "galled" by the "canker" [worm] of sexual license. Shifting metaphors, from the horticultural to the military, he warns that she must keep her "chaste treasure" out of "the shot of danger and desire." His thesis is "Be wary then: best safety lies in fear" (l. 43). Laertes is talking, of course, not about some wild affair but about the love between Ophelia and the prince of the realm. He concedes, "Perhaps he loves you now" (l. 14). But Hamlet's very rank is the basis for Laertes's distrust: "He may not, as unvalued persons do, carve for himself," he warns. His "choice" must be sanctioned by "the main voice of Denmark" (ll. 19–20; 28).

Politic and ambitious courtier that he is, Laertes presumes to know the limitations of Hamlet's choices. Later we see that, in fact, both the king and the queen would gladly have approved the match. In any case, "the safety and the health of the whole state" have already been hopelessly undermined by Claudius's regicide in a way that no marriage can restore. Laertes cannot know that, of course. But in his arrogance, he is oblivious to the insult he is giving both lovers: he is denigrating both the sincerity of Hamlet's love and the worth of the woman it is directed at. His final warning is:

> Fear it, Ophelia, fear it....
> ...weigh what loss your honor may sustain
> If with too credent ear you list his songs   [I.iii.33, 29–30].

In retrospect, this speech contains irony upon irony: in listening with too credent ear to *this* song, Ophelia loses not only honor but sanity. In the end, overwhelmed by fear, the only songs that she can hear will be her own mad ones.

At this point, though, Ophelia has the presence of mind to resist this ill counsel. She is very fond of her brother: she promises to write him often and she listens patiently to his advice. But, perhaps because of their closeness in age, she recognizes the source of his suspicions about other young men in his own loose behavior. She even slyly turns Laertes's flowery metaphor back on him, saying that she hopes that he is not preaching to her about taking "the steep and thorny way to heaven" while he himself treads "the primrose path of dalliance." (I.iii.48–50)

But if Ophelia can see through her brother's attempts to control her, she has no such perspicacity about her father's. Although she has assured Laertes that his advice is "in [her] memory locked" (I.iii.85), when Polonius demands to know what his son has been saying, Ophelia reluctantly acquiesces: "So please you, something touching the Lord Hamlet" (l. 89). He recalls the court gossip about the couple — "'Tis told me..." — and demands specific details: "What is between you? Give me up the truth" (l. 98). This is a father who spies on both his children, but his daughter he denies any semblance of privacy and independence. Polonius has no intention of letting Ophelia "ply [her] music."

Her innocent revelations spark a tirade on "my daughter" and "your honor": for him, the two are inseparable. When Ophelia protests that Hamlet has courted her "in honorable fashion," and pledged his love "with all the holy vows of heaven," the old man dismisses those words as "springes to catch woodcocks"— proverbially stupid birds. His concept of his daughter is cuttingly dismissive: "Pooh! You speak like a green girl / Unsifted in such perilous circumstances" (I.iii.101–02). Reducing her status still further, he cautions, "Think yourself a baby." Otherwise, he concludes, "you'll tender me a fool" (ll. 105, 109)— make *him* look foolish, perhaps by tendering (producing) a child out of wedlock ("fool" was an Elizabethan endearment for "baby").

Polonius echoes not only his son's sentiments on this subject but also his metaphors. Ophelia must "set [her] entreatments" at a higher rate than "a command to parley" (I.iii.122–23). The woman is pictured here in military terms, as a castle under siege. Like Laertes, he dismisses the vows that she believes are silver "sterling" as not, in fact, "true pay." His values are those of the market place, with the highest premium put on wiliness and material gain. Polonius can never resist multiplying his metaphors, and the one he adds in this case sullies the love still further: Hamlet's "holy vows" are, he claims, "brokers" and "bawds" (ll. 114, 127, 130)— procurers. Upon what does he base these degrading charges? Conventional wisdom and, he implies, his own past:

> I do know
> When the blood burns, how prodigal the soul
> Lends the tongue vows   [ll. 115–17].

Again, these are Laertes' precepts. But instead of merely concluding with a warning, this sermonizer issues an order: Ophelia is to cease all further "words or talk" (a typical Polonian redundancy) with "the Lord Hamlet." Giving the prince his title underlines the reason that Polonius believes the prince is simply toying with her. Ophelia seems deaf to his pomposity and venality alike. She makes no further protest to his devastating command: "I shall obey, my lord," she responds meekly — and does, to her ultimate destruction.

Nor does further experience teach Ophelia the foolishness of this counselor. The next time that we see her, she has sought him out to report a crisis: "O my lord, I have been so affrighted!" It is the voice of a child awaking from a nightmare. She has come to report on Hamlet's disheveled appearance in her "closet." Polonius immediately expresses what he sees as the only possible interpretation of such conduct: "This is the very ecstasy of love" (II.i.102). Then he turns on the frightened girl: Has she given the prince "any hard words of late?" Oh no, she assures him, "but as you did command, / I did repel his letters and denied / His access to me" (ll. 109–11). Clearly, he has forgotten all about the harsh order that she has been so scrupulous in carrying out. Now he admits his error — "I feared he did but trifle"— and regrets his officiousness. He claims that that fault is typical of the old, as "common" as "for the younger sort / To lack discretion" (ll. 116–17). Neither father nor daughter notes that he has learned nothing from his mistake: he continues to think in behavioral stereotypes. Nor does his egregious mistake make him cease to interfere in his daughter's life. His conclusion to her sad tale is another order: "Come, go we to the king." His intention is to report "the very cause of Hamlet's lunacy" and so make political capital of Ophelia's misery. She, too accustomed to subservience to make any protest, remains silent.

In the interim, Ophelia turns over to her father the love letters that Hamlet has written her and recounts the "time," "place," and "means" of all her lover's "solicitings" (II.ii.126–27). Like all the failed fathers in Shakespeare's plays, Polonius thinks of his daughter as his property; as he says to Claudius when he goes to relay the intimate details of her love affair: "I have a daughter (have while she is mine)..." (l. 106). He congratulates himself before the king and queen on her "duty and obedience," which have led her to give him the letters. He proceeds to read one sample aloud and to defile it further by mocking its style. The man who preached to his son that the chief value in life should be truth to oneself robs his daughter of privacy, respect, and integrity.

Polonius's next actions confirm his underlying motive: to make Ophelia a pawn in his ambition for political favor. Before he presents his plan for testing his theory that Hamlet's madness is caused by unrequited love, he demands of the king: "What do you think of me?" Claudius gives the expected answer: "As of a man faithful and honorable" (II.ii.129–30). Polonius, pleased, praises his own efforts at intervening in the "hot love" he has been so keen as to perceive and at warning her that the "prince" is "out of [her] star" (l. 141). "I went round to work" (l. 139), he reports complacently, and launches into a lecture against social climbing whose purpose is to advance his own status. His next scheme is to use Ophelia to prove his theory: When Hamlet walks through the lobby, Polonius will "loose [his] daughter to him." The verb, with its connotations of hunting, reflects his crass indifference to her feelings. He and Claudius will hide "behind the arras"—a hanging tapestry—and eavesdrop on the lovers. The plan recalls his scheme for having Reynaldo spy on Laertes. Here, Ophelia herself will serve as the "bait of falsehood" that will land what Polonius is convinced is the "carp of truth." When Hamlet suddenly appears, he begs to test the "mad" young man's mood: "I'll board him presently.... O, give me leave" (l. 170). He is nearly bursting with eagerness to show off and to gain favor.

A major effect of Polonius's tête-à-tête with Hamlet is to express outright what has been implied earlier: we get the hero's own word that the king's chief courtier is a hypocrite, a toady, and a fool. Under cover of madness, Hamlet scores one insulting point after another. In response to Polonius's probing questions about whether he "knows" him, the prince responds that he is "a fishmonger"—Elizabethan slang for a pander, and thus a glance at Polonius's treatment of Ophelia. He sharpens the needle with a warning that a man who has a daughter must guard her lest she "conceive," a frank allusion to Polonius's fears. Master of style that he is, Hamlet takes wry pleasure in mocking Polonius in his own idiom. He posits a stereotype of the Old Man, who is characterized by "a plentiful lack of wit" (II.ii.198). These barbs penetrate even Polonius's thick hide: "How pregnant sometimes his replies are," he muses, unwittingly alluding to his own greatest anxiety. When Hamlet finally gets rid of the would-be spy, he expresses his contempt outright: "These tedious old fools!" (l. 217) He reasserts that scorn each time they meet.

Before the "nunnery scene," Gertrude tells Ophelia: "I hope your virtues / Will bring [Hamlet] to his wonted ways again, / To both your honors" (III.i.40–42). But both women should divine that they are sanctioning a betrayal that will alienate him irreparably. Of course, neither knows at this point that Hamlet's beloved father was murdered, and by the despised stepfather who "now wears his crown." Still, they could not miss the hostility he expresses to Gertrude's precipitous second marriage. The first time that he vents his feelings in private, Hamlet hisses, "Frailty, thy name is woman" (I.ii.146). He shows that misogyny in every encounter with his mother and his lover. Ironically, Ophelia's fault is the opposite of "frailty": she is blindly, self-abnegatingly loyal—but to her father. At the same time she *is* frail: fragile and passive. The two men whom she expects will protect her are blind to her suffering. Her father is a fool and a social climber. Her lover is obsessed with his own father's return from the grave and his charge to exact revenge on the "incestuous, adulterate beast" who has taken his throne and his wife. Hamlet has vowed to "wipe away all trivial fond records" and to concentrate on "setting right" the disjointed time: a messianic enterprise that excludes such "trivial" and "baser matter" (I.v.99, 104) as Ophelia's well being.

The men in Ophelia's life — her lover, her father, her king — subject her to an encounter of excruciating humiliation. She has prepared a neat little set speech for returning Hamlet's letters and breaking off their affair. It concludes with a Polonian epigram: "to the noble mind / Rich gifts wax poor when givers prove unkind" (III.i.100–01). Hamlet, as usual, seizes the advantage in a verbal duel and breaks both the sententious mood and the meter. "Ha, ha! Are you honest?" he demands. The word meant "chaste" in Elizabethan parlance — the very issue that is preying on his mind in regard to his mother and that drove Polonius to make Ophelia break with Hamlet. Sadly, he concedes, "I did love you once," and blames his own faults and the corrupt state of the world for his fickleness: "I loved you not" (ll. 115, 119). Ophelia is confused by the contradiction and mortified by the knowledge that Polonius and Claudius, labeling themselves "lawful espials" (l. 32), are eavesdropping on this intimate talk.

Still, the exchange to this point has been fairly civil. Suddenly, with the question "Where's your father?" (III.i.130), Hamlet's mood shifts to sharply suspicious and bitter. The usual stage business at this point is to have his question provoked by an exposed shoe or sudden movement behind the arras. Stunned, Ophelia replies lamely, "At home, my lord." The feeble lie drives Hamlet over the edge. "Let the doors be shut upon him, that he may play the fool nowhere but in's own house" (ll. 132–33), he cries. What follows is a vitriolic tirade against women and marriage, ending with the "plague" he gives Ophelia as a "dowry": Even were she "as chaste as ice, as pure as snow," her fate would be "calumny." The only alternative he offers is the "nunnery" — Hero's other choice, proffered here as half a curse, half a prayer.

The poor girl is crushed. Her one inference is that he has gone mad: "O, what a noble mind is here o'erthrown" (III.i.150). Her manly ideal, the paragon of intellect, courtesy, and beauty, "th'observed of all observers," is "blasted with ecstasy." She can only pray weakly — "O heavenly powers, restore him!" a petition that provokes further vituperation. Hamlet stalks off after a final threat, directed at the eavesdroppers, against marriages in general and the life of one of those already married in particular. Ophelia collapses, describing herself as "most deject and wretched," beset by "woe" to "have seen what I have seen, see what I see" (ll. 155, 160–61). She is dazed and helpless as a wounded animal.

The king and his counselor emerge from hiding to comment on the prince's behavior. Claudius, the wily politician, recognizes that Hamlet has been showing neither "love" nor "madness." Polonius, reluctant to relinquish his pet theory, still insists that the "origin and commencement of his grief / Sprang from neglected love" (III.i.177–78). Ophelia, meanwhile, is forgotten. The one word spoken to the desolate young woman is her father's directive: "You need not tell us what Lord Hamlet said. We heard it all." On stage, this line is often supplemented by comforting gestures, but in the text it is brief and cold.

The focus of the men's exchange is on the political repercussions of the prince's threat. Claudius announces his plan to send his dangerous stepson abroad; Polonius, still convinced that Hamlet is mad, proposes spying on him once again, this time when he is summoned to his mother's chamber. Gertrude, supposedly "all alone," must "entreat" him to reveal the cause of "his grief" (III.i.182–83). If she cannot discover what troubles him, then Polonius concurs with the plan of sending him away. The wily king agrees in an abrupt about-face: "Madness in great ones must not unwatched go," he pronounces solemnly. Claudius has realized that Hamlet's "antic disposition," which he has just called feigned, might still be credited by the gullible and, thus, useful for his purposes. The tone-deaf lord chamberlain, busy with his own scheme, takes no note of the changed attitude. Neither man expresses a word of concern for the young woman they have just exploited. Ophelia makes no objection to her father's abuse. In fact, neither she nor Laertes ever questions his motives or his worth.

Ophelia is made to face further humiliation, this time in a more public arena. With the entire court assembled for the performance of "The Murder of Gonzago," Hamlet pointedly chooses to sit by her and then to address her as though she were a prostitute. "Lady, shall I lie in your lap?" (III.ii.107) he begins. When she objects to his crass language, he asks with assumed innocence, "Did you think I meant *count*-ry matters?" (l. 111, italics mine). His crude pun on the female sex organ is intentional. Quickly, Hamlet's lewdness becomes so explicit that Ophelia is driven to scold: "You are naught, you are naught. I'll mark the play" (l. 139). But she tries once more to divert him by appealing to his theatrical expertise: "What means this, my lord?" She succeeds only in evoking more obscenity: he pictures himself as the commentator on a scene of Ophelia and a lover "dallying" like "puppets." To her lame compliment that he is "keen," he responds lasciviously, "It would cost you a groaning to take off mine edge" (l. 240). Ophelia is hopelessly outmatched in this duel. Hamlet has on his side not only superior wit but a relish for public show. The young woman, shy, modest, keenly aware of what should be her proper role, has for defenses only simulated poise and feigned ignorance: "I think nothing, my lord." She does not stand a chance, either of controlling him or of preserving her dignity.

Directly after the disrupted play, Polonius appoints himself once more the eavesdropper on Hamlet's private conversation and assures the distraught king: "I'll call upon you ere you go to bed / And tell you what I know" (III.iii.34–35). Claudius, overwhelmed by the knowledge that Hamlet knows and has shown the entire court the precise manner of the regicide, absentmindedly agrees. He is all too aware of the real reasons for Hamlet's rage and he wants to be alone to pray and think. Polonius, oblivious as usual to anyone's feelings but his own, undertakes the new scheme with relish. He confronts the queen with a script that he has invented for the coming confrontation: "Tell him…," "Look you lay home to him…" (III.iv.1–2). This is the approach we have seen him use before, with his servant and his children. He loves playing the moral arbiter. Instead, he ends up not only ignominiously exposed but de trop. Polonius's death, accidental and unnecessary, turns the play irreversibly in the direction of tragedy. Its immediate consequence is the destruction of the daughter who has obeyed his every wish.

Hamlet's ruthlessness about his murder of Polonius is foreshadowed before the performance of "The Murder of Gonzago," when he mocks the chamberlain's youthful acting efforts. Polonius reminisces about the time that he played Julius Caesar and was duly killed by Brutus in the capital. The prince puns, "'Twas a brute part of him to kill so capital a calf"— Elizabethan slang for a fool. When Hamlet does in fact kill the old counselor, after mistaking the concealed Polonius for the king, his attitude is no less crass. His words to the corpse are ruthlessly contemptuous: "Thou wretched, rash, intruding fool, farewell! / Thou findst to be too busy is some danger" (III.iv.32–33). Later in the scene, somewhat calmer, he claims, to "repent," but still he sees the murder as "heaven's" means of punishing *him*, who "must be their scourge and minister" (l. 176). Noble, divinely ordained agent of God's will: it is a self-concept that does not permit remorse for the destruction of "baser natures" that come between "mighty opposites" (V.ii.60–62).

That lofty stand announced, Hamlet's tone switches back to sarcastic. He tells his mother, who has watched the murder in horror, "I'll lug the guts into the neighbor room." Then he turns his scorn once more on the dead man: "This counselor / Is now most still, most secret, and most grave, / Who was in life a foolish, prating knave" (III.iv.214–16). Neither then nor later when he evades Claudius's questions about where he has hidden the body with morbid puns does Hamlet express remorse.

More tellingly, it never occurs to Hamlet that his victim was the father of the woman he professes to love. At her funeral, he will insist: "I loved Ophelia" (V.i.256). There and in the letter that Polonius quotes to the king and queen, we have Hamlet's word for his devotion. But nothing in the play *shows* that regard. In fact, what we see is the aftermath of a seemingly shallow attachment. Never does Hamlet confide in Ophelia, appeal to her for aid, or profess his respect for her gifts: those roles in his life are fulfilled by his bosom friend, Horatio. The implication is that the young woman who can give an old busybody unquestioning devotion is too weak to be valued by "the son of a king." Ophelia's acquiescence in Polonius and Claudius's scheme to spy on Hamlet is the final proof in her lover's eyes of her unworthiness.

When Ophelia next appears, she has gone mad. Disheveled, speaking in double-edged non-sequiturs, breaking into snatches of song, she has been struck by the insanity that she believed afflicted Hamlet. Claudius pronounces the cause "the poison of deep grief," which "springs all from her father's death" (IV.v.75–76). Certainly that is the immediate cause. Ophelia "speaks much of her father" and sings about funeral rites and loss. She recalls "the grass green turf," the "stone," and the "shroud" (ll. 31–32) from his burial, and laments: "He is dead and gone, lady" (l. 29). The reference is clearly to Polonius: "His beard was as white as snow" (l. 193), she sings, and asks plaintively: "And will 'a not come again?" (l. 188). She answers her own question: "No, no, he is dead.... He never will come again" (ll. 190–92). It is the desolate wail of the lost child.

Laertes, called back from France, thinks, too, that this is the sole cause of Ophelia's breakdown: "O heavens, is't possible a young maid's wits / Should be as mortal as an old man's life?" (IV.v.159–60). But Ophelia herself suggests more complex causes for her insanity. "Lord," she muses, "we know what we are, but know not what we may be" (ll. 43–44). The other subject of her mad songs, besides bereavement, is seduction. In the Saint Valentine's Day ditty, the lover entices and then abandons the "maid" who visits his bedchamber, and "out a maid / Never departed more" (ll. 54–55). Is this an allusion to Hamlet's actual treatment of her? In Kenneth Branagh's recent film, the affair is made explicit, and some critics have speculated that Ophelia is pregnant. Or is this her projection of the seduction and abandonment that her father and brother warned her against? Perhaps it was a consummation that she devoutly wished but dared not pursue. The text is engimatic: The provocation for Ophelia's lewd ballad must remain ambiguous.

In any case, the sexual abandonment, so frequent a symptom of madness and so disconcerting to those who witness it, is short-lived in Ophelia's case. As Claudius says, excusing her shocking departure from decorum,

> poor Ophelia,
> Divided from herself and her fair judgment,
> Without the which we are pictures or mere beasts   [IV.v.84–86].

Ophelia has been too strictly trained to continue showing this "beastly" side. Throughout the play, she has been associated with flowers, fragile and transient, and in the end the extended metaphor takes on the force of prophecy. The adjectives most frequently applied to the mad girl are "sweet" and "pretty" (e.g., ll. 27, 57, 158). Her accusations of those who have harmed her are oblique: She speaks in the language of flowers, giving real or imagined "rosemary ... for remembrance" to her brother, "rue" to the guilt-ridden queen, and "a daisy," for "dissembling," to Claudius. She has no violets, which symbolize faithfulness, she explains, because "they withered all when my father died" (l. 183). A modern audience needs footnotes to interpret such innuendoes, but the Elizabethans were well versed in the symbolism of plants.

In her brother's eyes, Ophelia is herself a flower. Anguished by her deterioration, Laertes cries out to her, "O rose of May, / Dear maid, kind sister, sweet Ophelia!" (IV.v.157–58). He marvels: "Thought and affliction, passion, hell itself, / She turns to favor and to prettiness." He means this as a compliment to her womanly forbearance and refinement. We can look beyond that euphemism to her underlying frustration and hurt. Had Ophelia been encouraged to express her "passion" and "affliction" more openly, she might not have been driven to destroy herself. Instead, in the words of the gravedigger-clown, she achieves the paradox of "drown[ing] herself in her own defense" (V.i.5–6).

The process of Ophelia's death is entirely fitting for her repressed character: every aspect of her last moments is pretty and pathetic. While adorning herself with "fantastic garlands," the mad young woman slips into a stream. "Mermaid-like," she floats along, "chant[ing] snatches of old lauds," like "a creature native and endued unto that element," and oblivious to "her own distress" (IV.vii.175–79). By having Gertrude report this scene, instead of staging it, Shakespeare can put graceful distance on what would be an agonizingly painful struggle to witness. Everything in the account is tranquil, innocent, and passive. Ophelia does not actively commit suicide: her water-laden garments acted as murderers and "pull'd the poor wretch from her melodious lay / To muddy death" (ll. 181–82).

At her funeral, the prettification and the floral metaphor are sustained. Ophelia is "allowed her virgin crants [garlands], / Her maiden strewments" (V.i.219–20). The Queen sadly strews the flowers and utters a pretty epitaph: "Sweets to the sweet! Farewell" (l. 130). Laertes prays, "from her fair and unpolluted flesh / May violets spring" (ll. 226–27). But we have Ophelia's word that these symbols of faithfulness "withered all when [her] father died," and her own death is allowed no such pretty aftermath.

Her brother, as rash and aggressive as she is passive, is moved to violence by this final loss. He orders the gravediggers to "hold off the earth awhile" until he has given her body a last embrace, and then orders melodramatically that they bury him alive with his sister. Hamlet, who has been eavesdropping on this rite, is outraged by the affected style of Laertes's "grief." He steps forward to mock this "phrase of sorrow" that "conjures the wandering stars" (V.i.242–43). Although Hamlet claims to have "lov'd Ophelia" more than "forty thousand brothers" could have, his main preoccupation is not to mourn her but to challenge Laertes: "Dost thou come here to whine, / To outface me with leaping in her grave? / ... I'll rant as well as thou" (ll. 264–65, 271). And in he leaps. Within seconds, lover and brother are "grappling" in the grave, the corpse of the woman both profess to have loved forgotten. When the other members of the court break up the shameful scuffle, Hamlet professes puzzlement at Laertes' outrage: "What is the reason that you use me thus?" he demands. "I loved you ever" (ll. 276–77). Although Hamlet later expresses regret to Horatio that he "forgot [him]self" (V.ii.76) in this situation, at the time he seems as insensitive to the brother's suffering as he has been to the sister's.

In any case, Hamlet's disruption of the funeral provides the final spur to Laertes's revenge. Even before this confrontation, he vowed that he would willingly "cut [Hamlet's] throat i' th' church!" (IV.vii.125). Now his "speech of fire" turns to plans for dishonorable action. Laertes is again Ophelia's opposite, in imagery as well as in attitude: her element, we recall, is water. Fiery Laertes does not stop to reason or to question. He accepts Claudius's half-true claim that neither "by direct nor by collateral hand" (IV.v.204) is he responsible for Polonius's death. Spurred by hatred, Laertes betrays the highest principles of the chivalric code by which he has lived: honor in dueling and loyalty to the throne's rightful heir. He conspires with Claudius to win by using an unbated sword and doctoring the tip with poison. Claudius's contribution to this scheme, the poisoned cup, will prove his own undoing, but it is Laertes's dishonorable actions that will cheat the prince of life.

Before the duel, Laertes restates his old values, ironically in response to Hamlet's apology and attempt to make peace:

> In my terms of honor
> I stand aloof, and will no reconcilement
> Till by some elder masters of known honor
> I have a voice and precedent of peace
> To keep my name ungored   [V.ii.235–39].

Laertes is still looking to older authority figures for the definition of "honor." Only in his last moments will he admit that it is "almost against

[his] conscience" (l. 285) to win the duel by cheating. When that plot fails and he is stabbed with the poisoned rapier, he pronounces his own sentence: "I am justly killed by my own treachery." With his dying breath, Laertes exposes the king's plot and "exchanges[s] forgiveness" with the enemy he acknowledges as "noble" (l. 318). Hamlet uses his remaining moments to assure the political succession, restrain Horatio from suicide, and bid "adieu" to the "wretched queen" who has so preoccupied his overwrought imagination. He gives no thought to the young woman he berated and abandoned. Perhaps the final irony of the groundlessness of Polonius's fears about Hamlet's obsession with Ophelia is that, in the end, she is irrelevant to the prince's tragedy.

The ultimate effect of Polonius's parenting is devastation, of both his principles and his family. He had professed "honor" to be his major goal and had urged his son "above all": "To thine own self be true." But both father and son die ignominiously, in the course of treacherous acts. His daughter dies pitifully, sunken to insanity and suicide. Polonius equips neither of his children to see him objectively, to measure his homilies against his actions, or to question the role he has cast them in: son as clone, daughter as pretty possession. When he is killed, they are left desolate, Laertes desperately seeking a father figure to replace him, and burying his grief and fear in rage, Ophelia lost and helpless. Polonius has helped neither to develop a self to which to be true.

4

Plighted Cunning, Playing the Good Girl Role: *The Taming of the Shrew* and *King Lear*

> "Time shall unfold what plighted cunning hides."
>
> *King Lear*, I.i.120

Shakespeare, in his love of variations on a theme, depicted not only genuinely dutiful daughters but those who play that role. On first appearance, they are fair-spoken and subservient, to both fathers and suitors. But they soon reveal that "plighted cunning" hides manipulative, self-serving natures. Two plays that depict such daughters are otherwise markedly different in tone and depth: the early comedy *The Taming of the Shrew* and the majestic tragedy *King Lear*. In both plays, the fathers show preference to the hypocritical daughters and set down, by direct statement and implication, the public role that they want them to play. Both Baptista and Lear flatter themselves on being good fathers, and both see as the test of their effectiveness the daughter's compliance with her prescribed role. Above all, each man values reputation and status and eschews any word or act that reflects badly on his public image. The shallowness of their outlook is revealed by the presence of a sister who is the favored daughter's temperamental opposite. The disobedient daughter, disavowed and berated by her father, sees through her sister's Good Girl guise. This doubling of sisters is striking: in most of Shakespeare's plays, single daughters are the rule. The heroine's confidante is typically a friend or a cousin; her sibling, if she has one, as in *Hamlet* and *Twelfth Night*, is a brother from whom she is separated by circumstances. The pairing of sisters, with its juxtaposition of opposites, provides a telling look at the father-daughter relationship. What becomes clear by the end of both comedy and tragedy is the cost to the father of misjudging his children and to the daughter of abusing his trust.

The sister plots in *Shrew* and *Lear* are mirror opposites in tone and structure. The former play is a rousing farce, the latter a bleak tragedy; the differences in the daughters' motives and actions set the tone. In the comedy, the older sister is reportedly the unregenerate black sheep, causing her family public humiliation and herself insult and rejection. The younger sister, her father's "pretty peat" [pet], seems to him and her many suitors the ideal woman: eloquent, modest, and pliable, a "treasure" whose possession enriches their status. Her name, Bianca, Italian for "white," seems symbolic of the beauty and purity that all the men see in her. Only her rebellious sister, Kate, is aware of Bianca's petty, vindictive side — the ugly features that the pretty mask conceals. At the play's outset, Bianca's accomplished enactment of the Good Girl role seems to destine her for all the happiness that her unconventional sister lacks. Her gullible father is the main enabler of this sustained performance. He basks in the good impression that she makes and determinedly distances himself from the fractious Kate, refusing all blame for her behavior and intent only on "rid[ding] the house of her" (I.i.141–42). It takes the intervention of another man, someone who values Kate enough to teach her self-control and empathy, to break this cycle. By the end of the play, we have had ample evidence of Bianca's manipulativeness and Kate's integrity. True to the comic tone, the conflicts have been temporarily resolved in multiple marriages. Baptista, however, remains largely oblivious to his daughters' true natures: he has fixed Kate in the family stereotype of the shrew. But Bianca has begun to reveal, to husband and father, the claws and fangs beneath her white cloak.

In *Lear*, the sisters' roles are reversed: the elder are the accomplished hypocrites and the younger a model of integrity. Again, it is the youngest whom the father "love[s] the most" (I.i.290). Such doting, Shakespeare implies, does not necessarily spoil the child. Cordelia is deserving of Lear's favor. Like Bianca's, her name is symbolic, but this time the label is apt: the root word of Cordelia means "heart," suggestive of her compassion and unwavering devotion. The problem comes when the father posits a faulty image of ideal daughterhood, and the wily daughters use it to gain their own ends. In keeping with the play's tragic tone, the central issue is not the mere quest for a suitable marriage partner but the struggle for political power. The factor of loyalty between wife and husband does occur, but the focus is on the bond between father and daughter. As in *Shrew*, a private scene involving the sincere and hypocritical sisters shows us their true natures. This time, however, the schemers seek not merely praise and a large dowry but their father's title, wealth, and, eventually, his life. The honest daughter is excluded not only from the room but from the kingdom. The beset father suffers not just frustration and pique but exile and madness. Lear is granted a moment's reconciliation with his faithful child, but only a moment's. The ultimate price of his misjudgment will be the death of the daughter whose true worth he will come to acknowledge only when it is too late. His relationship with Cordelia, however, is matter for a later chapter. (See Chapter 6: "Daughters Who Forgive and Heal.") This one will focus on daughters who masquerade as paragons and fathers who abet them in playing that role.

The Taming of the Shrew

The Taming of the Shrew is broad farce from opening public spat to final raucous wager. At the same time, as in all of Shakespeare's best comedies, the main characters are drawn in psychologically realistic terms. The relationship between the wealthy burgher, Baptista, and his strikingly different daughters is evident from their first appearance. Flanked by Kate and Bianca, he announces the ground rules for their accessibility to two suitors and anyone else who cares to listen. He offers either man "leave to court [Katherine] at [his] pleasure," but restates his resolution "not to bestow [his] youngest daughter / Before [he has] a husband for the elder" (I.i.54, 40–41). The old father knows full well that the suitors, Hortensio and Gremio, have no interest in marrying "the shrew"—her type is specified in the cast list. Their predictable scorn of his offer only subjects her to ridicule, as she charges Baptista in her opening line: "Is it your will / To make a stale [laughing-stock] of me among these mates?" "Wonderful froward," even "stark mad," as she is, the suitors fear and disdain her. "No mates for you," Hortensio says sententiously, "Unless you were of gentler, milder mold" (ll. 59–60). Kate reacts with greater refractoriness, threatening to smash his head and claiming that the idea of marrying is "not halfway to her heart" (l. 62). The scene has such an air of the pageant wagon or the auction block that an onlooker, the newly arrived Tranio, mistakes it for "some show" (l. 47) designed to amuse him and his young master, Lucentio. The show is, of course, at Kate's expense.

Meanwhile, Bianca has been exhibiting the ideal of feminine decorum that the men exalt. Tranquil and quiet in the face of her sister's tantrum, she seems to the love-struck Lucentio the epitome of "maid's mild behavior and sobriety." Her father, who does not hear this aside, is in full accord with the sentiment. Calling her "good Bianca," he apologizes for having to separate her from her admirers and begs that it "not displease" her. He adds, "I will love thee none the less, my girl" (I.i.77). Kate hears this favoritism — she is *not* his "girl" — and reacts with a spiteful remark about Bianca as a "pretty peat" (spoiled papa's pet) who is feigning sadness. Soon, Kate vows, she'll see that her sister has good reason to weep. Bianca, breaking her silence at last, is inspired to heights of Good Girldom. First she urges Kate to be "content" with having caused her "discontent," and then she turns to her father to profess obedience and industry:

> Sir, to your pleasure humbly I subscribe.
> My books and instruments shall be my company,
> On them to look and practice by myself   [ll. 81–83].

The smitten Lucentio whispers to Tranio that this is "Minerva speak[ing]."

Bianca does not leave immediately, however, but lingers to hear Hortensio and Gremio praise her and lament that she must be "mew[ed] up" in "penance" for her sister's ill behavior. She also hears that sister subjected to such insults as "fiend of hell." Baptista defends himself as a "very kind and liberal" father, one who will provide tutors for his daughters "in music, instruments, and poetry" and devote himself to their "good bringing-up." Immediately, he makes clear which daughter he really means: "Katherina, you may stay, / For I have more to commune with Bianca" (I.i.100–01). He retreats into his house and the company of Bianca, abandoning Kate to more public humiliation. Kate refuses to be "appointed hours" and stalks off after him. Her anger thinly covers her hurt. Spoiled and unhappy, she would rather be berated than ignored. Her obnoxious behavior keeps escalating until she gets some acknowledgment.

Lucentio accuses Baptista of being a "cruel father" (I.i.182), but he is referring only to his seclusion of Bianca. He, like the other suitors, is oblivious to Baptista's cruelty to his elder daughter. The father has succeeded in preserving his own reputation, as, in Hortensio's words, "an affable and courteous gentleman" (I.ii.96) by exculpating himself from blame for Kate's "scolding tongue" and sour temperament. Hortensio again states the party line: Baptista has, after all, given Kate all the advantages, "brought [her] up as best becomes a gentleman" (l. 85). Since, in spite of such supposedly benevolent treatment, she has become a pariah, the men blame her. In the public eye and before eligible suitors, Baptista has declared Kate a hopeless misfit. Hortensio underlines the message that the father has conveyed: he "suppos[es] it a thing impossible, / For those defects ... before rehearsed / That ever Katherine should be wed" (ll. 120–22). Baptista has increased her humiliation by announcing his intention to use her younger sister's popularity and his wealth to better the seemingly impossible odds. Thus, at the same time that he has declared Kate's availability, he has jeopardized her one chance at the independence and status that only marriage could bring an Elizabethan gentlewoman.

The suitors stay behind to reiterate their scorn of her, though Hortensio reminds us that this is the marriage market, that Kate is the heiress to a fortune and there are men "would take her with all her faults, and money enough" (I.i.128). He and Gremio are in full accord with Baptista. They form a pact to find a suitor "that would thoroughly woo her, wed her, and bed her, and rid the house of her" (ll. 141–42). The lapse into prose underlines the crassness of their vow.

They go off, and Lucentio remains to pay starry-eyed tribute to Bianca, "that maid / Whose sudden sight thralled [his] wounded eye" (I.i.216–17). Cupid's little arrow has done its work. He utters exalted clichés about her "coral lips" and "perfumed breath" and declares: "Sacred and sweet was *all I saw* in her" (my italics, ll. 171–73). Her "modest" behavior and her "beauty" seem to him, as to her father, absolutes.

The first indication of the real Bianca comes when she is out of public view, away from her doting male audience. Kate, exasperated at the goody-goody way that she has behaved, has tied her hands. Bianca is not cowed by this bullying. Her first words are in her usual morally superior vein: "Good sister, wrong me not, nor wrong yourself.... " But immediately she drops sententiousness in favor of sarcasm, scorning the fetters as "gauds"—jewels. She threatens that if Kate does not free her, she will tear off all her clothes, down "to [her] petticoat" (II.i.5). She swears to fulfill this vow to "obey" Kate because she knows so well her "duty" to her "elders" (l. 7). The sarcastic tone, the mockery of her modest maiden persona, and the spiteful reminder of Kate's age suggest Bianca's true nature.

Her jabs work on Kate. She is clearly jealous and demands to know which of Bianca's suitors she "love[s] best." She adds, "See thou dissemble not," suggesting that she does not see her sister as a bastion of sincerity. Bianca responds by insulting Kate again, and at her sorest point: she offers to "plead" to either Hortensio or Gremio to accept Kate, adding with feigned disingenuousness: "Is it for him you do envy me so?" (II.i.18). The dart has a sharp point: both suitors have just told Kate to her face that they find her repellent. Kate, who loathes these men and claims to scorn marriage, nevertheless envies Bianca her popularity. She also sees through her Good Girl mask. In other words, the sisters have each other's numbers.

Into this spat steps Baptista, just at the moment when Kate *"strikes her"* (stage direction, II.i.22). All his sympathy is for the supposedly wronged innocent. He sees Bianca, bound and slapped, and makes no attempt to investigate the provocation for such treatment. "Poor girl, she weeps," he wails, and he turns on Kate, calling her a "hilding of a devilish spirit"—an evil-tempered good-for-nothing—and demanding: "Why dost thou wrong her that did ne'er wrong thee? / When did she cross thee with a bitter word?" (ll. 27–28). If Kate were calmer, she could answer both questions with ample examples, but instead she acts out her rage in another tantrum. Irrationally, she claims that it is Bianca's "silence" that "flout[s]" her, and she "flies after" her sister. This scene has been directed, rightly I think, so that Bianca, peeking around the shield of her father, makes faces at Kate, which he, of course, fails to notice. Kate cannot articulate how Bianca has provoked her because she is too humiliated and too hurt by her father's blatant favoritism. She confronts Baptista with the bitter truth about her position in the family: "She is your treasure, she must have a husband; I must dance barefoot on her wedding day, / And for your love to her lead apes in hell" (ll. 32–33)—the old maid's proverbial fate. The only bitter recourses she can envision are to "sit and weep" and to "find occasion for revenge" (l. 36)—depression or anger, both expressions of hurt. As usual, Baptista expresses no sympathy for this troubled daughter: "Was ever gentleman thus grieved as I?" (l. 37), he laments, his feelings entirely fixed on himself. Is it any wonder that this man has produced such self-centered children?

Alone with her suitors, Bianca reveals more of her true nature. Pretending to believe that the disguised Hortensio and Lucentio are genuine tutors, she first tells them categorically that she will not be subject to their authority: "I'll not be tied to hours nor 'pointed times, / But learn my lessons as I please myself" (III.i.19–20). The peevish tone sounds tellingly like Kate's. Bianca knows that the young men are using the disguise to evade her father's prohibition, and she enjoys both flouting the old man's authority and stringing them along. To Lucentio, her favorite, she gives a paradoxical message: "presume not ... despair not." Although she flirts so openly with him that Hortensio becomes suspicious, she relishes the double wooing. Bianca, unlike Kate, is a tease. Her parting words show her both playing the "sweet Bianca" role and leading the courtship dance with both partners at once:

> Take it not unkindly, pray,
> That I have been thus pleasant to you both   [ll. 55–56].

Provocative, self-satisfied, and naughty, this is *not* the "young modest girl" of Lucentio's romantic vision.

Nor is this the dutiful daughter of Baptista's fixed illusion. Because Bianca takes care not to disrupt that convenient image, Baptista assumes that he will maintain the usual paternal prerogative of choosing her husband. He conducts a contest between the rivals for her hand, unashamed of the materialistic grounds for victory:

> he of both
> That can assure my daughter greatest dower
> Shall have Bianca's love   [II.i.344–46].

Gremio, the "pantaloon," is "outvied" (l. 387) by Tranio, the servant disguised as his master Lucentio. The rules require the "assurance" of the fabulous marriage portion he offers, even if the groom should die. "If not," Baptista mandates, Bianca will be married to "signior Gremio." The father, then, will accept either husband, the stranger or the old fool: for all his favoritism and his pretty speeches about the requirement of winning the bride's love, he sees no need to consult her.

No matter. In *Shrew*, as in most comedies, youth is slyer than age. Bianca is more than a match for the father who has spoiled her. She has no qualms about deceiving him and eloping with a young man she barely knows. In fact, she has a better eye for the gold standard than the greedy old man, who is deceived into thinking that Tranio is the true Lucentio. In keeping with the comic mode, Bianca makes a fine match. But she does not go about it by kindly or decorous means. She could easily go straight to her father and plead the real Lucentio's case. Instead, she chooses the speedier and more exciting means of having her way. With Tranio still playing his master's role, the brash couple hire a traveling pedant to impersonate Vincentio. While they run off, he ensures that Baptista is distracted, "talking with the deceiving father of a deceitful son" (IV.iv.80–81) and "busied about a counterfeit assurance" (ll. 89–90). When they return from their elopement, Lucentio asks Baptista's "pardon," admitting, "I have made thy daughter mine / While counterfeit supposes bleared thine eyne" (V.i.105–06). The doggerel rhyme suggests his smugness. Baptista is infuriated into blustering prose: "But do you hear, sir? Have you married my daughter without asking my good will?" (ll. 122–23). But Lucentio is used to managing outraged fathers and, like Bianca, to having his own way. He reassures his bride, who "look[s] pale" at this first instance of her father's disapproval, that, his own identity revealed, "thy father will not frown" (ll. 126–27). Lucentio is well aware of Baptista's values. As the sole heir of a wealthy family, he is well qualified to meet the golden standard. Lucentio is also impervious to remorse. "Love wrought these miracles," he announces grandly, and adds: "Happily I have arrived at the last / Unto the wished bower of my bliss" (ll. 115–16). But Shakespeare does not end the play with this rose-colored vision.

If the shallow Bianca were the female lead in *Shrew*, the play would not have held the stage for four centuries. It is, however, her troubled sister who is the focal character. As Kate perceives, her father neither understands nor loves her. Baptista is afraid of her, embarrassed by her, eager to get her off his hands. When a willing suitor, Petruchio, does come along, drawn first by the promise of a large dowry and second by the challenge of "taming" a woman whose "wildness" matches his own, her father is at first incredulous and then baldly eager. He is blunt about her unworthiness. "She is not for you, the more my grief" (64), he tells Petruchio. But when the bold young man persists, within minutes Baptista is clapping up a bargain with him. He claims that the betrothal can be finalized only when "her love" has been "well attained ... for that is all in all" (II.i.128–29). In fact, as with Bianca, what he does is at odds with what he says.

The couple's first meeting is a duel of barbs and bawdry. But when Baptista inquires about how things have gone, Petruchio replies with one barefaced lie after another. "How but well? How but well?" he demands. All Kate's shrewishness, he maintains, has been feigned, and she is in truth "modest" and "temperate," a model of "patience" and "chastity" (II.i.295–98). He concludes his account with a Big Lie: "we have 'greed so well together / That upon Sunday is the wedding day" (ll. 299–300). Kate, appalled, immediately denounces him as "a madcap ruffian ... that thinks with oaths to face the matter out." Then she turns her attack on the man who has left her open to this latest humiliation:

> Call you me daughter? Now, I promise you
> You have showed a tender fatherly regard
> To wish me wed to one half lunatic...   [ll. 287–89].

Her response to Petruchio's assertion about their supposed wedding date is "I'll see thee hanged on Sunday first" (l. 302). The chorus of taunting suitors thinks that she has won. But Petruchio responds with more absurd fabrication about the "kiss on kiss" she has given him and their private "bargain" that she will act shrewish only "in company." Kate is shocked into silence, and Baptista quickly takes the stranger's word over his daughter's: "I know not what to say — but give me your hands. God send you joy. Petruchio, 'tis a match" (ll. 320–21). The lovers exit "severally" (separately), and the father stays behind with Bianca's suitors to jest about the sudden turn of events. He is unequivocal about his motives, frankly using the mercantile metaphor for marriage: "I play a merchant's part / And venture madly on a desperate mart." He admits further: "The goal I seek is quiet in the match" (l. 332). So much for his claims of the supreme importance of winning his daughter's heart.

Petruchio has promised to provide the trappings, at least, of respectability. He announces that he will travel to Venice "to buy apparel [for] the wedding day." He wants to "be sure," he claims, that "my Katherine" and he will "have rings and things and fine array" (II.i.324–25). Baptista can salve any qualms of conscience with the rationale that this suitor, however peremptory, is presentable and even caring. The wedding ceremony will destroy that pretense.

As part of his taming scheme, Petruchio has decided to put Kate through a series of trials designed to rid her of vanity, ill temper, and insensitivity. The method he adopts is to outshrew her, to act "curster than she" (III.ii.150). The humiliation and discomfort that he causes her and inflicts on others in her name are admittedly crude means for teaching empathy. But in this farcical world they work, not least because Petruchio has a keen sense of the carrot as well as the stick. At the same time that he torments Kate by acting out a caricature of her worst traits, he shows her an alternative to the "shrew" role in which others have cast her and she has acquiesced. He points out her "wondrous qualities," including "beauty" and "wit" (II.i.48–50). If she can learn to cultivate "affability" and "mild behavior" as well, he reasons, she will be both happier and freer. His ultimate promise is that she will thereby win the love of the one man who is her equal in intelligence and will. Unlike her father and sister, Petruchio does not want to avoid and reject Kate. He relishes her quick tongue and high spirits. Their first meeting is a duel of wits, in which they trade barbs and share blank verse lines. When Kate, glaring at him, claims that she sees a "crab," he demands, "Then show it me." Not missing a beat, she completes the line: "Had I a glass, I would" (l. 235). Petruchio is unfazed. He not only matches her jab for jab but keeps raising the stakes, threatening violence and waxing bawdy when she tries her usual tactics of striking and shocking men into submission. He goes so far as to turn a pun on "tale" and "tail" into a shocked protest against her supposed proposition of fellatio: "What, with my tongue in your tail? / Nay, come again, good Kate, I am a gentleman" (ll. 220–21). Kate is outraged but she is also fascinated. In mid-battle, she asks, "Where did you study all this goodly speech?" (l. 264). Her tone is only half-sarcastic. Like Petruchio, she senses that she has at last met her match.

It is very important that Petruchio finds Kate attractive. He keeps complimenting her looks, calling her "straight and slender" (II.i.256), "the prettiest Kate in Christendom" (l. 187). Unlike the feckless suitors of Bianca, who tell Kate that she is unworthy of marriage, he boldly claims at their first meeting, "I am a husband for your turn." He brushes aside her protests with the declaration: "I must and will have Katherine to my wife" (l. 282). The double verb reinforces his determination and, while it no doubt frustrates Kate, must also flatter her. The first man who has ever successfully opposed her has done so in the name of allying himself to her for life.

Petruchio is not only the lover but the parent-figure that Kate has lacked. Nowhere is that double role more evident than at their madcap wedding. Petruchio intends the next major round of his "taming" battle to be fought there. Kate, who claimed earlier that she wished never to marry, is dressed and ready, but the groom fails to appear. Baptista laments this stain on the family honor—"this shame of ours"—but expresses no sympathy for the abandoned bride. Kate, alert as always to her father's callousness, counters, "No shame but mine." First, she reminds him, she has been "forced / To give [her] hand opposed against [her] heart" to "a mad-brain rudesby.... Who wooed in haste and means to wed at leisure" (III.ii.8–11). Then she reveals the hurt that underlies this anger:

> Now must the world point at poor Kate
> And say, "Lo, there is mad Petruchio's wife,
> If it would please him come and marry her"   [ll. 18–20].

The proud Katherine "poor Kate"?! Kate is admitting not only that she feels humiliated but that, for all her protests, she wants this marriage. She "exits, weeping"—again, a first. This sudden revelation of her vulnerability evokes an equally unprecedented show of sympathy from her father:

> Go, girl, I cannot blame thee now to weep,
> For such an injury would vex a very saint,
> Much more a shrew of thy impatient humor   [ll. 27–29].

Kate, having gone off, does not hear these words. But we are left to notice that Baptista's pity does not alter his stereotyped view of her: she is not hurt but "vexed," and still, inevitably, the "shrew."

When news arrives that Petruchio is approaching, but in disgracefully ragged dress, Baptista's first reaction is relief: "I am glad he's come, howsoe'er he comes" (III.ii.70). The sight of his future son-in-law's get-up, however, is beyond the old gentleman's tolerance, and he pleads with him to "doff this habit," which he calls "shame to your estate, / An eyesore to our solemn festival" (ll. 96–97). But Petruchio, as the clever Tranio surmises, "hath some meaning in this mad attire"—namely, to force Kate to look beyond the externals of propriety and reputation. He responds calmly,

"To me she's married, not unto my clothes" (l. 113), and goes off to seek his "lovely bride." Baptista does not at this juncture stop the wedding, but merely follows, half stunned, half amused, to "see the event."

The ceremony, as reported by Grumio, is a travesty, with Petruchio acting the "mad-brained bridegroom" with manic glee. He swears, strikes the priest, throws the "sops" from the wedding toast "in the sexton's face," and kisses the bride "with such a clamourous smack / That ... all the church did echo" (III.ii.174–75). Kate "trembled and shook" and appeared "a lamb, a dove, a fool" compared to Petruchio. The scene, like those of Kate's later torments at the hands of her tamer, is both funnier and more tolerable for being an "unscene," reported rather than staged. Witnessing directly the sight of the priest being struck and Kate distraught would disrupt the comic tone.

Farce requires that the audience be reassured of the victim's essential resilience. Like the cartoon cat that rises flattened from beneath the rock that has squashed him and, with a shake, resumes his former shape, Kate reenters and soon displays her old shrewish form. Petruchio's next ploy is to refuse to stay for his own wedding banquet — this despite the family's trouble and expense in "prepar[ing] great store of wedding cheer" (III.ii.182), and also despite earnest entreaties by friends, father-in-law, and, finally, Kate herself. He offers only the vaguest excuse for his haste, and he tantalizes Kate by pretending to reward her new humility with acquiescence: "I am content," he pronounces grandly, but only, it turns out, that she "shall entreat [him] stay" (l. 198). He *will* leave, he tells her, "entreat me how you can." This latest disappointment is too much for Kate, and she reverts to her usual methods of getting her way. She dismisses him: "The door is open, sir, there lies your way." She herself, she declares, "will not go today / No, or tomorrow nor till I please myself" (ll. 206–08). Petruchio pleads with her not to "be angry"; she retorts, "I will be angry. What hast thou to do?" (ll. 211–12). Baptista, who with the rest of the company has witnessed this tantrum, says nothing. Whether he makes some gesture of protest at this point or Kate simply decides to aim at a familiar target, she snaps: "Father, be quiet, he shall stay my leisure." She concludes with the lesson she has learned about the wages of compliance: "I see a woman may be made a fool / If she have not a spirit to resist" (ll. 216–17).

This is the showdown, and Gremio assumes from past experience that Kate has won: "Now it begins to work" (III.ii.214). Petruchio, however, knows that a man, too, must show "a spirit to resist," especially against an adversary with a will as strong as Kate's: her past conquests are standing right before him. He brings out his full battery of sticks and carrots.

The crudest — and hardest for modern audiences to accept — is his relegation of the wife to a lower order: "She is my goods, my chattels ... my ox, my ass, my everything." Her tantrum is futile, he asserts flatly: "I will be master of what is mine own" (ll. 225–26). He also alludes to Kate's vulnerability as a virgin about to consummate her marriage, urging the others: "Carouse full measure to her maidenhead" (l. 221). This crass comment also has a positive aspect: it underlines Petruchio's attraction to Kate and reminds those present that, in marrying, she has raised her social status. However unconventional the wedding, she is now the wife of a well-to-do and bold gentleman. As such, she is under his protection. He takes advantage of that traditional concept to win the last round in the wedding bout: he orders the others to obey Kate's "command" to go on with the banquet and swears that he will "buckler her against a million" — i.e., fight for her honor and safety against all comers. Drawing his sword and issuing orders to Grumio to support him, he carries her off in a melodramatic flourish. We may guess from Kate's silence that she is too dumbfounded to protest. At the same time, for all the crudeness of his behavioral psychology, Petruchio has been teaching Kate hard lessons in self-control. He has also made her the focus of concern: instead of the peripheral, barely tolerated daughter, she has become the sought-after wife. If Petruchio were merely a bully and Kate a helpless victim — caricatures in which some recent critics have cast them — the play would not hold up. In this, as in all of Shakespeare's most successful comedies, the key relationships are complex and convincing. The secret of Petruchio's success is that he cares enough about Kate not to tolerate her hostile behavior, which has served in the past not to free her but to lock her into loveless isolation.

Her father's reaction to the confrontation recalls the mold in which the family has cast Kate. He only comments wryly, "Nay, let them go, a couple of quiet ones" (III.ii.236). Like Gremio, he could "die with laughing" at this contretemps, and like Bianca, he believes that Kate has gotten the husband she deserves: "being mad herself, she's madly mated." He turns with relief to his favorite child and proposes that, since the wedding banquet is already laid, "Bianca take her sister's room" and Lucentio (the disguised Tranio) "supply the bridegroom's place" (ll. 245–46). It is a symbolic moment. This is the substitution that Baptista has long wished to make: the intractable daughter gone and the one he sees as "apt to learn and thankful for good turns" (II.i.165) in her place. But Baptista's view of Bianca proves no more reliable than his opinion of Kate. Slyly, Shakespeare goes on to show how thoroughly the father has misjudged both his children.

Kate is unique among Shakespeare's rebellious daughters in that she does marry her father's choice of suitor against her will. She also grows to value her husband for reasons that the old man could never perceive. What Baptista sees in Petruchio, besides his willingness to court a harridan, is his eligibility. He has the pedigree and the independent means to qualify for Kate's hand. He is "Antonio's son, / A man well known throughout all Italy" (II.i.68–69). Baptista, pleased by the late gentleman's reputation, pronounces Petruchio "welcome for his sake." As Antonio's only heir, the son has "crowns in [his] purse ... and goods at home" (I.ii.55). Even so, Petruchio's initial motive for marriage is financial gain, as he boasts on his arrival: "I come to wive it wealthily in Padua —/ If wealthily then happily in Padua" (ll. 73–74). He claims that he would marry even a diseased "old trot with ne'er a tooth in her head ... so wealth comes withal." Yet this crass materialism proves largely bravado—chest beating before his fellow suitors. Once he meets Kate, the attraction of her wit and beauty and the challenge of subduing so formidable an opponent become his major incentives. While Bianca is eluding her father's vigilance, Petruchio is subjecting Kate to his own. By the end of the play, the younger daughter's shrewish side has been revealed, while the older has been transformed into a composed and affectionate being.

After the wedding, Petruchio devises more taming methods. Through a combination of deprivation to Kate and cruelty to underlings, he continues his scheme of acting "more shrew than she" (III.i.74). Bereft of food, sleep, and conjugal rights, Kate experiences physical suffering and the terrors of someone else's violent temper for the first time in her coddled life. As Petruchio intends, the treatment causes her to move beyond egotism to empathy. After crawling out from "under her horse," which has fallen on her in a "miry ... place," she "wade[s] through the dirt" not to complain but to intercede for the servant Grumio. Petruchio has pretended to blame him for the mishap and is beating him. When, back at the manse, the master berates and strikes the servants, Kate pleads, "I pray you, husband, be not so disquiet" (l. 155).

Shakespeare uses several means to soften the effects of this cruelty and to assure that the play remains comic. First, as in the wedding scene, he places the most painful episodes, such as Kate's fall from the horse, offstage. Second, he provides amused commentators on Petruchio's actions at every stage: the servants, who note wryly that he "kills her in her own humor" (IV.i.167); Hortensio, who observes Petruchio's feigned tyranny towards the tailor and the haberdasher; and both the principals in the taming. Between ploys, Petruchio soliloquizes on his scheme to "curb [Kate's] mad and headstrong humor" and on his main pretense, that "all is done in reverent care of her" (l. 191). Thus, he makes the audience his confidants and silent accomplices. He also subjects himself to the deprivations along with his victim. The 1992 Royal Shakespeare Company production, rather than showing Petruchio effortlessly in control, got hilarious mileage out of emphasizing the cost to the weary tamer of sacrificing his own food, sleep, and tranquility. Finally, although Kate is at first overwhelmed by the force of Petruchio's methods and "sits as one new-risen from a dream," she is far from broken.

In her tête-à-tête with the servant Grumio, Kate makes clear that she understands exactly what Petruchio is putting her through:

> ...I, who never knew how to entreat,
> Nor ever needed that I should entreat,
> Am starved for meat, giddy for lack of sleep,
> With oaths kept waking and with brawling fed   [IV.iii.7–10].

She makes clear, too, that she understands his method: "that which spites me more than all these wants, / He does it in the name of perfect love." This is no naive victim, crushed by abuse and baffled by her persecutor's aims, as some have argued. Kate knows Petruchio's game, and she still has plenty of fight left to oppose it, as Grumio soon finds. When he continues to taunt her, she "*beats him*" (stage direction, l. 31) and curses "all the pack of you / That triumph thus upon my misery" (ll. 33–34).

But Petruchio does more than simply make Kate suffer. He also keeps teaching her alternatives to tantrums as ways of asserting her will. Albeit crudely, he also teaches her manners. For example, he insists that she thank him before he will serve her the meat he has brought: "The poorest service is repaid with thanks" (IV.iii.45) he says sententiously — and then orders Hortensio sotto voce to "Eat it all up" (l. 50) before Kate can touch it. Petruchio knows that Kate, although subdued, is far from tamed. When the haberdasher arrives with the new cap that he has ordered for her, he pretends to be displeased with it. She protests; he says that she cannot have it until she is "gentle." Driven beyond her slender patience, Kate has another outburst:

> I am no child, no babe....
> My tongue will tell the anger of my heart
> Or else my heart, concealing it, will break   [ll. 74, 77–78].

She makes the mistake of taking the spoiled child's stance: "I like the cap, / And I will have it or I will have none"— the perfect opening for Petruchio to toss it away. The same kind of scene takes place with the gown that Petruchio has ordered, with him pretending to be displeased and abusing the tailor for incompetence, while telling Hortensio in an aside to "see the tailor paid." Although his announced purpose was to "return [Kate] unto [her] father's house" in style, wearing her new finery, and "revel it as bravely as the best" (IV.iii.53–54), he deprives her of that salve to her ego. Instead, he subjects her to another sermon on the insignificance of fine clothes and insists that she make the visit "even in these honest mean habiliments." "For 'tis the mind that makes the body rich" (ll. 167–69), he pronounces. Petruchio is determined to teach Kate humility, by main force if necessary.

The other lessons that Kate must learn take place on the long-delayed journey to her old home. One is the importance of maintaining a sense of humor—abetting rather than opposing Petruchio in his practical jokes. The first jest is his insistence that the sun is the moon. After trying her usual ploy of direct opposition, Kate joins in the game and teases back:

> …be it the moon or sun or what you please.
> An if you please to call it a rush candle,
> Henceforth I vow it shall be so for me   [IV.v.13–15].

The absurdity escalates when they meet old Vincentio, and Petruchio insists that he is a "fair lovely maid." This time Kate passes the humor test, embracing him as a "young budding virgin, fair and fresh and sweet" (l. 36), and thus topping Petruchio's claim with hyperbole. When he shifts tactics, berating her rudeness and expressing the hope that she is "not mad," Kate does not miss a beat. She apologizes prettily to the old man for her "mad mistaking" (l. 48). Vincentio takes the prank well and accepts the couple's invitation to travel with them to Padua. The newlyweds have arrived at a nearly complete sympathy of minds.

One more test of Kate's compliance remains. Having arrived home in Padua and witnessed Bianca's declaration of marriage, Petruchio demands that Kate give him a kiss if he is to remain for a visit. Kate is shocked: "What, in the midst of the street?" she demands. He asks if she is "ashamed of [him]." Kate relents: "Nay, I will give thee a kiss. Now pray thee, love, stay" (V.i.133, 136). This new Kate has reassured him of her affection, and she has entreated him. In turn, Petruchio softens his demeanor towards her. He makes a public declaration of his love, calling his bride "my sweet Kate." It is Bianca's old epithet, a preview of the plot's final ironic twist: the Shrew and the Good Girl are about to show that they are sisters indeed.

The final scene gives us the wedding banquet at last—officially, Bianca and Lucentio's but also in essence Kate and Petruchio's and, for good comic measure, Hortensio and the widow's. It begins with a pretty speech by the new groom in tribute to his "fair Bianca" and a "welcome to [his] house"

(V.iii.4, 8) for the other couples. The scene seems at first a resumption of old roles: Petruchio complaining and provoking controversy, Kate exchanging barbs with the company. But this time she is using her wit, mostly against the widow, in defense of her new husband and in protest to her reputation as a shrew. Petruchio does not oppose but supports her efforts, albeit crudely: "a hundred marks my Kate does put her down" (l. 35). Baptista does not notice the change in Kate and continues to mock Petruchio's choice of wife: "I think thou hast the veriest shrew of all" (l. 64), he gloats.

Bianca, a silent onlooker during the other women's duel of wit, speaks up at the end. Having achieved the desirable husband and the married status that she sought, Bianca drops her mask of the mild and innocent maid. Her first words are a bawdy pun about cuckoldry, which provokes a wry comment from her new father-in-law: "Ay, mistress bride, hath that awakened you?" Unperturbed, she retorts, "Ay, but not frighted me; therefore, I'll sleep again" (V.ii.42–43). She rouses herself from that bored daze to spar with her new brother-in-law: "Am I your bird?" she challenges Petruchio. If so, she taunts, he can "pursue" her; she is going to "shift [her] bush" (ll. 46–47)—the same bawdy allusion to the female sex organ that Celia makes in *As You Like It*. Sharp-tongued and petulant, this is the Bianca that we have seen in private but that she has heretofore taken care to conceal from father and suitors.

The grooms, meanwhile, decide to wager on their wives' obedience — their willingness to appear when summoned. Baptista, deaf as ever to his daughters' voices, is still so confident of Bianca that he vows to pay half Lucentio's stake, an offer that the proud bridegroom rejects. Both Bianca and the widow, however, refuse to come, the latter rightly surmising that the men "have some goodly jest in hand." Kate alone responds, pleasing her father so much that he doubles her dowry on the spot. He declares that "she is changed as she had never been" and therefore merits "another dowry to another daughter" (V.ii.119–20). Petruchio predicts that her altered character bodes "peace" and "love" and "quiet" life (l. 113)—not only desirable but mutual qualities in any marriage.

Another part of his credo, however, sounds highly objectionable to a modern audience: the insistence that marriage be based on the husband's "awful rule and right supremacy" (V.ii.114). In the controversial final vignette, Kate enters, driving the other wives before her as Petruchio has bidden her to do, and gives her now infamous speech on wifely duty. Her husband, she tells each woman, is "thy lord, thy life, thy keeper, / Thy head, thy sovereign" (ll. 151–52). His "painful labor" is given for her "maintenance" and she must in turn grant him "love, fair looks, and true obedience," all of which are "too little payment for so great a debt" (ll. 153, 159). The uncompromising tone and outdated tenets of this harangue are understandably distasteful to modern couples: the husband is no longer the only one to "watch the night in storms" while the wife stays "warm at home, secure and safe." With the upsurge of women's athletics, female bodies are not typically "soft and weak and smooth" (l. 170). And any woman with an ounce of self-esteem would take offense at being called an "unable worm" (l. 174). Certainly Kate goes too far in presenting her case.

In an effort to reconcile the speech to modern sensibilities, recent productions tend to distort the text in one of two ways. Either they dismiss its import by treating it as sarcasm or they present it with vocal inflections and blocking that show Kate as helpless and broken. The first ignores the context of the speech. Although Kate's tone may be exaggeratedly compliant, her thesis is meant to be taken at face value. The women whom she is addressing have, after all, just behaved to their new husbands as the "contending rebel[s]" and "graceless traitor[s]" (V.ii.164–65) that she is preaching against. Bianca has been especially cutting. She upbraids Lucentio for his pointless summons: "Fie, what a foolish duty call you this?" When he protests that she has caused him to lose money by wagering on her obedience, she counters: "The more fool you for laying on my duty" (ll. 130–34). Although the charge has grounds, this affront in public and on her wedding day is hardly tactful or considerate. In fact, Bianca is acting "peevish, sullen, sour"—the very traits that the reformed Kate counsels against. She already sounds nearly as bored and frustrated as Kate was at the play's outset, with little prospect of finding in her husband a match for her will. Coddled and paraded by her foolish father, Bianca has gone from willing conspirator in the Good Girl masquerade to incipient shrew. Her pretense has yielded her the image but not the substance of a happy marriage. In deceiving her father, she has also beguiled herself. Reading Kate's advice to the other women as sarcasm makes nonsense of the text.

Other productions take Kate's tone literally but show her as exhausted and bedraggled, broken by Petruchio's treatment into a dazed puppet of his views. That reading gives the play a bleakly pessimistic ending and turns exhilarating farce into pathos. More balanced productions have stayed truer to Shakespeare's text. Kate ends her encomium with a self-denigrating pronouncement that to "do [her husband] ease," a wife should be ready "to place your hands below your husband's foot." She offers herself as a model: "My hand is ready" (V.ii.182–84). If Petruchio were a brute, he would take her up on it. Instead, he acknowledges her as an equal and a mate: "Come and kiss me, Kate" (l. 185). Before the father and suitors who have insulted and rejected her, he claims her as a desirable wife. Together, they have achieved a social and emotional triumph. "Come, Kate, we'll to bed," he says, reminding us that the honeymoon is yet to take place. Petruchio gets in a last dig at Lucentio: "'Twas I won the wager, though you hit the white" (l. 191) — i.e., the supposed bulls-eye, "fair" Bianca. Then they go off, arm in arm, leaving the rest to "wonder."

Shakespeare himself outgrew Kate's categorical manifesto. Five years later, when he wrote his comic masterpiece on sparring couples, *Much Ado About Nothing*, he would end the duel of wit and will more equitably: the groom's only means of coping with his still-quipping bride is to "stop [her] mouth" with a kiss. But the earlier play, for all its crudeness, continues to hold the stage. Its popularity is due not only to its sparkle and quick pace but to its depth of human understanding. Petruchio treats Kate with the cunning of a behavioral psychologist. He shows her that she need not be obstreperous to get attention, that wit can be a more effective weapon than coercion, that compassion can be a sign of strength, that she is someone capable of attracting and giving love. He, not Baptista, is the knowing father figure in the play.

King Lear

Lear in his maddened state poses the play's central question about fatherhood: "Is there any cause in nature that makes these hard hearts?" (III.vi.75–76). He is referring to the cruelty of his elder daughters, Goneril and Regan, to whom he had ceded his rights in his kingdom. In this play, it is they who begin by playing the Good Girl role, while the youngest sister, Cordelia, refuses to make a pretense of love and obedience. The stakes are much higher than in *Shrew*, the prizes not dowries but kingdoms and the costs not pride and decorum but sanity and survival.

Bianca offends simply by evading her father's authority, and for an end of which he ultimately approves. But Lear's feigning daughters subject him to dire proofs of their opposition: insults, quarrels, exile, and, finally, open warfare. By mid-play, they have cast him out onto the heath in a raging storm and begun a battle to the death against the combined forces of father and younger sister. They defy not merely social norms but the natural order, destroying the "holy cords" (II.ii.69) that bind parent and child, human beings and God. Their conduct is condemned as "unnatural" by every virtuous character in the play. "Shrew" would be too mild a metaphor for such women; they are repeatedly reviled as "monster" and "devil." The Fool, Lear's jester and externalized conscience, comments wryly: "I marvel what kin thou and thy daughters are" (I.iv.173). Lear professes amazement that one father could produce such "different issues" as Gloucester's sons and his elder daughters. He is particularly puzzled because Goneril and Regan, unlike Edmund, have been "got between lawful sheets." He is obsessed with their "filial ingratitude" toward, as he describes himself to them, the "old kind father" whose "frank heart gave all" (III.iv.20). But a closer look at Lear's relationship with his children calls into question that self-flattering description and makes clear "what kin" Goneril and Regan are to him.

The play begins with a fairy tale situation: a king creates a public test of his children's mettle. He calls an audience to announce that he will divide his kingdom among his three daughters, the most "opulent" third (I.i.86) going to the one who says she "doth love [him] most" (l. 51). Granted that Lear is an old man weary of the burdens of office and that his daughters are young and capable. What is wrong with his plan? In a word, it ignores the realities of human nature. The king claims that his motives are altruistic — to forestall "future strife" over the division of power and land. He wishes only, he says, "To strike all cares and business from our age, / Conferring them on younger strengths, while we / Unburdened crawl toward death" (ll. 39–41). But the royal "we" and the melodramatic tone suggest Lear's penchant for self-aggrandizement. He may be tired of the responsibilities of kingship, but he loves the trappings. He reveals that attitude when he specifies the conditions of his legacy: "Only we still retain / The name and all th'addition to a king," including a company of "an hundred knights" (ll. 133–36) to serve him. He does not, in other words, mean to bestow this gift and retire, but to remain on the scene to bask in his former glory. This would be a formula for strife even in the most amicable of family enterprises. An additional proof of Lear's obtuseness is that he cedes power to children whom he should know would never willingly share it, with him or with one another.

The test that he devises virtually guarantees hypocrisy. Each daughter must publicly profess love for the father who dangles power and property before her as the rewards for saying what he wants to hear. Goneril, the eldest and so the first to respond, gushes the series of required hyperboles: she loves her father "dearer than eyesight, space, and liberty." In case that list is not enough to satisfy his vanity, she covers any possible omission with the claim that hers is "a love that makes breath poor and speech unable" (I.i.56, 60). The ploy works on Lear, who doles out "shadowy forests," "plenteous rivers," and "wide-skirted meads" to Goneril, her husband the Duke of Albany, and their "issue." Regan, who has been listening intently to this exchange, professes herself "made of that same mettle as my sister." Goneril, she claims, has "name[d] my very deed of love"—then, to top that performance, she adds, "only she comes too short" (ll. 71–72). These statements will echo ironically through the torments that the sisters later visit on their gullible benefactor. For the moment, however, he gobbles up the honeyed words and gives Regan an "ample third of our fair kingdom," of equal "space, validity, and pleasure" (ll. 80–81) to Goneril's portion.

Were this episode presented in isolation, we would have little cause to blame Lear for his credulity. Goneril and Regan's words, while excessive, seem appropriately formal in the context of the grand royal audience. Shakespeare provides, however, three means by which we can gauge their sincerity: the contrasting response of the third daughter, Cordelia; the outraged protest of the loyal counselor, the Earl of Kent; and the cynical commentary of Goneril and Regan themselves in the tête-à-tête that follows the big public scene. All exemplify one of the dramatist's favorite techniques—juxtaposition—for implying the contrast between what is said and what is shown.

The most important of these means for judging Goneril and Regan's sincerity is Cordelia's reaction. Her first line, delivered as an aside, is a vow to "love and be silent" (I.i.62). When the old king turns to her expectantly and asks, "What can you say to draw / A third more opulent than your sisters?" she takes him literally and says "Nothing" (ll. 85–87). For that motive—to win a richer prize than her sisters—Cordelia will not speak. With a willfulness that we are soon to see she has learned from Lear, she refuses to bend: "I love your Majesty / According to my bond, no more nor less," she asserts. She reminds him of what that "bond" means: he has "begot," "bred," and "loved" her; she, in turn, will "obey," "love," and "most honor" him (ll. 96–98). This bare statement does not satisfy the vain old man. Cordelia could have anticipated as much, but she stubbornly sticks to her principles: to eschew the "still-soliciting eye" and "tongue" that have won her sisters favor.

Technically, Cordelia is right, as the staunch Kent assures her. Candor, in fact, will emerge as one of the play's predominant values. In the final speech, Edgar, the long-suffering heir to the throne, urges that the great charge to the survivors of all this tragedy must be to "Speak what we feel, not what we ought to say" (V.iii.163). But another value that the play embraces, compassion, is in short supply in the opening scene. Cordelia does not show much empathy—or even tact. Perhaps she is so revolted by her sisters' "glib and oily art" (I.i.224) and her father's vanity that, with adolescent self-righteousness, she refuses to play their game. Cordelia must, though, be aware of Lear's vulnerability, especially in this moment of public exposure. She, his "joy," whom he has openly favored in the past, has mortified him. He confesses his anguish to Kent and the assembled company: "I loved her most, and thought to set my rest / On her kind nursery" (ll. 123–24). But as Lear will state later, his macho creed dictates that showing pain is both unkingly and unmanly. He covers his hurt with a burst of fury, depicting himself as a "dragon," breathing the fire of his "wrath" (l. 122).

The ostensible reason for summoning Cordelia had been to allow her suitors, the Duke of Burgundy and the King of France, to decide their rivalry for her hand. In the presence of these suitors and the entire court, Lear strips her of her dowry, reputation, and his "benison" (I.i.265) and banishes her from the kingdom forever. So sudden and extreme is his reaction that the suitors are stunned and Cordelia is forced to plead that Lear assure them that "no vicious blot, murder,... no unchaste action" (ll. 227–28) of hers has provoked this punishment. Lear is unbending in his rejection, and he cruelly uses the imagery of the marriage market to underscore her humiliation: Now that Cordelia is no longer "dear" (meaning both cherished and expensive) to him, "her price is fallen"; she is "Dowered with our curse, and strangered with our oath" (ll. 196–97, 204). Cordelia tells him that she is "glad" she lacks her sisters' hypocrisy, "though not to have it / Hath lost me in your liking." The old man's response is uncompromisingly vain: "Better thou / Hast not been born than not to have pleased me better" (ll. 232–34). Burgundy is so put off by the rescinding of the marriage contract that he cedes his claim to France, who gallantly takes up Cordelia's cause and Lear's metaphor to express her intrinsic worth: "She is herself a dowry" (l. 241). Before this final judgment, the loyal Kent, too, has expressed his shock and begged the king to "check / This hideous rashness" (ll. 150–51). His reward is to precede Cordelia in banishment.

The confrontation ends with Cordelia stripped of all honor and position, relegated to the protection of a husband she barely knows. The audience may still be wondering if she might have misjudged her sisters. In fact, students reading the play for the first time are often puzzled by her stubborn silence and by the ferocity of Kent's outrage. The final episode before her departure leaves no doubt that she, and not Lear, has read Goneril and Regan right. Alone with them, Cordelia says candidly that she sees through their mask of benevolence: "I know you what you are," though, being a "sister," she is "most loath to name [their] faults" (I.i.269–71). Her one request to them is for the welfare of Lear: "Love well our father." Reluctantly, she "commit[s] him" to their "professed bosoms" (l. 272)—hearts that express but do not feel love. She adds sarcastically that if she could, she would wish him in "a better place" (l. 274). Just before his own summary dismissal, Kent expressed the same doubt about the distance between Goneril and Regan's "words of love" and their "deeds." Neither he nor Cordelia accuses them outright nor quarrels: both recognize that the sisters are the ones in power now. In any case, Goneril and Regan are impervious to criticism. They dismiss Cordelia with haughty remarks about her "scanted obedience." Cordelia is not deceived: "Time shall unfold what plighted cunning hides" (l. 280), she predicts, and goes off with her new lord. She will never see her sisters again.

Goneril and Regan remain behind to comment and scheme. Letting their hair down at last — indicated textually by their lapse into prose — they agree that their father is a fool. He has always been "rash," even at "the best and soundest of his time" (I.i.294), Goneril clucks. Regan agrees that his latest decisions result from "the infirmity of age," but adds, "yet he hath ever but slenderly known himself" (ll. 292–93). His show of preference for them and his lavish bequests do not earn their trust or respect. In fact, they see his rejection of Cordelia as unnatural and self-destructive: "He always loved our sister most," Goneril says, matter-of-factly confirming Lear's own statements. She adds that his decision to "cast [Cordelia] off" is a gross proof of "poor judgment" (ll. 290–91). Any sibling jealousy that Goneril may have felt once has been converted to scorn and ruthlessness. She has not expected favor from her father; having received it, she recognizes the manipulativeness behind the gift and is not appeased. In fact, both she and Regan immediately suspect that they may be the next victims of Lear's rashness. Regan suggests that they "think further" about the turn of events. Goneril, older and harder, counters: "We must *do* something, and i' th' heat" (l. 306, my italics).

What Goneril does is to renege on her agreement to host Lear and his retinue of knights in the royal style to which he has been accustomed. She blames the king for her breach, complaining to her steward that the knights "grow riotous" and the "idle old man" censures her for "every trifle"(I.iii.6, 16, 7). Showing some of her father's temper, Goneril vows, "I'll not endure it" (l. 15). She orders her obsequious steward, Oswald, and his "fellows" to slight the royal party: "I'd have it come to question" (l. 13), she declares. Lear, meanwhile, has begun to perceive "a most faint neglect" (I.iv.65) in his treatment, but he has been reluctant to see it as a sign of "unkindness" (l. 67). In Shakespeare's day, "kind" meant "natural" as well as "compassionate": it is one of the words that echoes through the play. Lear, having been unkind in both senses himself, does not trust his own judgment of others' kindness. He cannot stand to hear that his Fool has "much pined away" at Cordelia's exile: "No more of that," he orders. "I

have noted it well" (ll. 71–72). He has been used to denying painful feelings, attacking the messenger and taking refuge in his privilege and rank.
Now that that fortress is gone, he begins to question the very identity he
had thought was his. When Oswald insults him, Lear demands angrily:
"Who am I?" The steward responds insolently: "My lady's father" (ll.
75–76). The disguised Kent is there to trip up the underling and reassert
the old king's sense of hierarchy. "I thank thee, fellow," Lear says. "Thou
serv'st me, and I'll love thee" (l. 83). That is the status quo that Lear has
always taken for granted. But his feeling of reassurance is transient. The
Fool enters to remind his old master that his world and his complacent
self-concept have changed irredeemably.

Thus, Lear arrives at one of the central questions of this restlessly
questioning play: Who am I? Is identity founded on rank? Office? Relationship? Or is it something intrinsic? How does it change with changes
in circumstance? The king, the Fool tells him wryly, is as much a fool as
his own jester: "All thy other titles thou hast given away; that thou wast
born with" (I.iv.142). Continuing to address the king in the familiar second person, the Fool offers proof: "Thou ... mad'st thy daughters thy
mothers ... gav'st them the rod, and put'st down thine own breeches" (ll.
164–65). He goes a step further and claims: "I am better than thou art
now; I am a fool, thou art nothing" (ll. 184–85). The Fool sugarcoats all
this bitter truth-telling with jests and colloquialisms. His use of the familiar "you" is a mark of the special privilege granted his office: as the king's
"all-licensed fool" (l. 191), he is free to say anything to his royal master
and not be charged with treason. (Jesters were assumed to be too simple-
minded and powerless to be taken seriously.) Naturally, Goneril loathes
him and, as the Fool notes, would have him "whipped for speaking true"
(l. 174). Candor, loyalty, perspicacity, all of which the Fool has in abundance, are her enemies. She silences him with threats and turns on her
father, accusing him of keeping knights "so disordered" by "epicurism and
lust" that they are turning her "graced palace" into "a tavern or brothel"
(ll. 232–35).

How credible is Goneril's accusation? The one knight who has a speaking role in this scene addresses Lear with eloquence and respect. Goneril's
other charge, "you strike my people," a reference to Kent's chastisement
of Oswald, is clearly exaggerated. Lear's opposing view seems more per-
suasive: that his soldiers are "men of choice and rarest parts, / That all par-
ticulars of duty know" (I.iv.254–55). Yet his reaction to Goneril's
accusation is so extreme that it repels sympathy for him. He is stunned
into questioning her identity and, again, his own: "Are you our daughter?" he demands, and then: "Does any here know me? This is not Lear ...

Who is it that can tell me who I am?" The Fool replies cuttingly: "Lear's shadow" (ll. 216, 220–21) — the shade of the powerful old sovereign.

Thwarted, Lear reacts with his old means of exerting his will: flying into a rage at the person opposing him. He calls Goneril a "degenerate bastard" (I.iv.244), and bestows on her a "father's curse" of the most vindictive sort. He invokes the goddess nature to "Dry up in her the organs of increase" and "convey sterility into her womb." Or "if she must teem" — the word suggests bestial procreation — to bear a child "of spleen," so malevolent that it is a "torment to her" (I.iv.270–74). Rather than "honor her," he prays that the child will "turn all her mother's pains and benefits / To laughter and contempt" (ll. 277–78). Clearly, this is Lear's view of his own treatment at Goneril's hands, and he flings at her his famous charge of filial betrayal: "How sharper than a serpent's tooth / It is to have a thankless child" (ll. 279–80).

Goneril reacts to Lear's fury with grim composure. Clearly, she has witnessed this mood before. She assures her shocked husband, the kindly Duke of Albany, that this is only her father's "dotage" speaking. She is no more moved when, defeated, Lear breaks down and laments the "hot tears" that he cannot hold back and admits "I am ashamed / That thou hast power to shake my manhood thus" (I.iv.287–88). In his impotence, he vows pathetically to "resume" his former royal "shape." Abruptly, he realizes his "folly" in rejecting Cordelia for her "most small fault." "I did her wrong," he says, the non sequitur suggesting the suddenness of his remorse. Yet, in spite of this momentary insight, Lear is as given to rashness as ever. He rushes off to seek solace from Regan, whom he is "sure is kind and comfortable" (l. 297).

In the face of this new torrent, Goneril remains coldly self-possessed. She tells Albany that her father's slights are imaginary, and that his wrath, backed by the armed knights, is dangerous to them. "I know his heart," she claims, and cautions her husband against his "milky gentleness" (I.iv.321, 332) toward the king. "Well, you may go too far," he objects. She snaps back, "Safer than trust too far" (l. 319), completing the blank verse line and getting the last word.

Distrust is a natural response to so temperamental and arrogant a father. In this new crisis, Lear obstinately maintains the rigid stance that has already caused him pain and loss. He has convinced himself that Regan loves him and will side with him against Goneril, whom he pictures as a "vulture" attacking him with "sharp-toothed unkindness" (II.iv.130). He makes this accusation to Regan herself in spite of his shock at finding the messenger that he has sent ahead, the disguised Kent, locked in the stocks at her palace. This form of punishment was usually reserved for "basest and contemned wretches" (II.ii.138), and is thus a marked show of disrespect to Lear. At first, the old king refuses to believe that Regan and Cornwall are responsible; then he goes to the other extreme of hyperbolic denouncement: "'Tis worse than murder" (II.iv.22), he proclaims. Regan insults him further by sending flimsy excuses for failing to greet him, and Lear angrily demands: "The *King* would speak with Cornwall. The *dear father* / Would with his daughter speak" (ll. 96–97, italics mine). When Regan finally appears, he tries by various means to force her to honor these former titles. Instead, she repeats Goneril's charges about "the riots of [his] followers" and says cuttingly that, as he is "old," he "should be ruled" (ll. 141–43). She urges him to ask forgiveness of Goneril. Lear's response is a bitter parody of that entreaty:

> Dear daughter, I confess that I am old. [*Kneels.*]
> Age is unnecessary. On my knees I beg
> That you'll vouchsafe me raiment, bed, and food   [ll. 149–51].

Regan calls these "unsightly tricks" and when he persists in cursing Goneril, she predicts: "So you will wish on me when the rash mood is on" (l. 164).

Lear responds by reminding her of her obligations to him, in the form of a description of his ideal daughter. But the comparison he makes is designed to deepen the sibling rivalry he has always fostered:

> 'Tis not in thee
> To grudge my pleasure, to cut off my train,
> To bandy hasty words, to scant my sizes,...
>   Thou better knowest
> The offices of nature, bond of childhood,
> Effects of courtesy, dues of gratitude....
> Thy half o' th' kingdom hast thou not forgot,
> Wherein I thee endowed   [II.iv.168–76].

Lear is committing his old mistakes: making service to his pride and comfort the test of love, and measuring love in quantitative and material terms. Not surprisingly, the sisters join hands, and forces, against him.

Goneril dismisses his perception of things: "All's not offense that indiscretion finds / And dotage terms so" (II.iv.191–92). Regan adds with sarcastic solicitousness: "I pray you father, being weak, seem so." Lear is again shocked: "I gave you all," he protests, and Regan, not missing a beat, completes his line: "and in good time you gave it" (l. 245). Determinedly rational and composed, the daughters ignore his humiliation and anguish and engage in a game of reducing his knightly complement by halves. The old man tries to intercede. Although he begs Goneril "O reason not the need"—the necessity to his self-esteem of retaining his train—he continues to gauge love quantitatively. Since Regan will allow him only twenty-five retainers, he will return to Goneril after all. Her offer of fifty doubles Regan's and so, he reasons, equals "twice her love" (l. 255). This conclusion takes no account of the poisonous words that have passed between him and his elder daughter.

Predictably, Goneril rejects the proposal, and the sisters take turns stripping Lear of all his remaining knights. His mood veers crazily between grief and rage. He begins mildly, saying sadly to Goneril: "I will not trouble thee, my child: farewell. / We'll meet no more, no more see one another" (II.iv.214–15). But within two lines, he is denouncing her as not his "flesh and blood" but "rather a disease that's in my flesh." He gets more graphic, calling her "a boil, a plague sore ... in my corrupted blood" (ll. 216–20). Like so many of Shakespeare's failed fathers, Lear sees his daughters not as separate entities but as aspects of his self, now tainted.

In keeping with this patriarchal mindset, Lear is haunted by the paranoid conviction that daughters who reject him so cruelly cannot be legitimate. Their mother (who presumably has long been dead) must have been "an adulteress," he accuses, and he calls on the gods to "divorce me from their mother's tomb" (II.iv.126–27). Later, on the heath, he will be obsessed with "lust" as the essential source of moral corruption. Recent readings that see this preoccupation as evidence of incest, however, distort the text. Jane Smiley's novel A Thousand Acres, a reconception of Lear's kingdom as a modern Iowa farm dynasty, goes so far as to depict both Goneril and Regan as innocent victims of their father's sexual abuse. There is no evidence in the play of father-daughter incest, a relationship that Shakespeare did not hesitate to make explicit, and to condemn, in Pericles. Lear is overbearing and chauvinistic, but perfectly willing to sanction and support his daughters' marriages.

The more likely explanation for Lear's revulsion toward lust is that he blames his passion for his late wife for creating such treacherous daughters. In fact, the one actually illegitimate child in the play, Edmund, does betray his father. But he at least repents in the end and feels remorse toward both the father and the brother that he has wronged. Goneril and Regan undergo no such softening. Perhaps their rigidity is a reflection of their father's. As we have seen in his earlier confrontation with his daughters, Lear despises his own grief, and its expression in tears, which he scornfully calls "women's weapons, water drops." He prays instead that the gods "touch [him] with noble anger" (II.iv.271–72). In Lear's chauvinistic conception, women cry, men take revenge. But he senses that the cost of so rigid a schematization may be self-destruction: before he will let himself "weep," he vows that his heart "Shall break into a hundred thousand flaws" (ll. 279–81). Although he has threatened to bring on his daughters "the terrors of the earth," the emptiness of the decree is clear even to him. Lear himself is the main victim of his helpless rage. He rushes off into the storm crying, "I shall go mad!"

Goneril and Regan stay behind to close the gates against their father and to rationalize their rejection. "The house is [too] little" to accommodate "the old man and his people," Regan begins. Goneril adds that the "blame" is all his, and Regan joins her on this moral high horse, saying sententiously "to willful men / The injuries that they themselves procure / Must be their schoolmasters" (II.iv.297–99). Their indifference and complacency are chilling. Still, were Goneril and Regan to stop at this show of defiance, they might merit the largest share of the audience's sympathy. It is Lear, after all, who has given them a model of vanity, obstinacy, and ruthlessness. He has stinted his love, favoring their sister and making any show of affection conditional. When they displease him, he curses them and their progeny. They have learned to emulate him all too well. Goneril emerges as the soldier, Regan the sovereign overlord; both are supreme politicians. Cordelia, in contrast, has not learned the means to power. Her essential qualities, compassion and loyalty, let her see beneath Lear's vain, stern surface to the feeling man, and she finds the means to help him recover, through gentle example rather than ruthless imposition of will, his better self. (For that account, and his bittersweet reconciliation with Cordelia, see Chapter 6: "Daughters Who Forgive and Heal.") But although Cordelia rescues her father's spirit, she cannot save his or her own life. Her sisters are much more adept in the ways of the world. Goneril and Regan's subsequent treatment of Lear, as well as of Gloucester and Albany, however, undermines any identification with their cause. By the play's end, we are moved to agree with the old king's self-pitying cry: "I am a man more sinned against than sinning" (III.ii.59–60).

What do the sisters do? Abandon their father to a fierce storm on a heath so barren that "for many miles about / There's scarce a bush" (II.iv. 296–97). Conspire to destroy his supporters, including the brave old Earl of Gloucester. Wage war against both father and younger sister, eventually imprisoning and, in effect, executing both. This is typical dynastic war, some have argued, brought on by Lear's short-sightedness. Yes, but the manner in which the sisters conduct it is ruthless to the point of sadism. For all his arrogance and insensitivity, Lear has never done them physical harm. In fact, he has provided well for their social and material needs. Proof of their essential barbarity is that once he has been defeated and is no longer their target, they turn on one another. Each has the same ambitions: to be sole ruler of Britain with the handsome young Edmund Gloucester as her consort. In the struggle, the sisters show no more mercy for one another than they have for their other kin. Like the gingham dog and the calico cat in the nursery rhyme, they eat each other up.

Early on, the sisters recognize their essential similarity. As noted above, Regan says in her opening speech, "I am made of that self mettle as my sister" (I.i.69), and Goneril, citing Lear's supposed faults as a house-guest, describes Regan as someone "whose mind and mine I know in that are one" (I.iii.15). Their bond stays intact while Cornwall is alive to part-ner Regan and while the sisters conspire against their father. At first, Goneril, the elder, leads and Regan follows. But during the torture of Gloucester, Regan shows her own capacity for authority and cruelty. Although her husband does the actual blinding, it is Regan who "*plucks his beard*" (stage direction, III.vii.34), a gross insult, urges Cornwall to put out *both* the old man's eyes, and kills the horrified servant who attempts to intervene. Throughout, her tone is ruthless and mocking. In mid-blind-ing, she says sarcastically, "One side [of Gloucester's face] will mock another. Th'other, too" (l. 71). Afterwards, she orders: "Go thrust him out of gates, and let him smell / His way to Dover" (ll. 93–94). Never does Regan show mercy or remorse. In fact, she later calls the decision to let Gloucester live "great ignorance" (IV.iv.9) because of the sympathy he invites wherever he goes.

Regan defies the Elizabethan conventions of feminine behavior. Not only does she not turn away from the violence, she relishes it. The servant, also ignoring the conventions of his station, tells her, "If you did wear a beard upon your chin, / I'd shake it in this quarrel" (III.vii.76–77). Regan responds to this reproach to by asserting masculine prerogatives. Demand-ing her husband's sword, she "runs at [the servant] behind" and stabs him in the back. Before he dies, he manages to wound his master mortally. Cornwall asks for Regan's arm to aid him as he staggers. The text gives her no lines at this point, and some productions have shown her turning her back on her dying husband. In any case, she does not mourn Cornwall long.

Goneril, too, sees kindness as weakness and especially despises it in men. When we next see her, she has joined league with Edmund. She openly expresses scorn for her "mild husband" and the "cowish terror of his spirit" in refusing to join the war against Lear. She frankly offers her-self to the young man, giving him a kiss and her "favor" to wear in bat-tle. He responds with the morbid pledge, "Yours in the ranks of death" (IV.ii.25). After his exit, she muses lasciviously, "O the difference of man and man. To thee a woman's services are due. / My fool usurps my body" (ll. 27–28).

Albany enters, transformed by outrage at the sisters' "vile offenses" to "a father, and a gracious aged man" (IV.ii.47, 41). He calls them "tigers, not daughters" and flings insults at his wife, calling her "barbarous" and "degenerate," a "monster" and a "devil." Albany longs "to dislocate and tear / [Her] flesh and bones," but says that her "woman's shape" shields her (ll. 65–67). Like the servant with Regan, he upholds the chivalric code even in the face of her defiance of it. For Goneril, as for Regan, that attitude is a matter for scorn. She calls him "a moral fool," a "milk-livered man, / That bears a cheek for blows, a head for wrongs" (ll. 58, 50–51). For his "manhood," she gives a Bronx cheer — "mew!" (l. 68). She, not Albany, will lead her forces in the upcoming battle. Although all the good characters in the play — Gloucester, Kent, Cordelia, and Edgar as well as Albany — take the side of the king, Goneril and Regan remain staunch in their determination to defeat him. As Albany tells her: "Wisdom and goodness to the vile seem vile; / Filths savor but themselves" (ll. 38–39). The villains' forces win, but their league does not last beyond the initial conspiracy. Victory achieved and the spoils at issue, the vicious pack begins to "prey on itself, / Like monsters of the deep" (ll. 49–50).

The main prize in contention is Edmund himself. Hearing of Cornwall's death, Goneril wastes no time in grief for her brother-in-law or pity for her newly widowed sister. Immediately, she concludes that since Edmund is "with her [Regan]," her sister will pursue him and bring Goneril's castles in the air tumbling down "upon [her own] hateful life" (IV.ii.86). This is one of the only hints that Goneril gives of the desperation and despair that fuel her drive to power. Possessing Edmund is even more important to her than military victory. Recklessly, she records her feelings in a letter that she sends by messenger into the precarious heat of battle. In it, she begs Edmund to "deliver" her from "the loathed warmth" of Albany's bed by "cut[ting] him off" (IV.vi.262, 259). She signs the letter "Your (wife I would say) affectionate servant." When Edgar intercepts the missive and shows it to Albany, it becomes a key piece of material evidence against the conspirators. Goneril feels neither remorse nor shame. In an aside that she utters just before the final conflict, she fairly hisses her single-minded determination: "I had rather lose the battle than that sister / Should loosen him and me" (V.i.18–19).

Regan is equally jealous and equally determined to have exclusive rights to Edmund's favors. As Goneril has surmised, she does not mourn Cornwall's loss. At her next appearance, she is attempting to bribe Oswald into revealing Goneril's feelings. "I know your lady does not love her husband," she tells him, and notes that she has seen the "most speaking looks" that have passed between her and Edmund. About her own situation, she is matter-of-fact: "My lord is dead, Edmund and I have talked, / And more convenient is he for my hand / Than for your lady's" (IV.v.30–32). Oswald refuses to "Let [her] unseal the letter" he is carrying—the one that Edgar will later intercept. So Regan orders him to report her feelings to Edmund, adding that should he meet "that blind traitor" Gloucester, he should kill him, since "Where he arrives he moves / All hearts against us" (ll. 10–11).

Like Goneril, Edmund, and all of Shakespeare's most skillful evildoers, Regan recognizes benevolent qualities but scorns them. They see altruism, empathy, and loyalty as alien and ridiculous, worth heeding only to manipulate the gullible. Their own feelings are cruder and fiercer: lust, jealousy, and violence are inextricably linked, as both the brothers Gloucester assert in their different ways. Edgar, having intercepted Goneril's letter, labels her and Edmund "murderous lechers" (IV.vi.270). Edmund, in soliloquy, muses on the sisters' duel over him: "Each jealous of the other, as the stung / Are of the adder" (V.i.56–57). Ruthless and unscrupulous, he concludes that "Neither can be enjoyed / If both remain alive" (ll. 58–59) and decides to let them battle it out, in a cat fight to the death.

Regan takes her case directly to the object of her passion, demanding to know if he has "found [Albany's] way to the forfended place"—Goneril's bed. Edmund pretends to be shocked at the thought, and, when she persists, swears by his "honor" that he has not. In a grim echo of Goneril's vow, Regan tells him, "I never shall endure her" (V.iii.15). The military battle won, her tactics shift from wheedling to bribery. Before the gathered victors, Regan proposes:

> Take thou my soldiers, prisoners, patrimony;
> Dispose of them, of me; the walls is thine.
> Witness the world that I create thee here
> My lord and master [ll. 75–78].

Immediately Goneril undercuts the romantic tone with lewd innuendo: "Mean you to enjoy him?" This before her husband, who provides sardonic commentary on the distasteful scene. He informs Regan that Goneril, "this gilded serpent," is already engaged to Edmund, and so he, "her husband," must "contradict" Regan's proposed marriage banns. "If you will marry," he says sarcastically, "make your loves to me. / My lady is bespoke" (ll. 88–89). Goneril remains brash and cool. "An interlude!" (a comic episode) she interjects. What she alone knows is that she has already defeated Regan: her weapon, poison. As the disguised Edgar appears to answer Edmund's challenge, Regan mutters that she feels "sick, o sick!" Goneril comments sotto voce, "If not, I'll ne'er trust medicine" (l. 96). The sister who was once her ally has become her victim.

Edgar's challenge to Edmund applies equally to Goneril:

> Thou art a traitor,
> False to the gods, thy brother, and thy father....
> A most toad-spotted traitor   [V.iii.134–35].

In fact, the list of Goneril's victims is incomplete. We will discover shortly that it included her younger sister, too. The dying Edmund confesses that he and Goneril devised the insidious plot to hang Cordelia, whom they have arrested, in order to make her murder appear a suicide.

Goneril's last ploy, her final act of "plighted cunning," is against herself. Edmund's defeat makes her furious. Instead of comforting her wounded lover, she berates him for his foolishness in meeting "an unknown opposite," which "th'law of war" had not demanded. "Thou art not vanquished / But cozened and beguiled" (V.iii.154–55), she charges. When Albany confronts her with her clandestine letter to her paramour, she rejects the rule of law that she has just invoked: "the laws are mine, not thine." She defies him and everyone else: "Who can arraign me for't?" (ll. 159–60). He persists, and she eschews all further human contact. "Ask me not what I know," she says, and rushes off. Her last line echoes that of another remorseless villain, Iago.

Albany knows Goneril's moods, and orders: "Go after her. She's desperate. Govern her." But he himself stays behind to manage the political business at hand. He has long since ceased sympathizing with the woman he once loved. Within minutes a messenger appears holding a "bloody knife," which he has just pulled "hot" and "smok[ing]" from Goneril's "heart." Albany pronounces her grim epitaph: "This judgment of the heavens, that makes us tremble, / Touches us not with pity" (V.iii.232–33).

It is left to Edmund to pay morbid tribute to the sisters' desperate resolve:

> Yet Edmund was beloved.
> The one the other poisoned for my sake,
> And after slew herself   [V.iii.240–42].

He sums up their sordid bond: "I was contracted to them both. All three / Now marry in an instant" (ll. 229–30). It is a menage-à-trois in perpetuity that both sisters would loathe: a No Exit hell of eternal jealousy. As Cordelia early predicted, "Time" has revealed what "plighted cunning" hid.

And the "cause in nature that ma[de] these hard hearts"? Certainly Lear is not faultless. He is far from the innocent victim he portrays himself as when he asks this disingenuous question. Advertently or not, he has trained Goneril and Regan in egotism and arrogance and ceded them the power to impose their wills. Yet the lengths to which the false daughters take their grievances against him are repellent and the effects dire. As Albany predicts, having cut themselves off from their "material sap," Goneril and Regan "wither" (IV.ii.34–35). They end by losing everything that once gave them pleasure and security.

The Taming of the Shrew ends with the false daughter revealed as an incipient shrew, petulant and rather bored with the marriage that she has manipulated father and suitors to achieve. But true to the comic mode, her marriage upholds the social order and affirms the family bond. The ritual of the wedding banquet signals Bianca's central place in the community. In the tragedy, the false sisters are revealed as "monsters." They break the bonds of humane sympathy and destroy the natural order and, in the process, cast themselves out of the human circle. Their end does not merit even the dignity of a funeral. They drop and are carted off, unmourned and reviled. We watching this bloody spectacle are, like Albany, moved to awe but not to pity. Making war on her father, the daughter destroys both him and herself.

5

Daughters Who Act in Their Fathers' Stead: Portia (*The Merchant of Venice*), Viola (*Twelfth Night*), and Rosalind (*As You Like It*)

"Truly the lady fathers herself."
Much Ado About Nothing, I.i.98

Three plays from the middle of Shakespeare's career depict daughters whose fathers are absent. In *The Merchant of Venice* and *Twelfth Night*, the fathers have recently died. In *As You Like It*, Duke Senior has been usurped by his villainous brother and banished to the Forest of Arden. Since the mothers are presumably long dead—none is even mentioned— the daughters are, for all practical purposes, orphans. At the plays' outset, each faces a crisis during which she must fend for herself in the world. Portia is compelled to conduct the contest that will determine her future husband, Viola believes that she has lost her only brother in a shipwreck that has landed her on a strange island, and Rosalind is banished from court on the whim of her malevolent uncle. In all, as Viola's brother Sebastian says of his own ill fate, the heroines' "stars shine darkly over [them]" (II.i.3–4). But that factor ends up being sauce for the comedy and spur to the young women's courage. None spends long indulging in self-pity. Quick-witted and resourceful, they deal with their sudden vulnerability by taking on, quite literally, the guise of their absent fathers. All dress as young men and enter a male arena—the law court, the duke's privy chambers, the greenwood. There they defeat older, more experienced men

125

in trials of wit and will and win, as ultimate reward, the husbands they desire.

Each woman is bold in pursuit of her beloved. The main purpose of her disguise is to gain access to his company and win his favor. Ironically, the cross-dressing makes each attractive to other women or, in the case of Portia, to other men as well. Perhaps Shakespeare is suggesting the charismatic nature of androgyny, as Marjorie Garber argues. Or perhaps he is implying simply that the best judges of what makes men attractive are women. It is not that the women become manly, in either appearance or attitude. Other characters are always remarking on how girlish and refined each of the "boys" looks. And they do not exhibit physical prowess: Rosalind faints at the mention of Orlando's wound, and Viola, the one woman who is forced to defend her honor with a sword, is brought to shame and danger and must be rescued by a stalwart male. A sure mark of the comic genre is that such coincidences occur in the nick of time. Another sign is the absurdity of the basic premise: that a person can switch genders and even those closest to them will not see through the disguise.

Yet for all the improbability of the basic situation, the psychology rings true: having been nurtured and valued by a strong parent, the daughter has the resources to cope with adversity. The father may be absent, but his influence continues to guide and sustain her. In all three of the comedies, his role is that of mentor, providing the daughter with standards for judging others and approbation for asserting her will. The ultimate proof and reward is her choice of husband. In each case, the daughter chooses a man her father would approve of. In fact, Duke Senior, the one surviving father, openly expresses that approval. As different as these daughter and father pairs are from one another, they reflect the conditions that Shakespeare implied are essential to healthy parenting: personal integrity and respect for children as individuals. These men may lack the supernatural resources of Prospero, but they share his capacity for loving his daughter and for showing her by example the means to earthly happiness.

The Merchant of Venice

Portia's late father is the most authoritarian of this group, literally designating the limits of her choice. She is described in the cast list as "an heiress," and the first references to her confirm the enormous wealth of her legacy. The enamored Bassanio describes her as "a lady richly left," whose "sunny locks" are like a "golden fleece" that attracts "many Jasons" (I.i.161–72). The metaphor, for all its pretty classical trappings, implies the disadvantage of Portia's state: she is a prize, and the motives of any suitor for her hand must necessarily be suspect. In his will, her father took pains to favor those worthy of her. Gradually, the terms of his bequest are revealed. He has set up a "lottery of [her] destiny" (II.i.15) with very strict rules: a suitor must choose among three "caskets," the winning one containing Portia's picture. Should he fail, he must comply with three conditions: to keep the results secret, to forswear marriage to any other, and "immediately to leave [Portia] and begone" (II.ix.15).

In her first appearance, Portia chafes at these hard terms, by which she "may neither choose who [she] would nor refuse who [she] dislike[s]" (I.ii.22–23). Thus, she says, is "the will of a living daughter curbed by the will of a dead father" (ll. 23–24). Her pun on "will" (both legacy and inclination) had still other meanings in Shakespeare's day. It meant not only "fervent longing" but sexual desire, and also the genitalia, male and female.* Portia is "weary" of these restrictions—this is her first word to Nerissa, her maid and confidante. She is bored and restless in her gilded cage, resentful that her father has "hedged [her] by his wit" (I.i.18) and longing to break out of her enforced passivity. At the same time, she feels honor bound to "perform [her] father's will" (I.ii.85–86), and she does not gainsay Nerissa's defense of him:

> Your father was ever virtuous, and holy men at their death have good inspiration. Therefore the lott'ry that he hath devised ... whereof who chooses his meaning chooses you will no doubt never be chosen by any rightly but one who you shall rightly love   [ll. 26–31].

In fact, the play reinforces the wisdom of his means. The contest brings the outside world to isolated Belmont, provides a stage on which Portia can demonstrate her gifts, foils unsuitable candidates, and ultimately yields her the suitor of her dreams.

Although Portia is frustrated by her situation, she is far from broken. In a society where the feminine model, as expressed by the chauvinistic Gratiano, is silent acquiescence, Portia is confident, witty, and resourceful. She has the strength not only to dominate the domestic sphere, as gracious hostess and desirable bride, but also to prevail in the traditionally male provinces of jurisprudence and finance. She wins every contest of wit, and she both adapts and surpasses the credo held by the men in her world. In short, Portia is no easy prize. Bassanio must not only win the contest, he must learn to deserve the woman he has won. Portia, in turn,

---

*In Sonnets 135 and 136, for example, Shakespeare puns on these bawdy meanings.

must strive to overcome all adversaries in order to secure his love. Those include not only her other suitors and Shylock, the rapacious lender of Bassanio's courtship expenses, but, less obviously, his too-devoted friend, Antonio. In all these situations, the "will" of Portia's father works to assure that she will be "chosen rightly" by a man whom she can "rightly love."

As the play opens, Portia is already in love with Bassanio, a "scholar and soldier" who first courted her "in her father's time" (I.ii.103–04). Left to her own devices, she would simply seek him out. She is "weary" of her other suitors, whom she mocks to Nerissa for every fault from stupidity to drunkenness. She longs to ignore her father's "will" and pursue her own, as she tells Nerissa in a wry proverb: to act the "hare" that is "madness the youth" and "skip o'er the meshes of good counsel the cripple" (ll. 19–20). But Shakespeare has shown us just enough of Bassanio to suggest that that impulsive course would be a mistake.

In some ways, he is worthy of Portia: he is handsome, gallant, and smitten with her. In a word, he is charming. But under that fair surface lurk some dark elements. Bassanio has "great debts" as a result, he admits candidly, of a "prodigal" lifestyle (I.i.128–29). He hopes to restore his fortunes with the rich marriage — the capture of the "golden fleece," a practical motive but hardly a noble one. To achieve his ends, Bassanio needs "means" to purchase clothes, gifts, and transport to "furnish [him] to Belmont, to fair Portia" (ll. 173, 182). He turns for funds to the friend to whom he is already deeply in debt, the rich merchant Antonio. Rather than upbraid the prodigal young man, Antonio agrees with alacrity: "My purse, my person, my extremest means / Lie all unlocked to your occasions" (ll. 138–39). The metaphor has a sexual innuendo, which Antonio echoes later when he protests against the practice of taking interest for loans: "When did friendship take / A *breed of barren* metal of his friend?" (my italics, I.iii.129–30). Antonio, in Solanio's words, "only loves the world for him [Bassanio]" (II.viii.50). He puts his offer in hyperbolic terms: "You do me now more wrong / In making question of my uttermost / Than if you had made waste of all I have" (I.i.155–57). These sentiments go beyond generosity to self-abasement, particularly since Antonio is short on liquid capital and must borrow the required sum. But Bassanio hears only what he wants to hear — that Antonio will supply the money — and dashes off to prepare for his departure.

It is not that Bassanio is ungenerous himself. Later, he will use some of Antonio's capital to provide "rare new liveries" for his servant Launcelot Gobbo (II.ii.101). He also has high standards of decorum. When the obstreperous Gratiano offers to accompany him, Bassanio warns him that he must curb his "bold ... voice" and "wild behavior" so that he himself will not be misjudged in Belmont and "lose [his] hopes" (ll. 67–75). Still, for all his boyish charm, as Bassanio leaves for Belmont, his motives are mixed and his personal history spotty. Meanwhile, the contest has been teaching Portia — and us— the importance of looking beneath the surface to discover true value.

These lessons, and the wisdom behind the lottery, are conveyed at the expense of Portia's other suitors. The egotistical Prince of Morocco believes that "blind Fortune" (II.i.36) determines the outcome, and prays that "some god direct [his] judgment" (II.vii.13). Portia, who finds him repellent, is tactful and politic. She invites him to dinner before he makes his "hazard" and, in his presence, acts the gracious hostess. She knows both how to please and how to keep an undesirable suitor at arm's length. She reminds Morocco that the choice is out of her hands: she may not be "solely led" by the preference of "a maiden's eyes" (II.i13–14)— implying that, if she could be, those eyes would favor him. The prince misses both the double meaning and the warning and uses his own "eyes" to judge by surface beauty. His choice, the gold casket, contains a death's head and the play's central caution: "All that glisters is not gold" (II.vii.65).

The second suitor, the Prince of Arragon, takes himself as the standard of value — "I will assume desert"— and chooses the silver casket. This time a fool's head — his own —confronts the failed suitor. After his dismayed departure, Portia comments wryly on such "fools" who "have the wisdom by their wit to lose" (II.ix.79–80). But she does not remark that, for all his disappointment, Arragon, like Morocco, has left amicably. His last words are: "Sweet, adieu. I'll keep my oath" (l. 76). The field has been left free for Bassanio. Portia, meanwhile, is unscathed and in charge. For all its stern strictures, the lottery is working in her best interests.

But Bassanio must still win, and be won. He fulfills Portia's every fantasy. In the enraptured words of Nerissa, he is "Lord Love" (II.ix.100), and Portia is giddy with desire. When he arrives at last, she makes a clumsy attempt at being subtle: "There's something tells me, but it is not love, / I would not lose you" (III.ii.4–5). Soon, although she chides herself for "speak[ing] too long," she is telling him outright that his eyes "have o'erlooked and divided me; / One half of me is yours, the other half is yours" (ll. 22, 15–17). She catches herself in this nonsensical arithmetic, but she does not take back the declaration. Like most of Shakespeare's daughters, Portia is bold in pursuit of her man. Still, she will not disregard the terms of her father's will. As she tells Bassanio: "I could teach you / How to choose right, but then I am forsworn. / So I will never be" (ll. 10–12). More than personal integrity is motivating Portia. On some level, she believes in the efficacy of the test. Pointing to the three caskets, she says: "I am locked in one of them; / If you do love me, you will find me out" (ll. 40–41). Having risked so much pride in admitting her love, she does not want to be lightly won. Nor does she want a husband whose values are at odds with her father's.

But Portia is nothing if not politic. In this trial, as in the literal one to come, she proves a brilliant manipulator of men and events, adept at both embracing and evading the patriarchal system. She is not above craftily bettering the odds in Bassanio's favor. Playing the neutral onlooker, she orders the members of her court to "stand all aloof," and she addresses him as "Hercules" braving a solitary "fray" (III.ii.60–62). But, while he contemplates his choice, she also gives the directive "Let music sound." The music is vocal, and the song contains several hints about the right answer. The first three lines are a triplet whose final word — "bred," "head," and "nourishèd" — rhymes with "lead," the metal of the winning casket. More important, the subject of the song is a warning against "fancy" — infatuation — which comes from "the eyes," rather than "the heart," and quickly ends. The chorus sounds "fancy's knell" — the death toll of superficial and transient physical attraction. Bassanio's reaction indicates that he has listened well. "So," he says as the last notes fade, and goes on to expatiate against the deceptiveness of "outward shows" and "seeming truth" (ll. 73–101). In the end, he chooses the casket made of "meagre lead" (l. 104); it contains Portia's picture and a scroll commending the man "that chose not by the view" (l. 131). In fact, Bassanio's choice does depend partly on "the view." He pays tribute once again to Portia's enchanting eyes and the "golden mesh" of her hair. Shakespeare never denies the vital role that sexual attraction plays in love. But at least it is the "outside" of the lady herself, not of her dowry, which Bassanio admires. He has, in Portia's words, fulfilled the terms of her father's will and earned the right to become "her lord, her governor, her king," ruling over "this house, these servants, and this same myself" (ll. 165–70).

For all these submissive words, however, Portia remains very much in charge. She speaks the words of the "coronation" ceremony and sets the conditions of the marriage. Bassanio is "bereft of all words" (III.ii.175), the passive role traditionally relegated to the woman. In a further reversal of the usual betrothal rite, it is Portia who gives him a ring symbolizing their union. She specifies that he must never "part from, lose, or give away" the token, "lest it presage the ruin of [his] love" (ll. 172–73).

The lovers have no sooner accepted joyous congratulations, compounded by the happy news that Nerissa and Gratiano have also made a match, than word comes from Venice that will put Portia to much harder tests of her mettle. Bassanio's mentor, the merchant Antonio, has lost his ships and is now subject to the terms of the usurer Shylock's bond. Bassanio is devastated by this news, rendered helpless with anxiety and guilt. Portia, in contrast, reacts to the crisis with vigor and imagination. First she requires that Bassanio read her the letter that has caused him to blanch and tremble. "I am half yourself," she declares staunchly, and thus insists on bearing half his grief. Portia immediately offers not only to pay "the petty debt" (III.ii.307), which is far beyond the impecunious Bassanio's means, but to double or treble the sum, and orders him away to carry out her wishes. Before he leaves, however, he must "go with [her] to church and call [her] wife" (l. 303). She will forego the honeymoon, and she and Nerissa "will live as maids and widows" (l. 310) until the grooms return. Lorenzo, who has brought the letter, praises her generous forbearance as "godlike amity" (III.iv.3). But Portia has sound practical grounds for her actions. As she tells Bassanio, she will not let him "lie by [her] side" with "an unquiet soul" (III.ii.305–06). A marriage founded on the suffering of his "dearest friend" would be doomed to fail. She will not have Bassanio until he is free to focus exclusively on *her*. She concludes with a wry pun: "Since you are dear bought [i. e., expensive], I will love you dear [deeply]" (l. 313). Bassanio may be the nominal "king," but Portia is the one giving commands and assigning values.

Nor is Portia content to play a passive waiting role while Bassanio is away. Her quick brain begins inventing a scheme for rescuing Antonio. She lies easily about going off with Nerissa to a monastery "to live in prayer and contemplation" (III.iv.28) — the traditional woman's role in a crisis. (That is the course planned for Ophelia, Hero, and Juliet, for example.) Once Portia has sent the men on their way, she begins making arrangements like the gifted leader she is. She puts Lorenzo in charge of her estate, sends to her cousin, the legal scholar Dr. Bellario, for "notes" and "garments," and orders her coach to take her and Nerissa to the ferry for Venice. She reveals to Nerissa only that they will soon join their husbands "accoutered like young men" (l. 63). This chance to break out of her enforced passivity fills Portia with mischievous elation. She delights in the details of the androgynous disguise, the chance to "speak between the change of man and boy," and "turn two mincing steps / Into a manly stride" (ll. 66–68). When Nerissa exclaims, "What, shall we turn to men?" (l. 78), Portia gives a bawdy retort. She promises to tell her "all [the] whole device" en route, and so creates suspense about her plan, both for her gentlewoman and for us. What is not in question is Portia's nerve. Given a chance to enter the male arena, she takes up the challenge with alacrity.

Portia has long been commended — or condemned — for her thorough defeat of Shylock. She carries out the scheme brilliantly. Has she gotten her knowledge of law from her father? Is her cousin Bellario a relative on the paternal side? We never find out. Her triumph is the more impressive because the Venetian men, privileged sophisticates at the hub of the power structure, are completely thwarted by the recalcitrant Jew. They are used to playing by their own rules, the Christian gentleman's credo, and their approach is to try to coerce Shylock into conforming to it. The Duke of Venice tries first to coax and then to bully him into dropping his suit. He asserts that "the world" and he, too, think that the bond is a mere bluff, a practical joke. He then portrays Antonio as an innocent victim, and pleads with Shylock to "glanc[e] an eye of pity on his losses" (IV.i.27). But the Duke is well aware of the "lodged hate" (l. 60) that Shylock bears the merchant. He knows, too, the bigotry and abuse that have caused such deep enmity. Evidence of that maltreatment comes immediately. The Duke insults Shylock, comparing him to such malevolent pagans as "Turks and Tartars" and ending what began as a plea for mercy with a threat: "We all expect a gentle answer, Jew" (l. 34). The admonition is the more demeaning for its punning glance at Shylock's religion (gentle / gentile). This approach seems calculated to provoke rage and defiance. Can the Duke really hope to change Shylock's mind, or is he so driven by arrogance that he loses sight of his goals?

In any case, Shylock responds by flinging insults of his own, and of the crudest sort. He compares Antonio to a series of animals— a rat, a pig, a cat — and says that the plea is no more efficacious than urging some men to love bagpipes when, at their sound, they "cannot contain their urine" (IV.i.50). Clearly, he is enjoying this public duel. Cleverly, he shifts the terms of the argument from personal to political: should the Duke fail to honor the bond, he will undermine the city-state's "charter" and " freedom" (l. 39), showing the world "There is no force in the decrees of Venice" (l. 102). Shylock has spoken in the language of commerce and the law, and the Duke is stymied. In desperation, Gratiano demands, "Can no prayers pierce thee?" Shylock shoots back: "No, none that thou hast wit enough to make" (ll. 126–27). Deaf to the young man's "rail[ing]," he says confidently: "I stand here for law." He has met his adversaries on their own ground and he has won. It takes another outsider, a woman, to both embrace and undermine his terms.

Although Portia comes "furnished with [Bellario's] opinion," based on research into Venetian civil law, she is on her own in the conduct of the trial. To some extent, she is making things up as she goes along — gauging her opponent, probing his weaknesses, and looking for an opening gambit. She begins by confirming that "the Venetian law" is on Shylock's side, which sends him into raptures of gratitude and self-congratulation.

Then, in her famous plea, she urges him to exercise mercy, not for Antonio's sake but for his own. Unlike the men, she is wise enough to appeal not to pity but to self-interest. Mercy benefits the giver more than the recipient, she argues, ranking him with "kings" and "God himself," and giving him the expectation of mercy when he himself has need. When Shylock remains obdurate, Bassanio urges her to bend the law and save Antonio: "to do a great right, do a little wrong" (IV.i.214). Portia is adamant: she will not weaken the legal system by establishing a bad "precedent," and Shylock is once more elated.

The tension in the scene is at its height. Portia has led everyone to assume that the eloquent plea for mercy was her only ploy. But just as Shylock is about to claim his bloody prize, she stops him with a word: "Tarry." Then she lets fall her series of swashing blows, trapping Shylock in his own rhetoric. She is even more absolute in her reading of the bond than he has been. It mentions "no jot of blood"; it requires "nor ... less nor more" than exactly "a pound of flesh" (IV.i.304, 323–24). Shylock quails at these exacting technicalities and offers to accept instead Bassanio's offer of triple the monetary value. Bassanio hastens to give it to him, but Portia stops him with the cold injunction: "The Jew shall have all justice" (l. 319). Shylock then tries, and fails, to reclaim merely his "principal" (l. 334). But Portia has a worse penalty in store: as an "alien" plotting the death of a "citizen," Venetian law prescribes that he be deprived of all his goods and of his very life. Obviously, Portia has had this backup threat ready should Shylock have thrown caution to the winds and chosen revenge. She feels no scruples about using his outsider's status against him. In fact, the "mercy" that she forces him to beg of the Duke contains little of the compassion that she has preached. It includes the conditions that Shylock bequeath half his fortune to the daughter who has betrayed him and her new Christian husband, and, hardest of all, that he convert immediately to Christianity.

Some commentators have argued that from the Christian point of view, Portia is showing Shylock mercy, by saving his infidel's soul. But the effect on him is not relief but devastation. Usually voluble, he says almost nothing. The bare line "I am not well" expresses his despair. That reading was reinforced in Olivier's 1970 production by a heart-rending cry from the wings after his exit. Our own feelings are conflicted. Shylock has been victimized, but, in revenge, he would exact cold-blooded murder. For all our understanding of the persecution that has warped him, we do not want to see him turn Antonio into a sacrificial animal before our eyes. We may not approve of Portia's ruthlessness, but we do see that it is the only means of countering Shylock's. Callow and untried as she is, she outplays the male cosmopolites at every turn. As Bellario's letter of introduction promised, seldom has there been "so young a body with so old a head" (IV.i.161–62).

Crucial as this contest of wit and will is for Portia's future happiness, it is not the only or even the major one that she must win. Not Shylock but Antonio is her rival for Bassanio's heart. Portia must rescue him from Shylock's deadly snare because Antonio is, in her words, "the bosom lover of [her] lord" (III.iv.17). Were the merchant to die, Bassanio's guilt at financing his courtship at the cost of his benefactor's life would poison the marriage. But Portia's description suggests her subtler and more complex task: to supplant Antonio in Bassanio's "bosom." From the first, she is wary of the attachment. As noted above, before she sends Bassanio to Antonio's aid, she asks to see the merchant's letter. Antonio's plea, on the surface humble and self-effacing, is in fact manipulative and narcissistic. He writes that he clears the young man of all debt "if I might but see you at my death," and adds that only Bassanio's "love" should "persuade [him] to come, not my letter" (III.ii.319–21). Poisoned darts of guilt and self-reproach wait in every line. It should be no surprise that Portia rushes to rescue so willing a sacrificial lamb. Whether Antonio is moved by homosexuality, as some recent productions have suggested, or simply the Renaissance male friend's strong bond with a protégé, he behaves like a possessive lover. It is a hold that Portia must break if the handsome, feckless Bassanio is to become her soulmate.

When we see Antonio under arrest, his masochism and self-pity are clearly evident. He describes himself to Bassanio as "a tainted wether of the flock, / Meetest for death," and "comforts" the distraught young man with the assertion that his most worthwhile course would be to live on and "write mine epitaph" (IV.i.114–18). Again, this is the guilt that binds. Bassanio is helpless before this onslaught. He offers—futilely—to give his "flesh, blood, bones, and all" (l. 112) to save Antonio. More practically, he offers Shylock double the cash value of the bond. He is no match for either merchant. Shylock cuts him off and Antonio proffers more specious comfort: "Grieve not that I am fall'n to this *for you*" (l. 264, my italics). He also urges Bassanio to ask his "honorable wife" to "judge / Whether Bassanio had not once a love" (ll. 271, 274–75). He concludes with a morbid pun: "if the Jew do cut but deep enough, / I'll pay [the debt] with all my heart" (ll. 278–79). Bassanio responds with a vow of his willingness to sacrifice "life itself, my wife, and all the world" to "deliver" Antonio (ll. 282–85). The disguised Portia, who overhears these words, makes a sarcastic retort on behalf of the "absent" wife. The dramatic irony of her presence lightens the tone. But the issue is a serious one: the ghost of the martyred Antonio would be an unconquerable rival for Bassanio's love.

Even after Portia has rescued Antonio from Shylock's clutches, she has not secured Bassanio's loyalty. While she is still disguised, she subjects him to the test of the ring. The gifted young lawyer demands as his fee the jewel that Bassanio has pledged never to remove. At first, the young husband holds off. When polite refusals fail, he is driven to telling the awkward truth about the ring's importance in his marriage vows. Portia pretends to be insulted, makes a sarcastic remark about false offers of generosity, and goes off in a supposed huff. Still, Bassanio has held his ground. Then Antonio interposes himself: "Let his deservings, and my love withal, / Be valued 'gainst your wife's commandment" (IV.i.448–49). This loading of the case is too much, and Bassanio gives in. It could be argued that Portia is too exacting: in this personal trial, as in the legal one, she is an absolutist. Nonetheless, she is not one to back off from a power struggle. She will let both Bassanio and his mentor know in no uncertain terms who passes the judgments and determines the relationships in her world.

When Bassanio returns home, bringing Antonio, Portia greets the merchant courteously: "You are very welcome to our house." But the plural pronoun is a reminder that she and Bassanio are a couple. When the greeting ritual is disrupted by the din of Nerissa and Gratiano's quarrel over the loss of his ring, Portia interrupts. "You were to blame," she pronounces, "To part so slightly with your wife's first gift" (V.i.166–67). She knows, of course, that Bassanio is equally guilty, and she enjoys turning the knife and watching him squirm. When he is forced to admit his own fault, she turns her accusations in a comic direction by pretending to be jealous of "some woman [who] had the ring" (l. 208). She denies him her bed until the token is recovered — a reminder to us that the marriage is still unconsummated. She taunts him with the threat of cuckoldry, and with the very "doctor" of laws who has received the ring. Bassanio tries to explain the forces of "shame and courtesy," the charge of "ingratitude," that would have sullied his honor had he not relinquished the ring. But he does not reveal that Antonio urged him to the act.

Antonio, who has been standing awkwardly by while his hosts quarrel, intervenes: "I am th'unhappy subject of these quarrels" (V.i.238). Portia wryly assures him that he is "welcome notwithstanding." Bassanio redoubles his effort to charm and apologize, but Portia is having none of it. She chastises him with having a "double self." On the surface, she is saying that he is a hypocrite, which she knows to be untrue, but her underlying charge holds: his loyalties are divided between his friend and his wife. When Bassanio swears by his "soul" to be true to her hereafter, Antonio again interposes. Reminding them that he once pledged his "body" for Bassanio's sake, he tries to offer Portia his "soul" as collateral "that your lord / Will never break faith advisedly" (ll. 252–53).

Firmly, Portia moves to break up this unwholesome triangle. The Renaissance conception was that two lovers completed one another. Their bond should form a perfect circle, symbolized by the wedding ring. A triangle is the wrong shape. She preempts both the lead and Antonio's claim and casts him in the role of guarantor of the couple's union: "Then you *shall* be his surety…. *Give* him this … and *bid* him…." (V.i.254–55, my italics). The imperative voice is the mark of a woman sure of her place and in firm command of her estate. Only after Antonio complies does she reveal her role in Shylock's defeat. She clearly relishes the company's shock. "You are all amazed," she gloats, and Antonio concedes, "I am dumb!" (ll. 266, 279). Portia's final ploy is to restore his financial security. She has withheld the news that three of his ships have come safely to harbor. "Sweet lady," he says, "you have given me life and living" (l. 286). Portia has taught Antonio to be grateful for the mercantile wealth and power — the Venetian domain — that he is entitled to. Bassanio's love, the province that she has captured by venturing abroad, she will keep for herself in Belmont.

While it is unlikely that Portia's father could have foreseen these complex results in establishing the test of the caskets, he did provide the means both to safeguard and to free his daughter. His legacy may also have included providing the model for her own strong character. We get no chance to see them together, but we do know that even in her isolated outpost Portia has somehow learned to gauge men and to lead. Wiliness and prescience, the defining qualities of her intellect, are also, by implication, those of the writer of the will. As the clown, Launcelot Gobbo, says, "It is a wise father that knows his own child."

Twelfth Night

Viola is the most father-bereft of these daughters. Her father, "Sebastian of Messaline" (II.i.15), died on her thirteenth birthday. How much time has passed since that sad event is unclear, but internal evidence suggests that it cannot be more than about three years. The plot of the play hangs on the fact that Viola and her twin bother, named for their father, look so young as to be androgynous. That father is mentioned only briefly in the course of the play, but the allusions are key to understanding the daughter. Her decision to present herself disguised as a page at Duke Orsino's court is based on her father's former acquaintance with the nobleman. When Viola lands in Illyria after a violent storm, she thinks that Sebastian has drowned and that she must make her own way in the world. She asks the captain who has rescued her who "governs" this place, and, at his answer, exclaims, "Orsino! I have heard my father name him" (I.ii.24, 28). In a seeming non sequitur, she adds, "He was a bachelor then." The captain confirms his single state but says that Orsino has been "seek[ing] the love of the fair Olivia," a countess. Viola's first plan is to apply for service with the lady Olivia. While that would seem the safer course, she abruptly decides instead that she will "serve this duke" (l. 55). Like Portia's, her preferred suitor is linked to a past time when her life was more secure. Is Viola seeking a father figure to replace the one that she has lost? Secretly piqued by the challenge of winning him away from Olivia? In any case, it is her father's commendation that serves as the catalyst for Viola's life-changing decision.

Her father's other function is as the parent of Sebastian, who, in name as in actions, stands in his place as protector and model. Viola believes in the woman's traditional need to be safeguarded by a strong male. Yet because she has been deprived of both her father and her brother, she makes the bold choice of taking on that role herself. Instead of turning to the Duke and asking for shelter, her impulse, on landing alone in Illyria, is to "conceal me what I am" until she is ready to be "delivered to the world" (I.ii.53, 42) — reborn, in a sense, in her female state. She hides her "maid's garments" (V.i.267) and strives to "imitate" her brother in "fashion, color, ornament" (IV.iv.362–63) and "voice" (V.i.208). Her effort is a resounding success. Ruby lipped and shrill-voiced, the twins seem to everyone in Illyria the same charming boy. As the sea captain Antonio exclaims when they are at last brought face to face: "An apple cleft in twain is not more twin / Than these two creatures" (ll. 215–16). Even Sebastian himself is fooled. When they meet at the end, he says, "Do I stand there? I never had a brother" (l. 218). By that point, Viola has discovered the truth, that he is still alive, but for much of the play she believes, as she tells Orsino, in her lone — and double — state: "I am all the daughters of my father's house, / And all the brothers, too" (II.iv.119–20). That heritage, and its accompanying responsibilities, stir Viola to new heights of boldness and imagination. Although more constrained than either the resolute Portia or the ebullient Rosalind, Viola, too, is freed by assuming male dress.

This is not to suggest that Viola becomes manly, in either appearance or physical aggression. Shakespeare is clear about the distinction between the genders, which overlap only in the guise of the handsome boy. His audience, of course, enjoyed an added fillip of dramatic irony: in the Elizabethan theater, the actor playing a girl playing a boy was, in fact, a male. For Viola, as for her cross-dressing Shakespearean sisters, male dress sparks her incipient gifts and provides her entry to the traditionally masculine provinces of chivalry and courtship. In choosing to assume the role bequeathed by the Sebastians, senior and junior, Viola takes risks and ventures actions that better the lives of everyone she loves.

Shakespeare reminds us of Viola's essential femininity in every instance of physical combat. Certainly she is no swordsman. When, provoked by the mischievous Sir Toby, Sir Andrew challenges "Cesario" to a duel, the youth "pants and looks pale" and protests weakly, "I am no fighter" (III.iv.275–76, 227). Sir Toby questions "his" right to wear a sword, claiming that a man must be ever ready, according to "the duello," to fight "for honor's sake" (ll. 286–87). In other words, valor is seen as a male virtue. Viola is so terrified that she almost reveals her true identity. Shakespeare keeps the play from veering into tragedy by making her opponent, the cowardly Sir Andrew, even more frightened than she is. They are spared by the comic device of coincidence: the timely intervention of two rescuers, first Olivia and later Sebastian's mentor Antonio. Olivia is indifferent to the duello and horrified by the attack on her beloved. She condemns Toby as barbaric, a "rudesby," who is "fit for the mountains and the barbarous caves" (IV.i.44), and orders him off, rescuing Viola in the process. The real Sebastian, in contrast, is valiant and feisty. Later, when the hapless Andrew, convinced that Cesario will not defend himself, mistakenly attacks her brother, Sebastian "*strikes*" him three times for his one blow. Sir Toby intervenes and "*seizes*" the young man, but Sebastian "*frees himself*," *draws* (stage directions, ll. 24–39) and challenges: "If thou dar'st tempt me further, draw thy sword" (l. 38). The familiar pronoun, from someone a third Toby's age, shows Sebastian's boldness. Olivia breaks up this confrontation, too, but later, off-stage, the two knights attack the boy again, and he proves more than a match for both men. In Sir Andrew's tearful complaint, Sebastian "broke [his] head across" and gave "Sir Toby a bloody coxcomb too" (V.i.169–70).

It is not that Viola is a coward. Simply, she has not been trained in fencing, and she does not have her brother's physical strength. But in the other masculine arena, courtship, "he" proves "masterly." Sent as Orsino's emissary to the cold Olivia, Cesario exudes an irresistible charm. The initial reason is physical: the countess is attracted to adolescent good looks. When her steward Malvolio announces that still another messenger has arrived from Orsino, Olivia is matter-of-fact in her indifference: "Tell him he shall not speak to me." But once she has provoked Malvolio into describing "his personage and years" as "in standing water, between boy and man" and "very well-favored" (I.v.149, 152–54), Olivia changes her mind. "Let him approach," she commands.

If good looks were Viola's only asset, however, she would not hold

Olivia long. Like all of Shakespeare's daughters, she is a gifted speaker. Although her first words as Orsino's messenger are conventional—"I can say little more than I have studied" (I.v.170)—she soon proves spontaneous and daring. Orsino has urged her to be aggressive: "Be clamorous and leap all civil bounds" (I.iv.20), courting Olivia with "fertile tears" and "groans that thunder love" (I.v.241–42). But Viola soon perceives that such self-dramatization repels Olivia. Cesario is a more subtle lover. When Olivia asks how he would court her, he responds:

> Make me a willow cabin at your gate
> And call upon my soul within the house;
> Write loyal cantons of contemned love
> And sing them loud even in the dead of night;
> Hallo your name to the reverberate hills
> And make the babbling gossip of the air
> Cry out "Olivia"! O, you should not rest
> Between the elements of air and earth
> But you should pity me   [ll. 254–62].

The speech pictures the lover not as an aggressor, leaping and clamoring at his mistress, but as a pilgrim worshipping at her shrine and a poet making music of her name. It is centered not on his needs but on his tributes to her, and it wins Olivia instantly. The countess, whom Viola has just frankly described to her face as "too proud" (l. 236), practically throws herself at the youth's feet and begins pursuing him with a single-mindedness that surpasses Orsino's.

How has Viola known what will win Olivia? First, because she is herself an unrequited lover, pining for the Duke even as she courts another woman in his name. But situation alone would not afford her such eloquence. In common with her Shakespearean sisters, the gift that Viola has in highly developed form is intelligence. In Sebastian's words, she "[bears] a mind that envy could not but call fair" (II.i.26). On the simplest level, Viola is witty, relishing every duel of words and matching her opposite — Andrew, Toby, Maria — idiom for idiom, riposte for riposte. As Andrew marvels after eavesdropping on an exchange between Cesario and Olivia, "That youth's a rare courtier" (III.i.83). The one verbal duelist who outfences her is the clown Feste, but Viola is sufficiently clever both to concede defeat and to philosophize afterwards on his gift: "This fellow is wise enough to play the fool" (l. 58).

Viola's greatest intellectual gift is prescience. Olivia praises that quick insight: "To one of your receiving / Enough is shown" (III.i.117–18). That compliment is substantiated when Olivia sends Malvolio after Cesario to return a ring that he supposedly left her. Viola quickly gets the underlying message. She reveals nothing to the peevish steward, but immediately after his exit, she exclaims: "Fortune forbid my outside have not charmed her" (II.ii.17). She sees the token for what it is—evidence of "the cunning of [Olivia's] passion."

The main use that Viola makes of her intellect is in the moral/emotional education of the Duke. At the beginning of the play, Orsino depicts himself as the resident authority on love, and its chief victim. He equates love with "fancy," the Elizabethan word for infatuation, a quality as changeable as the sea. He says that his desires are like "cruel hounds," pursuing and destroying him. He is convinced that the solution to his dilemma would be for Cupid's "rich golden shaft" to penetrate Olivia's heart, and make him the "one self-king" occupying all her "thrones" of passion (I.i.39). These fantasies are entirely self-centered. The main proof is that at the end of the scene, Orsino does not go to court the object of his devotion but to recline on "sweet beds of flowers" and conjure up her image — to indulge in masturbatory fantasies. It takes Viola, come from the sea, to show him the difference between infatuation and love.

Orsino is oblivious at first to both Viola's wisdom and her devotion to him. One of the funniest and most painful scenes in the play is their debate on the nature of the lover. Orsino claims to be the expert—"such as I am all true lovers are" (II.iv.16). They are, he asserts, constant in only one quality, their worship of the "image of the creature that is beloved" (ll. 18–19). This ideal should not be confused with mere "appetite," the Duke pontificates, the only sort of love of which women are capable. Barely pausing for breath, he then unwittingly uses that very metaphor to describe his longing for Olivia as "all as hungry as the sea" (l. 99). Viola counters by positing the case of a hypothetical woman in love with *him*. "You cannot love her," she continues, "you tell her so. Must she not then be answered?" (ll. 90–91). Viola has surmised that this would be the scenario should she reveal her own feelings. Rather than risk such humiliation and, perhaps worse, separation, she keeps her own counsel. The true lover, she argues, is selfless: better to "pine[ ] in thought" and "smile[ ] at grief" (ll. 111, 114) than offend by confessing a passion that would be rejected. We men, she continues, may "say more, swear more," but "our vows" surpass "our love" (ll. 115–17). This comes too close to home for Orsino—or Cesario—to dwell on. She cuts the exchange short by offering to renew the pursuit of Olivia, and Orsino seizes the chance to turn from discomforting thought to familiar action. On stage, a long — and longing — look may pass between the Duke and Viola at this point. He is strongly, disturbingly, drawn to the boy in whom he has confided so much and who understands him so thoroughly. Yet his soul mate, he insists, is the countess. For Orsino, as for Viola, the "strife" is too "barful" to resolve (I.v.40). Because this is a comedy, "Time" and happy, impossible coincidence will "untie" this knot (II.ii.39–40). But the cause of the conflict goes beyond that in Shakespeare's earlier confusion-of-twins play, the farcical *Comedy of Errors*. There, caricature is the mode and happenstance will do to sort things out happily. In the subtler comedy, changes in character must bring about the resolution.

The next time that Viola and Orsino come together is in the final scene of the play. There, she does what she has not dared do before: make a public profession of her love for him and be bold and courageous in its service. Orsino is outraged by what he believes is Cesario's duplicity in courting Olivia for himself. He threatens to kill first the countess and then the boy, proclaiming that his "savage jealousy" is noble and the murder of Viola a "sacrifice" of "the lamb that I do love" (V.i.124). Both his tone and his diction sound alarmingly like Othello's. His, too, is the language of egotism masquerading as love. Viola responds with self-denigrating devotion: "To do you rest, a thousand deaths [I] would die" (l. 127), she says fervently. And she announces to Olivia and all the rest of the court that she loves Orsino "more than I love these eyes, more than my life" (l. 129). Into this tangle of barbed emotions steps Sebastian, and, magically, the feelings of betrayal are soothed and the new matches made.

The proof of Viola's identity is her confirmation of her paternity. Sebastian instigates an exchange that proves her to be, like himself, the child of "Sebastian of Messaline," but daughter rather than son. Olivia must undergo the public humiliation of having courted "a maid." But the sting is lessened by having Sebastian himself treat that attraction as a joke. The greater sense of foolish exposure is Orsino's. He has been blind to both Viola's passion for him and his for her. With typical self-centeredness, he vows to "share" in the "happy wrack," and he turns to claim the woman who has so often professed her love for him. He commends her "service done him / So much against the mettle of [her] sex" (V.i.311–12) and promises that when she has redonned her feminine garb, he will make her "Orsino's mistress and his fancy's queen." (l. 377). These words, for all their prettiness, nonetheless imply Orsino's faults: he remains the chauvinist and the fantasizer. Still, he has learned to value Viola's courage and devotion. Is he a comparable prize for her? The play does not answer such a question; it is a comedy, after all, and we do not follow the couple beyond the plans for a joyous double wedding. The one ominous note is Feste's final song about the inevitability in life of "the wind and the rain."

For the present, however, Viola, like Portia, has fared very well in her father's absence. She has profited from his predilections and his example, continued in the person of his son. Alone, she has entered the male arenas of court and courtship and won for a husband the man she most desires. When Orsino commends Viola for having served him in ways "so much against the mettle of [her] sex," he is assuming, as she did at the outset, that the role of protector belongs to the male. Inadvertently, though, he is confirming that on her own Viola is intelligent and resourceful enough to have served in that capacity not only for herself but for him. Daughters, too, can inherit their father's strengths.

As You Like It

Rosalind, like her sister heroines, is made to fend for herself in the world. She, too, chooses male disguise as protection and release. Because her father is not dead but merely exiled, however, we get to see his influence at firsthand. More than the other two comedies, *As You Like It* anticipates the romances, particularly *The Tempest* and *The Winter's Tale*, in the idealization of a pastoral place where kindness and generosity prevail. The tone is more high-spirited and less nostalgic than that of these later plays, however. Perhaps the reason is that the focus is on the present generation, the resilient daughter rather than the yearning father. Duke Senior does not have Prospero's magic powers or his propensity to orchestrate his daughter's future. But, like the magician, he does act as benevolent overseer and well-wisher, as well as wise mentor of the man she loves. He, too, models the positive values that allow her to flourish in adversity and that help bring about the happy resolution of her conflicts. But it is Rosalind who dons the costume of son and heir and directs the course of her own future.

Like most of Shakespeare's comedies, *As You Like It* begins with a potentially tragic situation. Duke Senior has been banished by his "brother and usurper" (the description given is in the cast of characters). This is also the case in *The Tempest*, except that here the evil brother, Duke Frederick, has a daughter instead of a son. At first, Rosalind's lot is difficult but bearable. She is "no less beloved of her uncle than his own daughter" (I.i.103–04), and she and her cousin Celia are devoted to each other. In spite of her conflicting loyalties, Rosalind is reasonably content at Duke Frederick's court. Soon, however, the paranoid usurper turns against her. He banishes her, for no "fault" except, as he charges, "Thou art thy father's daughter, there's enough" (I.iii.42, 54). He ignores Rosalind's sensible objection: "Treason is not inherited, my lord." Her very "patience" under adversity, he argues, wins her favor with "the people," and so lessens his own daughter's popularity. Celia will "show more bright and seem more virtuous" (ll. 74–77) when Rosalind is gone, he says malevolently.

The duke has reckoned without the cousins' devotion, however. Celia, troubled before this outburst by her father's "rough and envious disposition," has already sworn to restore to Rosalind and Duke Senior what Frederick took "perforce" (I.ii.17). This, she stresses, is for her a question of "honor." Now, at the moment of crisis, Celia does not hesitate to side with Rosalind. She proposes that they flee the court together, following Duke Senior into the Forest of Arden. "Let my father seek another heir," she says defiantly, arriving at once at the surest way both to wound him and to assert her own will. In rejecting her own tainted legacy, Celia maintains boldly, she goes "To liberty and not to banishment" (l. 134). Rosalind, after a moment's demur, accepts the offer gladly.

The young women, though callow, are resourceful. They plan to take their "wealth" and their "jewels" to sustain them. They also plan to "steal" Touchstone, the court fool, to give them "comfort" (I.iii.125–26) on their travels. Still, they know that there is "danger" for "maids as [they] are" to leave the protection of the court (104–05). Both their riches and their "beauty" could tempt thieves, and the jester is no fighter. Rosalind, the taller, declares that she will "suit me in all parts like a man." Like Viola's, her male disguise will include a sword. Though in her "heart … lies hidden … woman's fear," she claims to be no weaker than many "mannish cowards" who have only "a swashing and a mannish outside" (ll. 115–17). This is the joke that Shakespeare develops more fully in Viola's disrupted duel with Sir Andrew. Rosalind, too, will come to a test of "masculine" prowess. But at this point in the play, her donning of "doublet and hose" gives her the swagger needed to "show itself courageous to petticoat" (II.iv.6–7). When, after hours of weary trudging, Celia loses heart, Rosalind — alias Ganymede — first bolsters her spirit with brave speeches. Then she takes the practical step of procuring them shelter. From a local shepherd, she buys "the cottage, pasture, and the flock" of his master, and so assumes the masculine prerogative of owning property.

But Rosalind's heart, like Viola's and Portia's, remains feminine. Her emotional life is focused not on her dire predicament or her banished father, but on romantic love. Shakespeare is careful to establish her mindset before she changes into male attire. When Celia bids Rosalind to "be merry" in spite of Duke Frederick's malevolence, the light-hearted topic that Rosalind proposes to distract them is "falling in love." At her first meeting with the handsome, stalwart young wrestler, Orlando, Cupid's arrow strikes with its usual speed. By the time that he has defeated the duke's champion, the brutish Charles, Rosalind is deeply smitten. She "*gives [him a] chain*" [stage direction, I.ii.226] and hints strongly that her heart goes with it. Orlando, although equally attracted to her, is paralyzed with self-consciousness. Years of oppression at his jealous brother's hands have deprived him of the courtier's easy eloquence. After Rosalind has gone off, he despairs that he has appeared before the lively young woman as "a mere lifeless block" with "weights upon [his] tongue" (ll. 232, 238). But the whole structure of the comedy works to confirm Rosalind's intuitive sense that Orlando is her rightful mate.

Crucial to bringing about their union is the influence of the benevolent father. That figure includes not only Duke Senior but also Orlando's late father and Shakespeare himself as creator and orchestrator. The first speech of the play is Orlando's, and its subject is his spiritual patrimony. As "the youngest son of Sir Rowland de Boys," he says, he has within him "the spirit of [his] father" (I.i.20). That legacy makes him chafe against the "servitude" in which Oliver, his cruel elder brother, keeps him. Oliver has seized his inheritance and refused to school or train him. Orlando confronts Oliver with these charges, whose response is to scorn and strike him. Orlando, more than a physical match for his persecutor, "seizes him" and threatens to throttle him. He refrains from carrying out the threat, however, partly at the behest of old Adam, the loyal family retainer, who pleads, "For your father's remembrance, be at accord" (ll. 58–59). Oliver, however, does not deserve accord. He is, as he soon accuses Orlando of being, "a secret and villainous contriver against his natural brother" (ll. 152–53). Hypocritical and envious, he arranges the wrestling match with the aim of having the burly Charles murder the young man. His motives are as baseless and as obsessive as Duke Frederick's toward *his* brother: "My soul, yet I know not why, hates nothing more than he" (ll. 152–53). This generation of brothers, however, will be redeemed: the spirit of Sir Rowland is moving events toward benevolent and happy ends.

First, Orlando wins the match, soundly defeating Charles and gaining Rosalind's admiration and love in the process. Obstacles only enhance this initial attraction. The paranoid Duke Frederick, while praising Orlando at first as "a gallant youth," sees his heritage as a reason to nullify all reward: "The world esteemed thy father honorable / But I did find him still mine enemy" (I.ii.206–07), he pronounces. Scolding Orlando for not having "another father," he sweeps off with all his train. Rosalind is stung into sympathetic defiance. She overcomes her maiden modesty to solace the young man: "My father loved Sir Rowland as his soul, / And all the world was of my father's mind" (ll. 216–17). Later, when Celia expresses amazement at Rosalind's falling so suddenly "into so strong a liking with old Sir Rowland's youngest son," Rosalind retorts with the same point that she made to Orlando: that her own father "loved his father dearly" (I.iii.25–28). Celia calls this a silly motive. But in Shakespeare's plays, as in real life, affinities often extend through the generations. Both absent fathers are giving a symbolic blessing to Rosalind and Orlando's union.

Old Adam is the living confirmation of Orlando's benevolent parentage. He addresses the young man affectionately — "O you memory / Of old Sir Rowland" — and commends him to his face as "gentle, strong, and valiant" (II.iii.3–4, 6). Adam has come to warn his favorite not to return to his brother's house. Oliver has reacted to the wrestling victory by cutting Orlando off entirely, and the young man can see beggary or theft as the only courses left to him. But Adam, emblem of "the constant service of the antique world," gives Orlando his life savings and pledge to go with him and defend him. The nostalgic strain that permeates the romances sounds in this episode: the longing for a "golden world" (I.i.111) in which such qualities as Adam represents, "truth and loyalty" (II.iii.70), can thrive. So Orlando, too, escapes from the corrupt court to the Forest of Arden. There the prevailing presence is another father, Rosalind's, who lives like "Robin Hood of England" in a spirit of amity and trust.

Unlike Prospero, Duke Senior does not have supernatural powers, nor does he act as a director of his daughter's courtship. But through both example and direct intervention in Orlando's plight, Duke Senior helps bring about the happy resolution. In the face of betrayal and exile, he has remained exuberant and resourceful. His first speech in the play contains the maxim that he lives by: "Sweet are the uses of adversity" (II.i.12). He tells his "brothers in exile," former courtiers who have joined him in the forest, that they are well rid of the "painted pomp" of the "envious court" (ll. 1–4). He extols the benefits of their pastoral life, friendship, simplicity, and integrity, and asserts that the message of the greenwood is to find "good in everything."

For all his optimism, the duke is no fool or weakling. He has drawn men to his service because he understands their needs and treats them justly. Those qualities are evident in his treatment of the desperate Orlando. The young man, in anguish at old Adam's collapse from hunger and exhaustion, invades the Duke's rural banquet "*with sword drawn*" and demands that the courtiers "eat no more" (II.vii.88). The sardonic Jaques responds with wry witticisms at the aggressor's expense. The Duke, in contrast, is perceptive and generous. He asks Orlando what has caused his lapse in "civility" — "distress" or "rude despis[ing] of good manners" (ll. 91–93). The young man responds that he is not brutish by nature; still, however, he is threatening them with death. Duke Senior teaches him a lesson in "gentleness." "What would you have?" he asks, and offers, "Sit down and feed, and welcome to our table" (ll. 101, 103). All the fire goes out of Orlando's rage. He expresses amazement at the Duke's courtesy. In an ironic reversal, he has found in the wild none of the savagery that he has come to expect at the court. The lesson takes instant effect: "I blush, and hide my sword" (l. 119), he says. Orlando then shows his own altruism by refusing to "touch a bit" (l. 133) of the food until he has fed Adam. He thanks the Duke and wishes that he be "blest" for his kindness. This first meeting between father and future son-in-law confirms their mutual sympathies and their shared belief in "sacred pity" (l. 123).

When Orlando returns with Adam, Duke Senior continues to play the spiritual guide and perfect host. He refrains from questioning the young man and provides music while the famished pair eat. The song that accompanies their feast concerns the lowest sin in the Duke's credo: "man's ingratitude." No "sting" of "winter winds" is "so sharp / As friend remembered not" (II.vii.174–76; 188–89). The scene taking place against that musical backdrop demonstrates the exact opposite: Orlando "whisper[s]" (l. 192) his story and the Duke recognizes his resemblance to Sir Rowland. Dropping the disguise of the forester, he confirms what Rosalind has said earlier about the friendship in the older generation: "I am the Duke / That loved your father" (ll. 195–96). All the humane values lacking in the bitter song — generosity, loyalty, gratitude — inform this new bond.

The Duke's influence extends beyond this initial meeting. It is in going later on "to attend the Duke at dinner" (IV.i.164) that Orlando stumbles upon the great test of the old values. The treacherous Oliver, having been ordered by Duke Frederick to capture Orlando "dead or living" (III.i.6), has gone into the Forest of Arden to hunt him down. But it is the "most unnatural" brother (IV.iii.123) who turns out to be in mortal danger. Orlando stumbles upon him asleep under a tree, menaced first by a "green and gilded snake" and then by a starving lioness. Orlando unwittingly frightens off the serpent, and then is twice tempted to leave Oliver to the beast's clutches. But "kindness, nobler than revenge" (l. 129), wins out, and he attacks the lioness with his bare hands.

Shakespeare wisely chose to narrate rather than dramatize this fairy tale rescue, and to have the would-be victim relate the "unscene." The battle between ruthless beast and dauntless young hero would be hard to stage convincingly. So too would be the idyllic outcome: Oliver's repentance and the reconciliation between the brothers. Some twelve years later in Shakespeare's career, in The Tempest, a parallel conflict is less perfectly resolved. Prospero forgives his evil brother, but Antonio does not repent and the wronged Duke admits that he remains perfidious. Despite the nostalgic tone of the romance, it is darker than the comedy, where the brother's conversion is instantaneous and complete. Again, the prevailing benevolent force in *As You Like It* is "the gentle Duke." In another off-stage scene, Orlando leads Oliver to his new mentor, who provides Oliver with "fresh array" and "commit[s]" him to his "brother's love" (IV.iii.144–45). Only then does the brave Orlando reveal the wound that he received. He also shows the newfound trust in his brother that the Duke has urged. He sends Oliver in quest of "his Rosalind," bearing the "napkin," "dyed in his blood" (ll. 155–56) as evidence of the reason for his missed appointment.

The encounter of messenger and recipient marks the turning point in the play. Rosalind, hearing from Oliver the story of her lover's courage and seeing the red sign of his suffering, "*swoons*" (stage direction, IV.iii.157). It is the undeniable proof of her love, her body's declaration of her bond with Orlando. While she does not then confess her true identity to Oliver, she cannot keep up her insouciant front, and he chides her with "lack[ing] a man's heart" (ll. 164–65). Celia, worried about her cousin's pallor, cuts short Rosalind's feeble pretense of "counterfeiting" and insists on leading her home to rest. So it is Duke Senior who has, wittingly or not, brought the lovers to this mutual sympathy. He has rescued Orlando, confirmed the young man's native integrity, sanctioned his heritage, and provided Oliver with the succor that leads to his repentance and the brothers' reconciliation. In all this time, he has not interacted directly with his daughter. Does he know of her plight?

The play offers only elliptical evidence. Rosalind recounts for Celia's amusement another unscene in which she met the Duke in the forest. He asked about her "parentage," she answered wittily it was "as good as his," and "he laughed and let me go" (III.iv.32–34). If he guesses her identity, he does not try to force her hand, nor does she, despite her precarious circumstances, choose to reveal herself and cling to him. To Celia, she claims to be bored with this subject: "What talk we of fathers when there is such a man as Orlando?" (ll. 34–35) she demands. Rosalind has her father's independent spirit and single-minded sense of purpose. She feels no need of his direct aid. In her pursuit of the man she loves, "truly the lady fathers herself" (*Much Ado About Nothing*, I.i.98).

What does Rosalind accomplish in donning the guise of Ganymede? She gets Orlando to let down his guard; after his isolated upbringing, he is comfortable with other men in a way that he cannot be with women. She has a chance to try out her theories, born of self-doubt, on the fickleness of romantic attachment. Most important, she can test the depth of his love for Rosalind. Seeing the trees of the forest laden with verses written in her honor, Rosalind cannot doubt that the writer is infatuated. The poems commend Rosalind's "beauty," "majesty," and "modesty." But, as she may sense, these are superficial qualities, their praise inspired by one brief meeting. Besides, Touchstone is present at their discovery to mock the "false gallop" of their faulty meter and to undermine their rapturous tone with a bawdy parody. Rosalind is equally contemptuous of the anonymous versifier — until Celia begins to hint that it is Orlando. For all of Rosalind's boyish bravado, she does not have, as she tells her cousin, "doublet and hose in [her] disposition" (III.ii.186–87). Usually the soul of wit, Rosalind loses all sense of humor on this subject. "The devil take thy mockery!" she exclaims to the bemused Celia, and then appeals to her sisterhood for sincere understanding: "Speak sad brow and true maid."

When Orlando himself appears, Rosalind's immediate instinct is to mask all these hopes and doubts. Ganymede's comic misogyny is the perfect disguise. In two parallel scenes, "he" lists the "giddy offenses" (III.ii.330) supposedly typical of women and defines love as "merely a madness": "changeable," "proud," "fantastical" (ll. 376; 385–86). Ganymede's avowed purpose is to cure Orlando of this insanity by posing as his Rosalind and enacting all the shallowness and inconstancy of his beloved. The actual effect of this daring game is to keep pushing Orlando to greater protestations of devotion without risking her own self-esteem. As Rosalind admits, in a delicious double entendre, a woman is more apt to believe her lover when he professes that he feels ardor "than to confess she does" (l. 367). She treats Orlando's protest that he will die if his love goes unrequited with sardonic dismissal. He is taking too exalted a view, she maintains mischievously. The accounts of the tragic fates of legendary lovers are "lies": "Men have died from time to time, and worms have eaten them, but not for love" (IV.i.96–98).

Rosalind even goes so far as to put Orlando through a mock nuptial, with Celia acting as parson. Ganymede undercuts every protest of constancy with arch jibes at both sexes. Men, she claims, are "April when they woo, December when they wed" (IV.i.134–35). Rosalind, she predicts, will welcome Orlando to her bed "and twenty such." She will then use her "wit" to exculpate herself, for, she warns, "You shall never take her without her answer unless you take her without her tongue" (ll. 157–59). Orlando is shocked by these quips, but his own constancy is unshaken. As proof, he promises her "with no less religion than if thou wert indeed my Rosalind" (ll. 181–82) to keep his vow of meeting her again at two o'clock — and goes off to his fateful rescue of Oliver.

Celia, a silent witness to these encounters, is outraged by Rosalind's "male" chauvinism: "You have simply misused our sex in your love-prate" (IV.i.185–86), she charges. But Rosalind is unrepentant — in, fact, exhilarated. "O coz, coz, coz, my pretty little coz," she chants, "that thou didst know how many fathom deep I am in love!" (ll. 189–90). For Orlando has passed every test of faith: he is as sincere and devoted as she could wish. Shakespeare implies here, as in *Much Ado*, that the woman's initial fears about infidelity are not groundless. The bawdy Touchstone and the cynical Jaques are present in the greenwood to remind us of the worldly take on romantic idealism. *As You Like It*, like all the comedies, is full of jokes about cuckoldry. Even the song about the killing of the deer, which follows the love scene, has as chorus a bawdy pun: "the horn, the horn, the lusty horn" (IV.ii.17), it reiterates, is every man's fate.

Rosalind's depiction of this worst-case scenario acts as a sort of charm against such cynical resignation. She is much more of a realist about love than her starry-eyed suitor. She wants to believe in Orlando's fidelity, but she will not allow herself to do so without proof. Her astuteness about the nature of love is shown in her reaction to the shepherd Silvius's infatuation with the scornful Phebe. Rosalind is frank about the marriage mart, advising the uncouth Phebe: "Sell when you can, you are not for all markets" (III.v.60). At the same time, she urges her to "thank heaven, fasting, for a good man's love" (l. 58). When Silvius meekly accepts Phebe's continued abuse, Rosalind reacts with scorn. She cuts short Celia's expression of sympathy. "He deserves no pity," she pronounces, and she berates him to his face as "a tame snake" (IV.iii.67, 71). The phallic pun suggests both Rosalind's worldly knowledge and her respect for manly assertiveness.

Orlando has appeared at first to fail the final test of his love by missing his appointment. In fact, the episode confirms every aspect of his worth. He has rescued his brother, borne his wound in silence, and remembered his vow to his beloved. His last conscious thought is of her: the reformed Oliver reports that Orlando "cried, in fainting, upon Rosalind" (IV.iii.150). Rosalind's corresponding faint at the sight of the napkin "dyed in his blood" (l. 156) is irrefutable proof of their bond.

When Rosalind meets Orlando again, he has regained his strength and she has recovered her insouciance. The news of Oliver and Celia's sudden infatuation — this is the play that cites Marlowe's line "Who ever loved that loved not at first sight" (III.v.81) — sets Rosalind happily scheming anew. First, she demands that Orlando swear by the sincerity of his faint: "If you do love Rosalind so near the heart as your gesture cries it out" (V.ii.59–60). Then she undertakes the role of "magician" when she claims to have means to grant each couple their hearts' desire. Rosalind is no Prospero; she does not possess actual magic powers. But the forces of both fate and inventiveness are with her. In this play, it is the daughter, not the father, who acts as matchmaker. Duke Senior plays a benevolent but supporting role.

At the ceremony, the Duke is still the nominal authority figure. He has been invited by Orlando, who gratefully recalls his forest host and offers to "bid the Duke to the nuptial" (V.ii.41). But it Rosalind who is in charge. Duke Senior again fails to recognize his daughter, still in disguise, though he does "remember in this shepherd boy / Some lively touches" of Rosalind (V.iv.26–27). Ganymede asks for his formal consent to the banns: "You say, if I bring in your Rosalind, / You will bestow her on Orlando here?" (ll. 6–7). But it is she who has arranged the quadruple wedding, of Oliver and Celia, Silvius and Phebe, Touchstone and Audrey, and, of course, herself and Orlando, and she who conducts the ritual. First she goes off to don her feminine garb. Then to each couple, she recites the terms of their marriage contract as a final test of commitment. To her own father and fiancé, she makes identical vows—"To you I give myself, for I am yours" (ll. 110–11), a reminder of what Desdemona calls the daughter's "divided duty."

Larger forces are present to second Rosalind's arrangement of these "bond[s] of board and bed": Hymen, god of marriage, appears to join "eight that must take hands ... in Hymen's bands" (V.iv.122–23). The joyous celebration is further blessed by the bounty of Providence. The third son of Sir Rowland de Boys, absent during the rest of the play, enters as messenger-ex-machina to announce the miraculous transformation of Duke Frederick. Entering the forest to exact revenge, the evil duke has come under Arden's benevolent influence and undergone a religious conversion. Deeply repentant, he restores his brother's usurped dukedom and retires to a life of prayer and contemplation. Duke Senior, bountiful as ever, promises that all will "share the good of [his] returned fortune" (l. 168). Even before this news, he has welcomed Celia, daughter of his treacherous brother, "in no less degree" (l. 142) than his own daughter. His warmth and optimism permeate the forest, which he celebrates as a place of things "well begun and well begot" (l. 165). He urges all to join in "our rustic revelry." Even the malcontent Jaques is moved to compliment his liege lord's "patience" and "virtue" as "well deserv[ing]" his "former honor" (ll. 171, 180–81). But it is Rosalind, in the Epilogue, who gets the last word. In *As You Like It*, the father is an essential supporting figure, but, like *The Merchant of Venice* and *Twelfth Night*, this is the daughter's play.

6

Daughters Who Forgive and Heal: Marina (*Pericles*), Perdita (*The Winter's Tale*), and Cordelia (*King Lear*)

> Thou ... beget'st him that did thee beget.
> *Pericles*, V.i.195

Another group of Shakespeare's daughters not only survive dire circumstances but also take the role, traditionally relegated to the father, of succoring and guiding their loved ones. Marina, in *Pericles*, Perdita in *The Winter's Tale*, and Cordelia, in *King Lear*, spend much of their respective plays exiled and, in the case of the first two, presumed dead. All have, in fact, found shelter with benevolent strangers and developed impressive reserves of daring and resilience. The daughters in the two romances are two-dimensional figures, paragons of virtue and optimism. Their simple natures are signaled by their label-names, which are linked to their situations: Marina, "of the sea," is lost and found in that element. Perdita, "the lost one," is "found again." The symbolic name of Cordelia, a more fully rounded personage, focuses not on her situation but her character: she is all "heart," a woman of prescience, compassion, and courage.

In the daughters' absence, their fathers have fallen into the depths of melancholy and despair. The degree of each man's blame for her initial loss proves to be directly proportional to the completeness of his recovery. In the simplest of these plays, the late romance *Pericles*, the title figure's suffering is caused primarily by fate: he is bereaved for the wife whom he believes died in childbirth during a storm at sea and the grown daughter who reportedly died in the care of those he left her with as an infant. In the more complex romance, *The Winter's Tale*, Leontes is anguished not only by grief but by bitter remorse. It was he who denounced Perdita, his newborn child, as illegitimate, and ordered her exposed to the elements and left to die. His tyranny caused his young son to die of grief, and his loss, in turn, was supposedly mortal to Leontes's innocent wife. Having realized that his charge of adultery was a product of paranoia, Leontes falls into a black abyss of depression. In the tragedy, Lear exiles not a baby he hardly knows but a young woman who has long been his best-loved daughter. At the outset, he denies any blame for Cordelia's suffering. Once his guilt penetrates his shell of vanity and self-righteousness, though, he is stricken to the point of madness. Not only his abuse at the hands of the corrupt daughters he has favored but his rash rejection of the loyal one create a howling "tempest in [his] mind." Only Cordelia's return and clemency can rescue him from its torments. In contrast to the healing in the romances, however, in the tragedy the daughter's cure is poignantly transient.

The tone of each play is determined largely by the nature of the father and daughter's reconciliation. In the romances, it is perfect and complete, leading not only to forgiveness but to the balm of restoration. Pericles and Leontes are blessed with the return not only of their daughters but their wives, and the family circle, long broken, is once again joined. The elegiac mood of each ending comes from the length of the family's separation — the irretrievably lost years covering the daughter's entire childhood. For the audience, it comes from the bittersweet recognition of the unlikelihood of such perfect reconciliation. The heartrending bleakness of *King Lear* rests on the brevity of the father and daughter's reunion. Lear has no sooner regained his balance and realized the unique preciousness of Cordelia's love than she is snatched from him and murdered at the hands of her cruel sisters. The old father's valiant efforts at rescuing her from the evil forces that he himself set in motion fail, and Providence looks on indifferently at her execution. His only comfort, expressed in his dying words, is the illusion that she is still alive. No icon of failed fatherhood is more poignant than Lear's pietà with the dead Cordelia in his arms.

Pericles

Pericles, the last written of the three plays, most resembles a fairy tale in the simplicity of its characterization and the idyllic nature of its denouement. The medieval poet Gower, who serves as chorus to the romance, underlines in his opening speech the ritualistic nature of the play: he has risen "from ashes ancient" in order "To sing a song that old was sung ... at festivals ... and holy ales" (I.Chorus.1, 5–6).* Its purpose is to celebrate the triumph of the virtuous — not to provide a subtle exploration of character but to serve as a dramatized exemplum, with Pericles as the type of the devoted husband and father. That role is made clear at the outset by contrasting the title character with the wicked King Antiochus, tyrant and incest-perpetrator, violator of every sacred family bond. Although his daughter looks so lovely that she seems "as [if] heaven had lent her all his grace," she is corrupt. Gower chastises both, but particularly the parent: "Bad child, worse father, to entice his own / To evil should be done by none" (I.Chorus.27–28).

To conceal the relationship, Antiochus has devised a spurious contest, supposedly to attract a husband for the princess, in which the suitor must either solve a riddle or lose his life. It is a malevolent form of the contest that Portia's late father establishes for her suitors in *The Merchant of Venice*. This riddle, however, is ridiculously transparent — it describes the incestuous relationship — and young Pericles, Prince of Tyre, deciphers it easily. Horrified, he soliloquizes on his revulsion for the king's "uncomely claspings with [his] child" and her "defiling of her parents' bed" (I.i.129, 132). He tells the king in a riddle of his own that he sees his "vice"; then, realizing the danger in his candor, he rejects the king's attempts at allaying his suspicions and flees for his life.

This picaresque tale of Pericles, brave and upright knight, favored of the gods, continues in the next episodes. The prince returns to his own land of Tyre, but fearing that the powerful Antiochus's vengeance will light on his people, Pericles flees again. By heeding his instincts and sense of honor, he escapes the assassination plot of the evil king. Having heard of a famine in Tharsus, he loads his ship with "corn" (I.iv.95) and seeks new refuge in that land. When he again senses Antiochus in pursuit, Pericles sets off once more. This time, his ship is "wrack'd and split" and he lands at Pentapolis, "having all lost" (II.Chorus.32–33). "Fortune," though, shines on him once again. The land is ruled by the virtuous Simonides, renowned for his "peaceable reign and good government." The timing is also propitious. It happens to be the eve of the Princess Thaisa's birthday, and Pericles learns from some fishermen that a contest is afoot, with "princes and knights come from all parts of the world to joust and tourney for her love" (II.i.107–09). Just as he is wishing for some means to compete, the fishermen draw up in their nets some flotsam from the shipwreck, "a rusty

---

* All quotations are from the Arden edition of *Pericles*, edited by E. D. Hoeniger (Methuen & Co, 1963).

armour." In keeping with the fable of the benevolent patriarch, this turns out to be Pericles' own suit, bequeathed to him by his dead father with the fond wish that it may be "a shield / 'Twixt [him] and death" (ll. 125–26). Pericles immediately feels revived by this good fortune: "My shipwreck's now no ill, / Since I have here my father gave in his will." He adds the fond recollection: "He loved me dearly, / And for his sake I wish the having of it" (ll. 137–38). Pericles' material fortunes may be at a low point, but his emotional and spiritual heritage is rich.

Thaisa is likewise blessed. Her father shows his love for her by holding "these triumphs" in "honour" of her birth and calling her by such affectionate names as "Beauty's child." She, in turn, shows herself worthy of his regard by embodying every virtue. Father and daughter agree on the worthiness of Pericles as a suitor. The king recognizes his "graceful courtesy" (II.ii.40) in spite of the rusty armor that he wears, and he chastises his courtiers' mockery of this "outward habit" (l. 56). Not surprisingly, "the mean Knight" triumphs in the lists. At first, in order to test Thaisa's love, Simonides denigrates these chivalric feats: "He's but a country gentleman; / Has done no more than other knights have done; / Has broke a staff or two; so let it pass" (II.iii.33–35). Still, Pericles, observing the whispered exchange, is moved by the king's resemblance to his own father. That sympathy is affirmed when Simonides privately declares: "by the gods, I pity his misfortune, / And will awake him from his melancholy." His values of piety and empathy align him with all of Shakespeare's positive characters. He bids the knights and ladies dance, gives Pericles Thaisa for his partner, pronounces him "the best" in this skill as well, and reserves the resolution of the contest for the morrow, to make the prize the sweeter.

To underline Simonides's role as the good father, promoter of the match between his beloved daughter and a virtuous suitor, the scene shifts to Tyre, where news is brought of the sudden death of Antiochus and his daughter. While "seated in a chariot / Of inestimable value," they have been struck by "a fire from heaven" that "shrivell'd up / Their bodies" (II.iv.7–10) and created so great a stench that their erstwhile followers have refused to bury them. The courtier who brings the news pronounces this fate "but justice," the apt "reward" for so much "sin" (ll. 13, 15).

Meanwhile, back at Pentapolis, Thaisa informs her father by letter that "she'll wed the stranger knight," and he privately approves their concord of taste: "'Tis well, mistress; your choice agrees with mine; / I like that well" (II.v.18–19). He also notes her willfulness and, sounding like Prospero, is amused and gratified by it: "how absolute she's in't, / Not minding whether I dislike or no! / Well, I do commend her choice, / And will no longer have it delay'd" (ll. 19–22). Again, like the magician in *The*

Tempest, he pretends to oppose the match, taunting Pericles with having "bewitch'd" his daughter and accusing him of lying when he swears that he has not courted her without permission. Stung, the prince protests, "My actions are as noble as my thoughts" (l. 58). Privately, Simonides "applaud[s] his courage" and professes himself "glad on't with all [his] heart." Aloud, he berates her: "Will you, not having my consent, / Bestow your love and your affections / Upon a stranger?" (ll. 75–77). This time he sounds like a feigning echo of Brabantio chastising Desdemona. Simonides works the charade to a high pitch with the threat, "Either be rul'd by me, or I'll make you —" and concludes slyly "Man and wife." Delighted, they consent in chorus, "If it please your majesty" (l. 90), confirming the good children that they are. Although critics commonly agree that Shakespeare had little hand in the first two acts of *Pericles,* these courtship scenes with the blocking senex contain several echoes not only of *The Tempest* and *Othello* but also of *A Midsummer Night's Dream* and *The Merchant of Venice.* This play, however, presents *two* generations of loving fathers and resourceful daughters.

At first it seems as though Pericles' fortunes have taken a permanent turn for the better. He and Thaisa quickly conceive "a babe," and, the threat of Antiochus past, Pericles is called home to be restored to the throne of Tyre. The pregnant Thaisa, Gower tells us in the chorus to Act III, insists on accompanying him. Pericles' family crest, we discovered when he donned his rusty armor, is "a withered branch, that's only green at top," the motto Latin for "In this hope I live" (II.ii.42; footnote 43). To this point, that green hope seemed to be represented by his bride. But Pericles will prove to be a king and knight who needs to be rescued twice, first by his wife-to-be and later by their daughter.

The second rescue becomes necessary in this saga of cataclysmic events and doleful consequences when a storm comes up at sea that proves the undoing of the young family. Panicked, the queen goes into labor and, despite her husband's earnest prayers, apparently dies in childbirth. Her nurse, Lychorida, enters carrying the newborn and declares: "Here's all that is left living of your queen, / A little daughter" (III.i.20–21). Pericles, distraught, nonetheless has room in his heart to pity the child, "poor inch of nature!" and to wish that the storm "be quiet" (ll. 35, 42) for her sake. Rather than proceed to Tyre, he decides to return to Tharsus, the kingdom that he aided earlier during the famine, "for the babe / Cannot hold out to Tyrus," he says anxiously. With the storm still raging, the superstitious sailors insist on throwing Thaisa's body overboard, claiming that the "sea" and "wind" "will not lie till the ship be cleared of the dead" (ll. 47–49). Reluctantly, Pericles agrees. But first he mourns over her corpse, addressing his dead wife with heartbroken tenderness: "A terrible childbed hast thou had, my dear" (l. 56). He laments having no time "to give thee hallowed to thy grave" and orders that the body be put to sea with all the ceremony and luxury he can muster: He calls for "spices," "jewels," and "ink and paper" (ll. 65–66) for him to write a description of her rank and story, and he orders the chest in which she lies to be "caulked and bitumed" (ll. 70–71) against the sea's incursion. No husband could be more caring and compassionate.

Next occurs one of the miraculous coincidences peculiar to Shakespeare's romances. The coffin, so carefully made watertight, washes up in Ephesus. There it is found by Cerimon, a pious nobleman, who, ordering it opened, finds not only the body "shrouded in clothes of state" and "entreasured with full bags of spices" but bearing a "passport" (III.iii.67–68). This is the scroll that Pericles wrote in the throes of the storm, declaring the victim a "queen, worth all our mundane cost," and pleading with whoever finds the body to bury her and keep "this treasure for a fee" (ll. 74, 76). Moved by the enormous care that Pericles has taken and the "woe" of his tale, Cerimon stares pityingly at Thaisa and realizes suddenly that she is not dead but "entranc'd" (l. 96). With such simple remedies as "fire," dry clothes, and "still and awful music," he revives her. Her awakening, reminiscent of Lear's and Juliet's, is announced with her dazed questions, "Where am I? Where's my lord?" Cerimon's response affirms both Pericles' love and her special qualities: "fair creature, / Rare as you seem to be" (ll. 105–06). With his triumphant announcement to his household, "Gentlemen, this queen will live," everything seems set for the happy reunion of the little family. But, unaccountably, both wife and husband make decisions that prolong the separation and anticipate the pathos of the denouement.

When next we see Thaisa, she has recovered physically, but decides, with uncharacteristic passivity, to remain ignorant of Pericles' final fate. Although she admits to having no memory of the voyage, she apparently assumes that he has perished at sea. Saying that she "ne'er shall see [him] again," she vows to assume "a vestal livery" in a nearby shrine to Diana and "never more have joy" (III.iv.8–10). Does it never occur to her to seek news of the shipwreck? To return to her beloved father? Her reaction seems more melodramatic plot device than convincing motivation.

The like is true of Pericles' decision to leave his "gentle babe Marina," whom he has so named because "she was born at sea," in Tharsus. After a year with the king, Cleon, and his queen Dionyza, Pericles has been called back to Tyre, locked in a "litigious peace" (III.iii.3) and desperate for leadership. The need for his return is clear, but his reasons for leaving his little daughter are not. Is it because his country is on the brink of war?

Because Dionyza has a child Marina's age and this is a family while he is a single father? In this two-dimensional characterization, his motives are never explained. Clearly, he is not moved by lack of love for his child. In an echo of his "priestly farewell" to the supposedly dead Thaisa, he makes the Biblical vow not to cut his hair "till she be married" (l. 27). He forbids her faithful nurse Lychorida, in whose care he leaves the infant, parting tears, and commands: "Look to your little mistress, on whose grace / You may depend hereafter" (ll. 39–40). This assertion will prove more prophetic for Pericles himself than for Lychorida.

As in *The Winter's Tale*, the abandoned daughter manages not only to survive but also to emerge as a paragon of talent and grace. In this play, too, the chorus serves as "winged time" to fly over the years of Marina's childhood and present her as a young woman, grown into "the heart and place / Of general wonder" (IV.Chorus.10–11). She is "absolute Marina," who "gets all praises" (ll. 31, 33–34) with her lute playing, singing, and erudition. But before we even see this wonder, Gower relates the dire results of all her accomplishment: the queen, "cursed Dionyza" (l. 43), is consumed with "that monster envy" because her own daughter is in Marina's shadow. As Act IV opens, she is already plotting her young charge's murder. Pericles is about to return, and Dionyza is in haste to dispatch Marina before he arrives. She commands her servant Leonine to do the deed, cutting short his reluctance to harm the "goodly creature" with the cynical quip, "The fitter then the gods should have her" (IV.i.9–10).

The girl, meanwhile, has been left entirely defenseless. She enters, bearing flowers and "weeping" for the newly dead Lychorida, and bemoaning her ill luck in losing first her mother and then her nurse. "This world to me is as a lasting storm" (l. 19), she laments. Yet she greets the falsely pitying Dionyza with gratitude and reluctantly accepts the queen's command that she walk along the seashore with Leonine, supposedly to improve her appetite. Modest, eloquent, and lovely — we have the jealous queen's word for the girl's "excellent complexion, which did steal / The eyes of young and old" (ll. 40–41) — Marina is the classic fair maiden. She soon shows, though, that she also has courage and spirit, which she attributes to her father's heritage. She begins by recalling Lychorida's account of her violent birth at sea and his stalwartness in the storm:

> My father, my nurse says, did never fear,
> But cried "Good seamen!" to the sailors, galling
> His kingly hands, haling ropes   [ll. 52–54].

When Leonine reveals his nefarious purpose, she first asserts her innocence and then makes a heartfelt appeal to his "well-favored" look and, she hopes, corresponding "gentle heart" (ll. 85–86). Undeterred, he "seizes her"— at which moment, pirates enter, cry "A prize! A prize!" and snatch her from him; "*Leonine runs away*" (stage direction, l. 92). This is the standard fairy tale plot: stereotypical evil and virtuous characters, dire events stopped by chance on the verge of realization, the heroine spared by means of her own spirited resistance and the aid of fate. The play depicts a more sordid world, however, than is typical for a fairy tale. Leonine returns to speculate lasciviously that the pirates may simply "please themselves upon" (l. 100) Marina and then abandon her, at which point he would finish his own murderous work. The lack of pity for the innocent victim is reminiscent of Lavinia's rape in *Titus Andronicus*.

In *Pericles*, however, lust anticipated is but lust delayed. The pirates do not rape Marina, but instead sell her to a brothel in the seaport of Mytilene. The house of ill repute is kept by three unscrupulous rascals, two called by the label names of Bawd and Pandar, and the third, his servant, by the bawdy pun Boult. Presumably the name alludes to one who "bolts" the door after customers enter or who bolts down any superfluous favors from the prostitutes. The latter definition is suggested when he reminds the Bawd that it was he who "bargained" with the pirates for the "joint" of Marina, and she responds: "Thou mayst cut a morsel off the spit" (IV.ii.130). These keepers are completely contemptuous of their "creatures," complaining that they have but a "poor three" and those are already "rotten" with disease (ll. 7–9). They joke about the "poor bastards" they have "brought up" and then "brought down" again—forced into prostitution at the age of eleven. Their only concern is how much money they may have lost in the "mart" by "being too wenchless" (ll. 4–5). Naturally, such crass exploiters are interested in Marina only for the price she can command. The Bawd orders Boult to hawk her "complexion," "age," and the "warrant of her virginity" with the cry, "He that will give most shall have her first" (ll. 54–56).

This is utter degradation, particularly harsh for one so delicately raised, and Marina's first reaction is to regret that neither Leonine nor the pirates murdered her. The Bawd is amused at such scruples. "Why lament you, pretty one?" she demands. She tries to sway the girl with titillating promises of "pleasure" with "gentlemen of all fashions" (IV.ii.72, 74–75). But when the pious Marina pleads, "The gods defend me!" and expresses her own high principles, the Bawd becomes irritated. "You're a young sapling, and must be bow'd as I would have you," she threatens. The means, she agrees with the lascivious Boult, is to "quench" her "blushes" with "some present practice" (ll. 123–24). The hapless girl vows suicide to keep her "virgin knot … untied" and prays to Diana for aid. "What have we to do with Diana?" (l. 148) the Bawd responds scornfully. But we know what she does not: the exiled Thaisa has become a votaress of the chaste goddess, and her daughter's prayer will not go unheeded.

The immediate rescue for which Marina prays is coming just too late: the scene shifts to Tharsus, where Pericles is expected any moment to "fetch his daughter home" (IV.iv.20) at last. Dionyza, believing that the murder has been carried out, is unrepentant. Lady Macbeth–like, she blames Cleon for his "coward spirit" and congratulates herself on having poisoned Leonine, the only witness to her crime. She has prepared a fine show of sorrow to fool the bereaved father: a lavish monument, complete with "epitaphs / In glitt'ring golden characters" (IV.iii.43–44), a hypocritical analogue to the heartfelt gift of the gold statue of Juliet that Montague offers Capulet. Her ruse works, as we see in a dumb show and chorus. At the tomb, Pericles *"makes lamentation, puts on sackcloth, and in a mighty passion departs"* (stage direction, IV.iv.23). The chorus steps in to describe the "tempest" of the father's grief: "in sorrow all devour'd," he reembarks for Tyre, vowing "Never to wash his face, nor cut his hairs" (ll. 25, 27–28). Summarizing rather than staging this reaction increases the fairy tale simplicity of the plot. That quality is further emphasized by the stark contrast between the good and evil parent. Dionyza calls the murder an act of love, "an enterprise of kindness / Perform'd to [her] sole daughter (IV.iii.38–39). She is the epitome of malicious jealousy. Pericles, in contrast, is the well-meaning victim, helpless in the face of such duplicity. With the distancing devices of dumb show and chorus, it is easy to miss the blame that he bears for Marina's fate. Like Macduff's, his absence has left his child prey to those who would harm her. Because, in contrast to the tragedy, Pericles' reaction is not staged, we do not see either the suspicion of the perpetrators or the remorse for his own neglect that deepens Macduff's characterization. The chorus sums up his gullibility and passivity: "Let Pericles believe his daughter's dead, / And bear his courses to be ordered / By Lady Fortune" (IV.iv.45–47). Marina, meanwhile, has again been left alone to cope with the "unholy service" (l. 50) into which she has been sold.

Back in Mytilene, scenes at the brothel prove the girl a marvel of daring and resourcefulness. She faces three tests of her will, each with an adversary more determined than the last to take her virginity. The first occurs off stage. Two gentlemen enter from the brothel, so struck by the "divinity" that she has "preached" that they swear off "bawdy-houses" forever and vow to devote themselves to "anything ... that is virtuous" (IV.v.4–8). The brothel keepers are exasperated by her powers of conversion: "She's able to freeze the god Priapus," the Bawd complains, and Boult swears the ironic oath: "Faith, I must ravish her, or she'll disfurnish us of all our customers" (IV.vi.3–4, 11–12).

The Bawd prepares Marina for the second, harder test. Lysimachus, "the governor of this country," has come for his usual pleasures. If Marina will "treat him kindly," the Bawd promises, "He will line her apron with gold" (IV.vi.57–58). Lysimachus is a jaded roué, intent on despoiling "a dozen of virginities" and concerned only that this one be truly fresh and therefore free of disease. He begins by treating Marina as a common prostitute, venturing that she began plying her "trade" at "five or at seven." Her aloofness, he thinks, is due only to her knowledge of his rank and her hope for greater profit. The girl goes quickly from arch denial to indignation, calling the brothel "this sty," "this unhallowed place" where "most ungentle fortune" has confined her. She wishes that "the gods / Would set [her] free," even if that meant being transformed into "the meanest bird" (ll. 96–101). She swears that she is a "maid" and challenges Lysimachus: "If you were born to honor, show it now" (l. 91). These fairy tale allusions trigger a correspondingly fabulous transformation. Lysimachus is charmed by her fervor and eloquence: "I did not think / Thou couldst have spoke so well," he marvels, and professes his "corrupted mind" "alter'd" by her speech. He gives her gold and more gold, pronounces her "a piece of virtue" (an echo of Prospero's description of Miranda's mother), and urges: "Persever in that clear way thou goest" (l. 105). Then he turns on Boult, just coming in to check on the assignation, and berates him in the lowest terms.

Again, the servant condemns Marina's "peevish chastity" and turns to his mistress for support. His is furious that Marina has spoken "holy words to the Lord Lysimachus" and "sent him away as cold as a snowball; saying his prayers too" (IV.vi.139–40). "O abominable!" the Bawd clucks. The self-righteousness of the lewd gives the scene a dark comic edge reminiscent of Measure for Measure. Marina's success against Lysimachus, though, sparks the third and most difficult test of her virtue. The Bawd reinforces Boult's lust and thirst for vengeance with her crass command: "Use her at thy pleasure. Crack the glass of her virginity, and make the rest malleable" (ll. 141–43).

Left alone with this callous lecher, Marina uses her vaunted eloquence not in prayers but in insults as coarse as those that have been directed at her: "Thou art the damned doorkeeper to every / Coistrel that comes inquiring for his Tib" and "Thy food is such / As hath been belched on by infected lungs" (IV.vi.164–65, 167–68). But she is too clever to limit her weapons to those that offend. Sensing that Boult is more intent on making a profit than on satisfying his lust, she gives him a practical course of action. When he claims that he has no choice but to earn his living as a pander, she offers her services as an artist and teacher and urges him to hawk those rather than her sexual favors:

> Proclaim that I can sing, weave, sew, and dance.
> . . . .
> I doubt not but this populous city
> Yield many scholars   [ll. 182–86].

She reinforces this assertion by giving him some of the gold that she has earned in her encounter with Lysimachus. When he hesitates, she switches again to his crass idiom: "Prove that I cannot, take me again, / And prostitute me to the basest groom / That doth frequent your house" (ll. 188–90). Incredibly, Boult accepts. He promises to place her "amongst honest women" and to persuade his "master and mistress" to approve the new contract. Marina has dared to wager her virginity and her honor, and in the gutter language of those who would exploit her. Her goodness is not weak or passive: in feistiness and resilience, she is a spiritual sister to Juliet and Rosalind.

Gower comes on to confirm that Marina has made good on her claims. She has proven such a "goddess-like" singer, dancer, and embroiderer that she has won over even "people of noble race" and paid off the "cursed bawd" (V.Chorus.9–10). Meanwhile, the fates are operating again to protect and reward her. Pericles, "driven before the winds," happens to anchor off the coast of Mytilene, and Lysimachus hospitably sails out to welcome him. The king, however, is in a deep state of depression, "unkempt and clad in sackcloth," eating almost nothing and, for three months past, totally mute with grief "from the loss / Of a beloved daughter and a wife" (V.i.29–30). His loyal courtier, old Helicanus, despairs of reaching him, but one of the local lords thinks of "the maid in Mytilene" to cheer him with "her sweet harmony" (ll. 42, 44).

Marina, soon summoned, demands to be left alone with the sufferer. She attempts to rouse him from his lethargy by singing and then addressing him, but he refuses to "mark [her] music" or even look at her, and, when she speaks, only pushes her away with an inarticulate exclamation: "Hum, ha!" Undeterred, the girl gives him a long description of one who has, she says, "endur'd a grief / Might equal yours, if both were justly weigh'd" (V.i.87–88). Hers, she persists, is that "time hath rooted out [her] parentage." Although her irony is unwitting, she has sensed a connection with the melancholy figure and confesses aside that "something" urges her to remain with him "till he speak" (l. 96).

Pericles *has* been listening, and the word that rouses him to respond is "parentage." Dazed, he demands if that has indeed been her choice of word, asks Marina to look at him, and blurts, "You're something like that — " (V.i.102). The wavelength between father and daughter is reestablished, and he bursts into an eloquent recollection of his "dearest wife," so "like this maid." Marina's pedigree is written in her beauty and talent: her "brows," "wand-like" carriage, "jewel-like eyes," and "silver" voice. For all her beauty, she looks "modest as Justice," the essence of "Truth" (ll. 108–22). He is especially struck by her self-possession. In contrast to his collapse in the face of suffering, she has remained the picture of Patience, conquering Extremity with a stoic "smile[ ]" (ll. 138–39). Pericles himself has stressed this reversal of roles in an ironic simile. He compares her courage to that of "a man," and accuses himself of "suff'ring like a girl" (ll. 136–37). Eagerly, he questions her heritage. She responds with the talisman: "My name is Marina." He is indignant and incredulous, sure that the gods are mocking him. She must play the parent who restores him to composure by chastising him: "Patience, good sir, / Or here I'll cease."

Marina then resolves his doubts in a moving exchange, reminiscent of Lear's reunion with Cordelia. She is "a king's daughter," "call'd Marina, / For I was born at sea" (V.i.155–56). It remains only to recount her miraculous escape from "cruel Cleon and his wicked wife" and to give the final proof of her identity: her mother's name. Pericles, who has not seen his child since she was a baby and who has believed her dead, is overwhelmed. He questions her reality: "But are you flesh and blood? / Have you a working pulse, and are no fairy motion?" (ll. 152–54). Reassured, he calls this the "rarest dream" imaginable. He weeps unrestrainedly and is so overcome that he demands of Helicanus: "Give me a gash, put me to present pain," lest he "drown" in the "sweetness" of "this great sea of joys" (ll. 191–94). The image is reminiscent of Gloucester's reported end: the heart that "burst smilingly" at his discovery that his beloved son was alive and guiding him. This, however, is Shakespearean romance, rather than tragedy, and Pericles is experiencing not death but rebirth. In fact, he describes his daughter as the parent in that process: "Thou beget'st him that did thee beget." Still using the tender second person, he reiterates her vital role: "Thou hast been ... another life to Pericles thy father" (ll. 206–06).

Pericles goes "wild" with elation. He calls for "fresh garments," cries "O heavens bless my girl!" addresses her fondly as "my Marina," and claims to hear "the music of the spheres" (V.i.213–28). Suddenly exhausted, he slips into a "thick" and healing slumber. Again, the echoes of Lear's cure by Cordelia are apparent — but this play is Lear made happy. To increase the joy, Pericles is visited in his sleep by a vision of the goddess Diana, the confirmation that the heavenly music he alone heard was not the result of delusion. He had intended to go first to Tharsus, to punish "inhospitable

Cleon," but he piously agrees instead to follow the goddess's command. The act ends with Lysimachus reappearing and hinting at a "suit" he will present later. Pericles anticipates it and grants his wish: "to woo my daughter, for it seems / You have been noble towards her" (ll. 260–61). The former reprobate, impressed by the news of Marina's noble parentage and reformed by her example, has been magically transformed into a worthy suitor. He requests Pericles's "arm," the father beckons the daughter to join them, again using the tender possessive "my Marina," and the trio go off in a pageant of fatherly blessing.

Only one strand remains to make the fairy tale denouement complete: the "dead" mother must be reunited with her long-lost husband and daughter, so that, as the Chorus puts it, "Wishes fall out as they're willed" (V.ii.16). The marks of identity, for mother as for daughter, are clear intellect, stainless principles, and boundless affection. Thaisa's "own most clear remembrance" (V.iii.12) allows her to recognize instantly Pericles' "voice and favor," and her unchanged love causes her to faint with joy. Recovered, she needs reassurance that this is truly Pericles, so that she will not mar her "sanctity" by giving way to "licentious" (l. 30) longing. The daughter's piety has a clear source.

At hearing her speak, Pericles cries, "The voice of dead Thaisa!" (V.iii.34). He is overwhelmed by a new joy so enormous that he can compare it only to death: He wishes that at their first kiss he "may / Melt and no more be seen," and urges her, long "dead," "O come be buried / A second time within these arms" (ll. 43–44). The morbid hyperbole strikes a chord in Marina, too. Not missing a beat, she completes her father's blank verse line and echoes his figure of speech: "My heart / Leaps to be gone into my mother's bosom" (ll. 44–45). She is wishing at one and the same time to be unborn and reborn. Instantly, Thaisa pronounces her "Blessed and mine own!" As in *The Winter's Tale*, the family circle is made complete by the efforts and saving graces not of the father but of the daughter and mother. This play, though, bears no taint of the paternal remorse that darkens the earlier romance. Pericles is simply overcome with gratitude, pronouncing his "past miseries" mere "sports" in the face of the gods' "present kindness" (ll. 40–41). His last act is to announce Marina's betrothal, a decision in which he consults neither wife nor daughter. Presumably the blocking would show that Marina is in accord, and Thaisa poses no objection. She reveals that her father has died, and Pericles decrees that he and she will go to rule his kingdom of Pentapolis, while Marina and Lysimachus will reign in Tyre. He will further "grace [the] marriage day" by shaving the fourteen-year beard that he grew as "ornament" of his suffering (l. 73). Marina, it is thus revealed, is the same age as Miranda and, like her, the embodiment of her kingdom's and her father's future.

The play ends with an epilogue by Gower, who returns to resolve the final plot element and to underline the moral. When the conspiracy against Marina's life is revealed to the people of Tharsus, "wicked Cleon and his wife" are attacked in their palace by the outraged citizenry and burned to death. Thus he, like the incestuous Antiochus, receives "his due and just" punishment, while Pericles and his family earn a happy fate: "Virtue preserved from fell destruction's blast, / Led on by heaven and crowned with joy at last" (Epilogue, ll. 65–66). Pericles, although responsible for leaving his daughter with caretakers who prove unfit, is not guilty of either Lear's or Leontes's tyranny. Rather than sentencing his daughter to banishment or, worse, death, or accusing his wife of adultery, he loses them through cruel fate — a tempest at sea. He also puts their welfare first in the crisis, lavishing tender care on both his supposedly dead wife and his newborn child. Thus, he is restored to both of his lost ones, and, as in *The Winter's Tale*, the family circle is not only rejoined but enlarged by the addition of a worthy son-in-law and the promise of future progeny. Only in the tragedy does the father's cruelty result in the total destruction of the family.

In contrast to the complexity that concludes *King Lear*, *Pericles* has the stylized flatness of an exemplum. With its two-dimensional characters, wooden professions of noble motives, and miraculous rescues, it is more fairy tale than exploration of character. Yet the main element of psychological realism animates the scenes that most commentators attribute to Shakespeare, those that depict the family reunited. In that fable of the resurrection of the beloved daughter and the forgiven father, Shakespeare once again taps the deepest sources of drama's capacity for healing ritual.

The Winter's Tale

At the beginning of *The Winter's Tale*, Leontes, King of Sicilia, is a man who has everything: a peaceful, ordered kingdom, a loving and accomplished wife, a precocious, affectionate son and heir, a lifelong friend who is a kindred spirit, and the happy anticipation of a second child. Wantonly, recklessly, he destroys all these worldly blessings through rashness and arrogance. He accuses his faithful wife and loyal friend of adultery, orders her arrest and plots his murder, and declares his newborn child illegitimate and condemns her to death by exposure. Not even the defense of the innocents by the Oracle of Apollo can dissuade Leontes from this cruel course. The consequences are dire and immediate: his young son Mamillius pines away from grief for his mother; at the news of his death, Hermione collapses and is declared dead; the baby girl, the king's only remaining relative, has been spirited away, and Leontes falls into an anguished state of remorse and despair. Since the play is a romance, not a tragedy, this situation is not irremediable. The king's actions do, however, exact a terrible cost: the loss of Mamillius and sixteen years of bitter loneliness. Only the fulfillment of the Oracle's prophecy, predicting the restoration of his lost daughter, can console the bereft man. The play is the story of Leontes' long lesson on the supreme value of trust, love, and forgiveness.

Leontes conceives his jealousy from the slimmest of evidence: watching his wife pay the courtesies that he himself has commanded to their guest Polixenes, King of Bohemia and his lifelong friend. The fact that she is nine months pregnant and that Polixenes has been resident in the court of Sicilia during that time adds to Leontes' irrational suspicion. Everyone from his most trusted advisor to his wife's upright lady-in-waiting tries to persuade Leontes that his accusations are groundless—a "sickness" (I.ii.384) and a "folly" (l. 429) that will prove "most dangerous" (l. 298) to his own happiness. Leontes himself compares his paranoia to the "venom" felt by one who, previously oblivious, suddenly becomes aware of a poisonous spider that has fallen into his cup: "I have drunk and seen the spider." But he concludes that his "mistrust" must be confirmation of what is "true" (II.i.45, 48).

Polixenes, warned by the benevolent courtier Camillo of Leontes' plot against his life, sees the fatal intensity of the jealous triangle: the more "precious" and "rare" the wife, the greater the jealousy at the betrayal. The belief that the lover is not a stranger but "a man which / Ever professed" friendship must make his quest for vengeance "more bitter" (II.i.452–57). Leontes' "mighty" power gives him the means to make such vengeance "violent." The one hope for curbing Leontes's tyranny, expressed by the lady-in-waiting Paulina, is that he will "soften at the sight o' th' child" (II.ii.38). The baby, whom Hermione has borne "something before her time" due to the shock of Leontes' accusation and harsh treatment, is "a goodly babe, / Lusty and like to live" (ll. 24–25). Paulina hopes that her "pure innocence" will move the king.

Paulina tries to convince Leontes that the baby is a tiny "copy" of him. In answer to her plea for his blessing of "the Princess," however, he hisses: "This brat is none of mine, / It is the issue of Polixenes" (II.iii.79, 93–94). He orders that both "the bastard" and "the dam" (the term for a maternal animal) be "commit[ted] to the fire!" (ll. 95–96). When Paulina protests, Leontes threatens next to "dash out" the "bastard brains" (l. 140) with his own hands, an echo of Lady Macbeth's sadistic vow. He will not, he rants, "live to see this bastard / Kneel and call me father," and adds, "Better burn it now / Than curse it then" (ll. 155–57). But something holds Leontes back from acting on his rage, and, at the plea of the kindly courtier Antigonus, he changes the sentence to exile and exposure. Antigonus is to take the baby to "some remote and desert place" and "without more mercy" abandon it. Helplessly, Antigonus agrees, though he protests that immediate death would be "more merciful" (ll. 176, 185).

Hermione, who has remained the essence of integrity and dignity throughout these trials, tries to warn her husband of his folly: "How this will grieve you / When you shall come to clearer knowledge" (II.i.96–97). She does not give way to scorn or fury at this most unjust of husbands, but she does say ominously: "I never wished to see you sorry, / Now I trust I shall" (ll. 123–24). Leontes had earlier predicted that his supposed cuckolding and its "issue" would "hiss me to my grave: contempt and clamor / Will be my knell" (I.ii.188–90). Hermione, firm in her faith in both her own "honor" and the "powers divine" (III.ii.110, 28), sees instead that children are the great hope for the future, that Leontes is cutting off his own posterity. In this conviction, she is supported by the Oracle of Apollo, which pronounces the somber judgment that Hermione is "chaste," Polixenes "blameless," and "the innocent babe truly begotten." The corollary is "The king shall live without an heir, if that which is lost be not found" (ll. 132–36). Leontes, incorrigibly obstinate, rejects even the divine testimony as "mere falsehood." Instantly, the heavens exact retribution for his hubris. A messenger announces that the ailing Mamillius, who had begun to recover, has died of a heart "cleft" by anxiety and sympathy for his "gracious" mother (ll. 196, 198). The queen "swoons" and Paulina immediately says that this news has been "mortal" (ll. 47–48) to her.

Leontes instantly repents his "injustice" to his family and "great profaneness 'gainst [the] oracle" (III.ii.154). He prays that the queen will recover and begs that Paulina and her attendants "apply to her / Some remedies for life" (ll. 152–53). They carry off the unconscious Hermione. Moments later, Paulina returns and grimly pronounces that the heavens' "vengeance" has been dire. She reviews in detail Leontes' sins against family and friends and cruelly advises: "betake thee / To nothing but despair." Leontes, stricken by "shame perpetual," vows that he will visit "once a day" the graves of wife and son and spend his life in "shed[ding] tears" (ll. 238–39) of grief and remorse.

Were the play a tragedy, that would indeed be the sad end of Leontes's story. But the romance form allows for the faint hope expressed by the oracle to bear fruit. The kindly Antigonus, pitying the "poor thing, condemned to loss" that he has been ordered to dispose of, prays: "Some powerful spirit instruct the kites and ravens / To be thy nurse!" (II.iii.186–87). Immediately, his prayer is answered. Hermione appears to him in a vision and tells him to take the child to Bohemia and, because "the babe / Is counted lost forever" (III.ii.32–33), to name her Perdita. Antigonus obeys. He leaves the infant with a "scroll" and a "bundle" that offer proof of her identity and riches to raise her and provide a legacy. This action is reminiscent of Pericles' care for Thaisa, but this time not to provide means to bury the loved one but to sustain her. With the affectionate wish, "Blossom, speed thee well!" (l. 46), he leaves the child to fate. Minutes later, he hears the "savage clamor" that marks his own fateful end, and runs off, *"pursued by a bear."*

Immediately, Antigonus's prayer for Perdita is answered. An old shepherd happens along, sees the "pretty barne," and "take[s] it up for pity" (III.ii.70, 76). He thinks her a "changeling," complete with "fairy gold." His son, witness to the bear's attack and to a storm at sea, comes in and reports the deaths of Antigonus and of the mariners who brought the baby to Bohemia. "Thou metst with things dying, I with things new-born," the old shepherd says, and proclaims: "'Tis a lucky day, boy, and we'll do good deeds on't" (ll. 113–14, 138–39). Providence has intervened to spare the hope for Leontes' future — a child who, as Mamillius once did, can "make old hearts fresh" (I.i.39). In the last happy talk between mother and son, the boy had requested prophetically that she tell him "a sad tale," as being "best for winter" (II.i.25). When we next see Perdita, sixteen years have passed, spring has come to Bohemia and the new season's blessings are at hand.

In keeping with the fairy tale shift of setting, Perdita has not been harmed by her banishment. Time, appearing as the play's chorus, "slide[s] / O'er sixteen years" and presents a young woman "now grown in grace" (IV.i.5–6, 24). Despite her upbringing by a "most homely shepherd" (IV.ii.38), she looks and speaks like the princess that she is by birth. Even Polixenes, disgruntled at his son's passion for the "low-born lass," concedes her "rare" beauty and carriage: she "smacks of something greater than herself, / Too noble for this place" (IV.iv.156–59). His faithful courtier, Camillo, also marvels at her "prett[iness]" and "breeding," so marked that although she "lacks instruction," she could serve as a teacher "to most that teach" (ll. 582–83). We have only to compare Perdita to some of Shakespeare's conventional country lasses, "greasy Joan" in *Love's Labour's Lost* or simple-minded Audrey in *As You Like It*, to note the impossibly idealized outcome of Perdita's deprivations. Cut off from every source of refinement and education, she nevertheless emerges as graceful and well spoken, with a naturalness to her manners that makes them the more winning.

Of course, something more than ordinary time is operating here. Providence has intervened, not merely to rescue Perdita from sordidness but to put her in the way of the young prince who will change her estate. Florizel, aptly named for the spring flowers that represent his fresh and hopeful nature, "bless[es] the time" that he met Perdita, when his "good falcon" happened to fly across the old shepherd's grounds (IV.iv.15). He is not merely handsome and gallant but utterly smitten with Perdita. She reminds him (in perfect blank verse) that she is but a "poor lowly maid" in contrast to his "high self," and she "tremble[s]" (ll. 7–9, 18) at the chance that the king will discover his son's love. But Florizel is determined to evade his father's will, not to seduce and abandon her but to treat his "fair belov'd" with "honor" and "faith" (ll. 34–35) and to keep his "oath" to marry her (ll. 491–92). From this risky defiance of his father, Florizel assures her, he "apprehend[s] / Nothing but jollity" (ll. 24–25). In keeping with the ambience of Bohemia and the workings of benevolent fate, this will indeed prove the outcome of the lovers' forbidden passion.

Perdita and Florizel serve as the means in this generation to reconcile their fathers' breach and to provide hope for the future. Polixenes, who has gone in disguise to break up the romance, pronounces with ironic aptness the traditional hope behind a father's marriage blessing: "All whose joy is nothing else / But fair posterity" (IV.iv.408–09). His sudden vengeful shift in tone is reminiscent of Leontes', although at least this time there is justification for the wrath. Perdita, as "mistress of the feast," has given Polixenes and the faithful Camillo "rosemary and rue," flowers that maintain color and aroma "all the winter long" (l. 75). We know from Ophelia that rosemary stands for "remembrance" and rue for remorse. But Polixenes does not respond to the language of flowers, any more than to the heartfelt pleas of the lovers that he would separate. Threatening Florizel with disinheritance and Perdita with death should they continue their romance, he stalks off.

Fortunately, Camillo is present to rescue the couple. He counters Florizel's desperate plan to run away to sea by advising them to "make for Sicilia" and ask for refuge from Leontes. He presents a vision of Leontes' open-armed "welcome" of the prince, a plea for "forgiveness" and a means of vicarious restitution for his past "unkindness" (IV.iv.549, 552) to the young man's father. Delighted, Florizel proclaims Camillo "preserver of my father, now of me, / The medicine of our house" (ll. 586–87). But the faithful old counselor has further restoratives in mind. Although the young people believe that they have escaped unnoticed, Camillo plans to tell Polixenes of their flight and to join him in pursuing them to Sicilia. His ultimate purpose is to bring the two former friends together and create "almost a miracle" (l. 534) of reconciliation. Again, Providential as well as human benevolence will aid him in that effort.

The agent of Providence is the sly Autolycus, itinerant pedlar, thief, and, as he is designated in the cast list, "rogue." He overhears the old shepherd and his son discussing the "secret" of Perdita's past and determines to use the information for his own gain: "Though I am not naturally honest, I am sometimes by chance" (IV.iv.712–13), he confides to us. He escorts them and their circumstantial evidence — the contents of the "scroll" and "bundle" left with the abandoned infant — to Sicilia, to reveal the true identity of "the changeling." Even without this confirmation, Perdita's royal heritage, like Marina's, is evident in her appearance. Three Gentlemen at Leontes' court discuss her arrival and reunion with her father, which has taken place off-stage. The young woman's "nobleness," which "shows above her breeding," the "majesty" that is evident in her resemblance to her supposedly dead mother, "proclaim her, with all certainty, to be the King's daughter" (V.ii.37–39).

Leontes is clearly overwhelmed by this turn of events. Just before the reported scene, we see him for the first time since he defied Apollo's Oracle. His courtier Cleomines describes the king's "penitence" and "saintlike sorrow" and urges him: "forgive yourself." But Leontes is prey to bitter remorse for actions that have left his kingdom "heirless" and destroyed "the sweet'st companion that e'er man / Bred his hopes out of" (V.i.10–12). Paulina is there to rub salt in these old wounds: "she you killed," she amends harshly. She reminds him of Mamillius's death, which Leontes recalls with fresh anguish, and repeats the Oracle's decree: "King Leontes shall not have an heir / Till his lost child be found" (ll. 39–40). She believes, however, that the "infant" has "perished." The one hope that she holds out is for him to marry again, someone of her choosing, though she says in an ironic riddle that that will happen only "When your queen's again in breath; / Never till then" (ll. 83–84). Into this impasse come the exiled lovers.

Leontes is touched by their youth, beauty, and obvious devotion. Calling them "a gracious couple," he says benevolently: "Welcome hither, / As is the spring to th'earth" (V.i.134, 151–52). He wishes wistfully that he could have "a son and daughter" so "goodly" and confesses the "folly" that lost him such a pair, when "the heavens," in "angry note" of his "sin," "left [him] issueless" (ll. 172–74). In a tragedy, this would be the outcome of Leontes' wrongs, his restitution and consolation only vicarious. But the renewal and fertility of the season are at hand. As Autolycus says at the sheep shearing fest, the spring is "the sweet o' the year," when "the red blood reigns in the winter's pale," and Perdita is "mistress of the feast" (IV.iii.2–4; 40). So lovely is she that the passion roused nearly takes a wrong turn, when Leontes is momentarily attracted to her. The austere Paulina reproaches him: "Your eye hath too much youth in it" (V.i.225). But it is the girl's resemblance to Hermione that has moved Leontes, and, in any case, Florizel, "his father's image," is on hand to complete the couple. Leontes is no Antiochus—incest is not his bent. As the Gentlemen report, when Perdita's identity is revealed, Leontes is recalled to his role as benevolent father and bereft husband:

> Our king, being ready to leap out of himself for joy of his found daughter, as if that joy were now become a loss, cries, "O thy mother, thy mother!" [V.ii.49–52].

He embraces the couple and his long-lost friend and again asks forgiveness of Bohemia. At the account of her mother's supposed death, Perdita "bleed[s] tears" of empathy and anguish. All go off to view the wondrously lifelike state of Hermione wrought, according to Paulina, by a "rare Italian master" (l. 97). These melodramatic scenes, which would be hard to credit if staged, Shakespeare wisely confines to report. As one of the Gentlemen notes: "The news ... is so like an old tale that verity of it is in strong suspicion" (ll. 28–29). The playwright saves for direct presentation the more subtle and affecting scene of Hermione's restoration.

Perdita's role in this episode is minor but crucial. She it is who first moves to kiss the statue, addressing it as "dear Queen, that ended when I but began" (V.iii.45). Paulina, who has long planned to engineer Hermione and Leontes' reunion, knows that it is he who must first touch his wife, and she stops the girl with the excuse that the paint on the statue is still wet. Leontes' first reaction has been some dismay that, for all its resemblance to the dead queen, the statue is "much wrinkled" and "aged"—effects of the "wide gap of time" (ll. 28, 154) that has separated the couple. At last, at Paulina's direction, the statue "comes down," and Leontes "presents [his] hand." His wife forgives him with an embrace and "hangs about his neck" (ll. 107, 112). The lady-in-waiting then calls attention to the boon that neither she nor her mistress had dared to hope for: "Turn, good lady, / Our Perdita is found" (ll. 120–21). Hermione reveals that it was this hope, conveyed by the Oracle, that her daughter remained alive that gave her the will to go on: "preserve[ ] / Myself to see the issue" (ll. 127–28). Fittingly, the last word is a pun, meaning both "outcome" and "child." Religious faith and familial loyalty have combined to save the wronged queen. As in *Pericles*, the family circle has been restored, mother and daughter safely returned, and father rendered beside himself with joy. Generosity and sympathy reign. Polixenes wishes that he could have taken some of the family's long grief on himself. Leontes not only does not blame Paulina for her duplicity and his sixteen years of penitence but makes a match between her and Camillo. Paulina urges everyone: "Go together, / You precious winners all" (ll. 130–31).

Perdita does not speak again during all these events. Her role, as she herself says, is to "stand by," a "looker-on" (ll. 84–85) at her parents' reunion, and a representative of future peace and fertility. She has the heavens' blessing on her own plighted troth. Of course, Florizel can never replace Mamillius, nor can Leontes regain the years of his daughter's youth and his once idyllic marriage that his tyranny obliterated. This is, after all, a "winter's tale," but one that ends with the blessings of spring perhaps all the more cherished for their rarity.

King Lear

King Lear's initial rejection of Cordelia, recounted in Chapter 4, is crueler than Leontes' of Perdita. Lear exiles not a baby whom he suspects of being illegitimate but a young woman who has proven not merely blameless but admirable. By his own admission, she had hitherto been his favorite daughter. Furthermore, the presence of her treacherous sisters should have been warning enough of how irrational he is acting. Nothing, however, deters Lear from his rash and vain decree, and he orders Cordelia into exile, charging her never to cross his path again. She would be fully justified in taking his command literally and cutting herself off forever from the father who has misjudged and rejected her. Instead, when next we hear about Cordelia, it is clear that her filial love has remained steadfast.

Although exiled to France, the kingdom of the husband who has provided her succor, Cordelia has continued to follow Lear's fortunes through the agency of the loyal Earl of Kent. The league between the old king's supporters is revealed when Kent, disguised as a servant, is arrested by the treacherous Regan and Cornwall. Thrust humiliatingly into the stocks, he comforts himself with a clandestine letter from Cordelia. Later, searching for the mad king in the storm, Kent confides to a "Gentleman" who has also remained loyal Cordelia's support for her father's cause. Through a network of spies disguised as servants, she has watched the "hard rein" of her sisters "against the old kind king" (III.i.27–28). Now she is leading "a power" from France, an invading force come "on secret feet" to aid him. Kent asks the Gentleman to give her the token of his signet ring to show his continuing support and to verify his message that Lear is in desperate straits, suffering "unnatural and bemadding sorrow."

The scene shifts to the heath, and we see the sad proof of Kent's description. Lear has gone completely mad, refusing to take shelter from the terrible storm and instead challenging the elements, the "winds," "cataracts and hurricanoes," that rage around him. He is obsessed with the theme of "filial ingratitude" (IV.iv.14). In his rage, he tries to shift all blame for his state on Goneril and Regan, picturing them as "two pernicious daughters" and himself as "the kind old father, whose frank heart gave all" (III.ii.22, 20). He says that he has been reduced to their "slave," "a poor, infirm, weak, and despised old man" (III.ii.19–20). He works himself up to the self-pitying defense: "I am a man more sinned against than sinning" (ll. 59–60).

One of Lear's responses to this treatment, in keeping with his mind-set at the start of the play, is to long for raw, violent revenge. Rather than "weep," which he denigrates as effeminate, he vows to "punish home" (III.iv.16). He conducts an illusory trial in which he arraigns the "she-foxes" and imagines an attacking army, wielding "a thousand red burning spits," attacking Goneril and Regan. He even takes his fantasies of vengeance so far as to will, with Macbeth-like nihilism, the destruction of all humankind: "Crack Nature's moulds, all germains spill at once, / That makes ingrateful man" (III.ii.8–9).

Were this hardened bitterness Lear's only reaction, there would be little for Cordelia to redeem, and her continued loyalty to her father would seem Pollyanna naiveté, even masochism. But in the midst of his suffering, Lear is discovering hard truths about empathy, the feeling for others' suffering from which his former power and pride insulated him. As the mocking jingle of the Fool suggests, Lear has brought this pain upon himself:

> The man that makes his toe
> What he his heart should make
> Shall of a corn cry woe
> And turn his sleep to wake   [III.ii.31–34].

Lear must reconnect with his own heart, and the daughter who represents it, if he is to move beyond this state of arid bitterness. He begins that change through his treatment of the other "child" he has always loved, the Fool, whom he habitually addresses as "boy." Drenched and forlorn, the king thinks not of himself for once but of his jester: "How dost, my boy? Art cold? / I am cold myself" (ll. 68–69). This is the process of achieving empathy through one's own suffering, reduced to its simplest terms. The childish vocabulary and the familiar second person make it a moment of startling intimacy. Lear goes further than this single encounter, coming to sympathize with all the "poor naked wretches" that "bide the pelting of [the] pitiless storm" (III.iv.28–29). He sees his own responsibility for his needy subjects, and laments, "O, I have ta'en too little care of this!" He rejects "pomp" in favor of experiencing such misery, so that one may feel directly the plight of the poor and act to aid them. Again, he practices this new principle on the Fool. Coming to a hovel, the erstwhile Me-Firster urges the jester, "In, boy; go first" (l. 26).

Inside the hovel, Lear's meeting with the supposed Bedlam beggar, Edgar disguised as "Poor Tom," provokes further realizations. Deprived of rich attire, he exclaims, man is merely "such a poor, bare, forked animal" as the wretched beggar. Later, with the blinded Gloucester, Lear takes such insights still further. "Robes and furred gowns" can hide the "vices" so evident through "tattered clothes," and even "a dog," given power, will be unquestioningly "obeyed" (IV.vi.161–62, 155–56). His older daughters, in fact, treated him just that way, he says, "flattered me like a dog," said "ay and no to everything that I said," and "told me I was everything." Now that he has been "wet" by the rain and made to "chatter" by the wind, he realizes that they lied and he is "not ague-proof" (ll. 96–104). He is revolted by Goneril and Regan's "stench" and "corruption," but he acknowledges that his own hand "smells of mortality" (l. 132). Suffering, physical and emotional, has taught Lear his own limitations as well as the restricted worth of wealth and power. He "see[s] how this world goes"—like the blind Gloucester, "see[s] it feelingly" (l. 147). Yet Lear's clarity is incomplete, and he has achieved it at the price of his sanity. He is still spouting "reason in madness" (l. 172), still confused and tormented, and still intent on bloody vengeance. He reverts to the wish to lead a surprise attack on his treacherous daughters and sons-in-law and "Then kill, kill, kill, kill, kill, kill" (ll. 183–84). It will take Cordelia's intervention to soothe his corrosive rage and give him a basis for gratitude and hope.

Earlier, Kent has puzzled that one couple, such as Lear and his late wife, "could ... beget / Such different issues." Only the "stars" (IV.iii.32–35) could be responsible, he maintains. Yet we have the bastard Edmund's scorn of astrological influences to counter such a theory. Moreover, the nature of the bond between father and child is shown to be clearly a product of the parent's treatment. When he visits Lear in the hovel, Gloucester laments, "Our flesh and blood is grown so vile / That it does hate what gets it" (III.iv.136–37). He thinks that he is describing the betrayal of his heretofore loyal son Edgar. But Edgar, wronged by his bastard brother, is looking on in his Poor Tom guise to provide a silent ironic commentary on this charge. It is Edmund, long scorned and rejected by Gloucester, who has gloated over the benefits for him of the conflict between the generations: "The younger rises when the old doth fall" (III.iii.23). Edgar and Cordelia, the children their fathers have long and deeply loved, put all their efforts into comforting and restoring them even after those fathers have wronged them. Being loved has taught them to reciprocate, and they set about repairing the "holy cords" of the parent-child bond that the unloved children have tried to sever.

The first time that we hear of Cordelia again is in an unscene reported by the Gentleman to Kent. Her reaction to hearing of Lear's desperate state is to shed "ample tear[s]" of "patience" and "sorrow" (IV.iii.12, 16). Rather than be, as Kent fears, "moved ... to a rage" (ll. 15–16) against her father, Cordelia shows only pity and compassion. Her outrage is directed against her malevolent sisters, "shame of ladies," who have subjected him to humiliation and peril. "'What, i' th' storm, i' th' night?'" the Gentleman reports that she cried, "'Let pity not be believed!'" (ll. 28–29). The person who is feeling shame at this point is not one of the "dog-hearted daughters," however, but the father, who is mortified by "his own unkindness" at having "stripped" Cordelia of "his benediction" and cast her off. The Gentleman concludes: "These things sting / His mind so venomously that burning shame / Detains him from Cordelia" (ll. 45–47). The king has been stricken by the serpent's tooth of his own thanklessness and has sentenced himself to separation from the beloved child he has wronged.

Cordelia will not be deterred from aiding him by such niceties of conscience. The first time that she reappears (she has been absent from the play since the opening scene), she is ordering her knights to "search every acre in the high-grown field" for the afflicted Lear. She is quick to assert that, as head of the French forces, traditional enemy of the British, she is not motivated by political "ambition" but by "love, dear love, and [her] aged father's right" (IV.iv.27–28). Her indulgent husband, "great France," has "pitied" her "importuned tears" (ll. 25–26) and therefore provided means for the invasion. He has been called back on urgent business, and Cordelia is left alone to lead her adopted country's army against the "British pow'rs" (l. 22) led by her sisters. She implies again that her main goal is personal, not military, as she signals when she offers "all [her] outward wealth" to anyone who can help restore Lear's "bereaved sense" (ll. 9–10). The word is a pun, meaning both "riven" and "beset by grief," a sign that only Cordelia herself can heal this broken mind. She wishes that benign herbs could "spring with [her] tears" (l. 17) to cure his madness, but it is the tears themselves that will prove the crucial balm.

Lear is found, new clothed, and made to sleep long. At the attending Doctor's urging, Cordelia rouses him, praying that she can "repair [the] violent harms" that her sisters have done him with the "medicine" of her "kiss" (IV.vii.2). On one level, this is a fairy tale cure. But in symbolic terms, such forgiveness and sympathy are the surest means to soothe and heal this "child-changed father" (l. 17). At first, the king is too distraught to understand or credit her kindness. He believes that he has died and been forced from his grave but that he remains in hell, "bound upon a wheel of fire," and in such an agony of despair "that [his] own tears / Do scald like molten lead" (ll. 46–48). He thinks Cordelia a fellow "spirit," but a visitant from heaven, "a soul in bliss." When he tries to "kneel" to her, she asks instead for *his* "benediction." The effect of these first shows of love is to snap Lear back to reality, and to a humble admission of his reduced status. He pleads:

> Pray do not mock me.
> I am a very foolish fond old man,
> Fourscore and upward, not an hour more nor less;
> And, to deal plainly,
> I fear I am not in my perfect mind   [ll. 59–63].

The man once obsessed with image and power has become movingly open and vulnerable.

Still too abashed to address Cordelia directly, he asks again that the onlookers "not laugh at" his wild speculation: "For, as I am a man, I think this lady / To be my child Cordelia" (ll. 68–70). He has described their bond in its most basic terms, and Cordelia responds with a touchingly childlike affirmation: "And so I am! I am!" Addressing her for the first time, the old father asks in amazement, "Be your tears wet?" (l. 71). The proof of her sympathy is in the actuality of her tears— not feigned but "wet" on her cheeks. He still believes, however, that she wants revenge. "I know you do not love me," he says. He reasons that her sisters, despite his generosity to them, "have (as I do remember) done me wrong," whereas, he tells Cordelia, "You have some cause" (ll. 73–75). She counters with another magnificently simple expression of forgiveness: "No cause, no cause." In these lines, Lear is not only clear-headed but unusually mild-mannered. As the Doctor notes, "The great rage is killed in him." His wishes have become strikingly simple and concentrated on Cordelia: "You must bear with me. / Pray you now, forget and forgive. I am old and foolish" (ll. 83–84). He has lost all his former pretense and vindictiveness. Like Edgar, the other loyal child in the play, Cordelia has "known the miseries of [her] father" by "nursing them," "bec[o]me his guide, / Led him, ... saved him from despair" (V.iii.181–82, 191–92). Could Lear's story end there, it would not be the stark tragedy it becomes.

Cordelia is no soldier, and all too soon Edgar reports to Gloucester the defeat of her forces: "King Lear hath lost, he and his daughter ta'en" (V.ii.6). Brought in with Lear as a prisoner, Cordelia tries to remain philosophical about their defeat, assuring him: "We are not the first / Who with best meaning have incurred the worst" (V.iii.3–4). But she feels "cast down" for his sake and proposes seeing — and facing down — "these daughters and these sisters" who have betrayed them. But the once vengeful Lear is adamant about avoiding their sight. "No, no, no, no!" he insists, and claims to welcome imprisonment so that it be with her. "We two alone will sing like birds i' th' cage," he says. He imagines a process of mutual benediction and forgiveness, but with the reversal of the usual father/daughter roles: "When thou dost ask me blessing, I'll kneel down / And ask of thee forgiveness" (ll. 9–11).

Clearly, Lear has come to feel that Cordelia's benison and pardon would be ample compensation for all his misery. He presents an idealized vision of their future life: "we'll live, / And pray, and sing, and tell old tales." It is an idyll of devotion to the tenets of religion, art, and family love. In turn, he would eschew his former values of wealth, power, and ambition. He and Cordelia would "laugh / At gilded butterflies," the "packs and sects of great ones" that so quickly "ebb and flow." Political grappling, "Who loses and who wins, who's in, who's out" would be matters of utter indifference to them. They would be intent on higher goals: to "take upon's the mystery of things / As if we were God's spies" (ll. 12–17). Clearly, Cordelia sees the danger of their situation as well as the nobility of these attempts to cheer her, and she weeps afresh. "Wipe thine eyes," he urges, and vows that his enemies will never make them weep — his old claim to Goneril and Regan but made now in the name of honor, not vanity. That Lear is aware, however, of the dire nature of their predicament is evident from his ominous metaphor, meant to comfort Cordelia: "Upon such sacrifices, my Cordelia, / The gods themselves throw incense" (ll. 20–21). When next we see him, he is feeling the full effects of that grim designation.

It is the vindictive Goneril and Edmund who conceive the insidious plot to "hang Cordelia in the prison" and to "lay the blame upon her own despair" (V.iii.254–55). Mortally wounded and repentant at last, Edmund confesses the scheme to Albany, who dispatches an officer to the prison with the prayer, "The gods defend her" (l. 257). In this stark tragedy, however, the gods do not intervene: cruelty wins the day and the human misery is absolute. Before Albany's messenger can return, Lear enters "with Cordelia in his arms." "Howl, howl, howl," he cries, reduced to a state of animal agony. The onlookers, Kent, Albany, and Edgar, three men who have fought selflessly for good, are appalled. Kent says, "All's cheerless, dark, and deadly" (l. 291), and Edgar calls this sight the "image of [the] horror" of doomsday (l. 265).

Lear is in such a state of shock and anguish that he barely knows what he is saying. One of his last sensible remarks is on the supreme preciousness of this beloved daughter. If she were to revive, he says, that fact would "redeem all sorrows / That ever I have felt" (ll. 267–68). He tells the dead woman proudly that, old as he is, he managed to "kill the slave that was a-hanging thee" (l. 275). His whole focus is on her — he barely recognizes the faithful Kent, and he cannot take in that Goneril and Regan "desperately are dead" (l. 293). He goes back and forth between the bitter realization that Cordelia is gone forever and the vain hope that she is still alive. "Why should a dog, a horse, a rat have life / And thou no life at all? Thou'lt come no more, / Never, never, never, never, never" (ll. 307–08). The relentless repetition recalls his former vow of vengeance — "kill" — now converted to despairing incredulity. Pathetically, his last words express the delusion that she has revived: "Do you see this? Look on her! Look her lips, / Look there, look there —" (ll. 311–12).

Stretched "upon the rack of this tough world," Lear must lose everything in order to realize the emptiness of what he once valued — ceremony, pomp, and rank — and the supreme worth of what he rashly scorned — candor, loyalty, and love. Like Marina and Perdita, Cordelia does forgive and heal the father who wronged her. But in the bleak world of *King Lear*, the benefits of her kindness are devastatingly brief.

Conclusion

The ending of *King Lear* devastates the audience as well. No play creates a clearer sense of a plunge into the abyss. At the same time, *Lear*, like Shakespeare's other tragedies, gives us the luxury of experiencing such feelings vicariously. At the curtain's drop, we can walk away from the battlefield, the heath, the death chamber, saddened but also enlightened. In gentler ways, the comedies, too, can teach us about the choices and forces that drive and shape our lives. While the consequences in the lighter plays are not so intractable or dire, the characterization in those plays, too, is complex and psychologically realistic, grounded in Shakespeare's remarkable insight into the human mind and heart. In Carol Rutter's words, "The reason we still go to see these plays is that they continue to inform us who we are."* This book has argued for the benefits, aesthetic and practical, of knowing a key cross-section of Shakespeare's characters: from daughters who seem to be their father's ideal children, to those who reject or feign that role, to those who have grown beyond their early nurture to assume the parental role themselves; from fathers whose prescience and generosity make them model parents to those who dictate and restrict, to those who become the beneficiaries of their daughters' wisdom and love.

Why does Shakespeare focus on the father-daughter relationship, and on the moment when the daughter is poised to leave her father's home and try her own wings? Because that is the moment of truth, when the father's convictions and hopes, his conception of his daughter and of himself, undergo the crucial test. At that point the daughter makes her choices: what she wants, whom she loves, and how she feels about her father's approbation or disapproval. The plays remind us that parents cannot reinvent the children that they have borne. Instead, their aim should be to understand who they are and to give them room to grow: to nurture their

---

* *Clamourous Voices: Shakespeare's Women Today*, ed. Faith Evans (New York: Routledge, 1989), p. xi.

gifts, resist crushing their spirits, and then get out of the way, except to be open to what they can teach their elders. It is a process that requires infinite empathy and hope, and that pays the highest rewards or, if we get it wrong, exacts the direct consequences.

Unlike small children, who are likely to tell adults frankly what they think, adolescents, like Juliet and Bianca, are sophisticated enough to know what their parents want to hear — and to say the words that we signal to them that we expect, whether or not they mean them. If communication breaks down further, they may stop confiding in us altogether and take upon themselves decisions about matchmaking or even survival. Children have to be willing to reach out, to risk telling a parent what is troubling them, and to explain more fully if the adult gets it wrong. But often it is the parent who, like Capulet who rants and threatens or Baptista who plays favorites and dotes, squelches the attempt at communication. Some of the worst mistakes that parents make, in Shakespeare's plays and in life, come when they act out of embarrassment or vanity. Both are signs that the parent is focused on his own needs, not the child's. Shakespeare takes that idea to an extreme when he has King Lear say, "Better thou / Hadst not been born than not t'have pleased me better." Of course, the irony is that he is berating Cordelia, his one loyal daughter. Shakespeare was a father, too.

Time and again, these plays teach us that the daughters cannot be fooled about fairness or sincerity or love. Adolescents have a reputation for being rebels, but, in Shakespeare's day as in our own, they are also idealists. The plays urge us to credit their strengths, to treat them as individuals — beware the shadow of the favored sibling — and, most important, to model for them the qualities that we want them to develop. The most attentive witnesses to our character are the young people in our care, who learn moral lessons, positive and negative, from what we say and do, whether or not we offer them wittingly. Shakespeare's daughters are watching as their fathers deal with an unfavorable turn of fortune, address an authority figure or an underling, or react to a fault in their behavior. They know how Duke Senior bears up under exile, how Polonius kowtows to his king, what evokes Lear's rage or Prospero's tenderness. They relish their father's praise, and all but the most hardened of them hate feeling that they have not measured up to his expectations. At the same time, Shakespeare shows us the need to signal to our daughters that we do not see them simply as the sum of their gifts and achievements — the traits that reflect well on us — but as uniquely, intrinsically precious. Loving one's children does not mean absolving them of responsibility, however, and support does not mean license. Shakespeare's good fathers hold themselves and their daughters to high standards of accomplishment and integrity. Prospero, Duke Senior, even Portia's dead father whose strengths are revealed chiefly in the terms of his will, expect their children to be diligent, trustworthy, loyal, and loving, and they demonstrate those qualities by their own example.

Ultimately, Shakespeare teaches us, parents cannot do better than to bless their child's imminent departure from the family home with Prospero's wish. He is speaking to Ariel, the "airy spirit" that he has cherished like a son: "To the elements / Be free, and fare thou well." That old-fashioned pronoun may need some glossing: Prospero does not say fare *thee* well — good-bye, so long — but fare *thou* well — may you prosper. Of course, Ariel is supernatural. With human children such as Miranda, the end should be a beginning. The great hope for the self-sacrificing and bereft old magician, as Shakespeare well knew, is the wonderful secret at the other end of child-rearing. Beloved children, like Miranda, Rosalind and, all too briefly, Cordelia, return, and in the form of their parents' best young friends. As Carol Gilligan notes, the tales of these heroines' struggles for selfhood have the force of myth. In an age when we are groping for standards and guidelines, when the bases for individual identity can seem ephemeral and social coherence precarious, Shakespeare's plays offer deep roots of human understanding and emotional health.

Index